A

BIOGRAPHICAL SKETCH

OF

THE LIFE OF WILLIAM B. IDE

A

BIOGRAPHICAL SKETCH

OF

THE LIFE OF WILLIAM B. IDE:

WITH

A MINUTE AND INTERESTING ACCOUNT OF ONE OF THE LARG-
EST EMIGRATING COMPANIES, (3000 MILES OVER LAND),
FROM THE EAST TO THE PACIFIC COAST.

AND

WHAT IS CLAIMED AS THE MOST AUTHENTIC AND RELIABLE
ACCOUNT OF " THE VIRTUAL CONQUEST OF CALI-
FORNIA, IN JUNE, 1846, BY THE BEAR
FLAG PARTY," AS GIVEN BY
ITS LEADER,

THE LATE HON. WILLIAM BROWN IDE.

The Rio Grande Press, Inc.
GLORIETA, NEW MEXICO · 87535

A RIO GRANDE CLASSIC

First published in 1880

LIBRARY OF CONGRESS CARD CATALOG
67-30871

1967

GLORIETA, NEW MEXICO · 87535

SCRAPS

OF

CALIFORNIA HISTORY

NEVER BEFORE PUBLISHED.

State of California

GOVERNOR'S OFFICE

SACRAMENTO 95814

RONALD REAGAN
GOVERNOR

FOREWORD

The Bear Flag Revolt, although short-lived, is one of the most well-known incidents in California's colorful history, largely because of the subsequent adoption of the revolutionists' banner as California's state flag.

Like the California Republic, which it symbolized, the original Bear Flag was official for less than a month. It was superseded by the raising of the American flag at Monterey on July 7, 1846, when Commodore John D. Sloat's naval forces captured the Mexican headquarters there. By July 9, the Stars and Stripes had been raised at Yerba Buena and Sonoma as well.

Preserved for many years in the custody of the Society of California Pioneers in San Francisco, the original Bear Flag was destroyed during the earthquake and fire of 1906. Its earlier display on Admission Days and the use of the same emblem by the Native Sons in their ceremonies throughout the years eventually led to the Legislature's action in 1911, adopting the Bear Flag as the official flag of the State of California.

Because the design and colors varied depending on the flag manufacturers, the Legislature acted again in 1953 to provide exact legal specifications for the dimensions, design detail, and colors to be used.

Although California school children can undoubtedly recite most of these facts, the history of the Bear Flag Revolt and the Bear Flag Party is not so clear-cut. The personalities, motives and actions of the individuals involved have been subject to conflicting interpretations by historians and students alike. Simeon Ide's books, *A Biographical Sketch of the Life of William B. Ide* and *Who Conquered California?* have been recognized by prominent historians as pristine source material on the Revolt and its leaders. The current reprinting of these rare and valuable volumes will be of particular interest to those students of California history who enjoy conducting their own research rather than merely accepting the conclusions reached in contemporary textbooks. Future generations of historians, scholars and booklovers may well be deeply grateful to the publishers for the ready availability of this first-hand biography of the author's brother--William B. Ide, the only President of California.

RONALD REAGAN
Governor of California

Sacramento, California
August 4, 1967

WALSWORTH PUBLISHING COMPANY, INC., MARCELINE, MISSOURI

PUBLISHERS PREFACE

ABOUT THIS BOOK, AND SOME
ACKNOWLEDGEMENTS

Only two states in the American Union were republics in their own right. One was, of course, Texas. The Lone Star Republic began as a rebellion of citizens against Mexico in 1836; the battle of San Jacinto and the siege and fall of the Alamo are events in American history well known and voluminously documented The Republic of Texas survived its fiery birth and lived for 10 ever-increasingly prosperous years; apparently, it could have gone on into time and history as a stable and powerful independent nation.

Less well known, and certainly not as well documented, are the lives of the men and the events that led to what historians sometimes refer to as "the Bear Flag Revolt" that made California a Republic for 25 days in 1846. We can't describe it better than historian Osgood Hardy did in Scribner's Dictionary of American History, Vol. 1, P. 170-171:

"*...Some color indeed was given to this fear... when the settlers learned of the Hawk's Peak episode and Frémont's expulsion from California in March, 1846...(and)...the rumors that the government (of Mexico) planned to seize and expel all foreigners in the province (of California).
"...Uneasiness gave place to alarm when the news came (later proved false) that 250 Californians were advancing on Sacramento. The Americans immediately repaired to Frémont's quarters at the Marysville Buttes where, in the middle of May, he had encamped on his return from Oregon. This much criticized defiance of the local authorities by Frémont was declared by him to be "the first step*

*in the conquest of California." The next step was
the seizure, early in June, by Ezekial Merritt and
a dozen other Americans of a large band of government horses which General Castro had obtained from
General M. G. Vallejo at Sonoma and which were
being driven to San José by way of Sutter's Fort.
This was an act of war and it was decided that the
third step must be the capture of Sonoma, the chief
stronghold of the Californians north of the Bay
Region. The actual capture of the quiet little pueblo
at early dawn, June 14, 1846, was a rather ludicrous
affair; "To whom shall we surrender?", demanded the
kindly general's wife. After a scene of no little confusion and considerable imbibing of Vallejo's wine,
simple articles of capitulation were arranged for
and signed.*

*"...Then followed the erection of the Republic of
California under the leadership of William B. Ide.
To signalize it, William Todd designed a flag from
a piece of unbleached cloth five feet long and three
feet wide. Facing a red star was a grizzly bear which
gave both the flag and the republic its familiar name.
A proclamation setting forth the justification and
purposes of the revolution was prepared, but before
the new government could get under way, July 10,
1846, the American flag was officially sent to
Sonoma.*

*"...The actual accomplishments of the Bear Flag
Revolt were thus of little importance, but had not
the Mexican War intervened, either "Ide or Frémont might have stood out as the creator of a new
republic, the Sam Houston of the Pacific Coast."*

Thus the events that began in 1836 in Texas led directly to the Mexican War and in the end, to the admission
of California to the American Union in 1850.

Most of the history of those turbulent times was
written by participants in the form of letters, journals
and sometimes newspaper articles, and since then, most of
these surviving publications have disappeared into private
collections and the locked vaults of great libraries. The
main source of information about the Bear Flag Republic
has always been the two small volumes published in 1880
by Simeon Ide--the volumes we have now reprinted, facsimile,
in this one edition.

William B. Ide, a native of New England, was the leader

of the Bear Flag movement in 1846. John C. Frémont, then nearing the height of his fame as 'The Great Pathfinder' for his noted explorations of the West, was the captain of a party of U. S. Army troops in Northern California, near Sacramento. General Stephen W. Kearny commanded the Army of the West as its bedraggled men and officers made their weary way into Southern California from the New Mexico and Arizona deserts.

The nearly-simultaneous development of the Bear Flag force and the appearance of the U. S. troops in the north and south made for a monumental confusion in the Mexican province of California, and led eventually to the downfall and humiliation of President William B. Ide, to the famous (or infamous) court-martial of Capt. John Frémont for insubordination, and to the deflation of Gen. Stephen Kearny's popular image as a military hero. Charges and counter-charges were printed in newspapers across the country, and "Who conquered California?" became one of the most argued and discussed questions of the day.

Mr. Ide never said much publicly before he died December 19, 1852. It wasn't really until 1880 that Simeon Ide, at the age of 85, put his brother's name forward as the real and true conqueror of California. The old gentleman Simeon, no doubt with hand trembling and eyesight fading, put together a handset account of the era entitled *Scraps of California History Never Before Published; a Biographical Sketch of the Life of William B. Ide, with a Minute and Interesting Account of One of the largest Emigrating Companies (3000 miles Over Land) From the East to the Pacific Coast, and, What is Claimed as the Most Authentic and Reliable Account of "The Virtual Conquest of California, in June, 1846, by the Bear Flag Party," as Given by its Leader, the Late Hon. William Brown Ide.* Maybe the typesetting *was* faulty, and perhaps the proof reading *could* have been improved, but to complain about such human failings of an old man is nitpicking on a grand scale; better faulty typesetting and proofreading, in a case like this, than no book at all.

Simeon printed some of these books on a primitive hand-operated press in his New Hampshire home, and began distributing copies to friends and subscribers.

About this time, he learned of William's letter to Senator M. M. Wambough, found among the effects of the lately-deceased James Ide, another brother. Whereupon Simeon put together a second volume, entitled, *Who Con-*

quered California? *Read the Following Pages, and then you will Know; for they Contain the Most Particular, the Most Authentic, and the Most Reliable History of the Conquest of California, in June, 1846, by The "Bear Flag Party", ever before published, Written by its Organizer and Leader, the Late Honorable William Brown Ide.*

He apparently bound some of the second volume into what he had left on hand of the first volume, and the remainder of the second volume became a second book in its own right. The number of copies of the first title was probably no more than 250; of the second title, perhaps 150. No one knows how many Simeon bound together of the two volumes, but those that remain in existence today are, as one might suppose, excessively rare.

Physically, pages 5 through 133 of the second title are *almost* identical to pages 88 through 212 of the first title, but not quite. There are enough differences in the text of each sequence of pages to justify our printing both titles, *en toto*, and putting them together in one volume as we have done here. This will allow students and scholars, as well as armchair adventurers, to see at once and compare easily both the similarities and the differences between the two rare volumes without further search for whichever title might not be at hand.

We have meticulously indexed our edition, largely by proper names, in a manner we believe will be of most help to those using the book. For those who might complain because we did not index ideas and incidents, as well as proper names, we point out that we *did*, to some extent, but it simply is not possible to please everyone. This comprehensive index we have prepared should, however, please all but those most difficult to please anyway.

We are aware that a small collector's edition of the Ide papers was reprinted (not facsimile) in 1944, and still another collector's edition (again, we understand, not facsimile) more recently. But our purpose is to make the full text of both books easily and inexpensively available in their most interesting and comprehensive form to the libraries and general public of the country. For that reason, we are not publishing this newest addition to our basic source documents of American history as a "limited edition" for book collectors only. We like to see everyone reading and using the Beautiful Rio Grande Classics. To us, it makes little sense to publish a book to be seen, but not used.

When we decided to reprint this fine, rare source book, we wrote to Governor Ronald Reagan, of California, and advised him of our intention. At our request, Governor Reagan graciously prepared for the book what we publishers call an "overview" foreword, presented here in the pages immediately preceding these. We are most grateful to the Governor, and to his Assistant for Education, Manuel Servin, for the chief executive's contribution to history. In this connection, we must also mention our thanks for the cooperation we received from Mr. Lorrin Morrison, publisher of the esteemed *Journal of the West;* his help was invaluable.

We have wondered just how to adequately express our thanks to Benjamin Franklin Gilbert, Ph. D., Professor of History at San José State College in, of all places, San José. Dr. Gilbert is one of the country's foremost authorities on the Bear Flag Republic, and his scholarly but highly readable introduction set forth in the following pages is only a sample of his painstaking and wide-ranging research on the subject.

The facsimile reprints of these two first editions would not have been possible without the extraordinary cooperation of the California State Librarian Carma R. Leigh, and of Mr. Allan R. Ottley, Supervisor of the State Library's California Section. The philosophy of service of the California State Library is that the function of a library is not only to collect and preserve books and rare documents, but also, wherever possible, to disseminate the knowledge their treasures make available. We appreciate enormously the cooperation of this great institution and its fine staff.

We therefore have the honor, and the privilege, to offer the present and future generations of America this perfectly splendid 'basic source document of American history'; it is the 35th in our continuing line of Beautiful Rio Grande Classics.

Robert B. McCoy
President

John T. Strachan
Vice President

Glorieta, N. M., 87535
November, 1967

INTRODUCTION

by

Benjamin Franklin Gilbert

Six flags flew over California before the American conquest came in 1846. The flag of Spain was the first, for she
discovered the area in 1542, erected the first mission and
presidio there in 1769, and ruled until 1822. Prior to actual
Spanish settlement, Sir Francis Drake had raised the English
standard at Nova Albion in 1579. From 1809 to 1841 the flag
of the Russian American Company flew over several posts
north of San Francisco Bay. The pirate Hippolyte Bouchard
sacked the capital at Monterey in 1818 and hoisted the flag of
Buenos Aires. The Mexican ensign warily guarded the turbulent territory from 1822 to 1846. The Bear Flag of the California Republic was the sixth to fly over California before the
United States flag was officially unfurled atop the custom
house at Monterey.

The first Americans were attracted to California by the
sea otter, seal, hide and tallow, and fur trade. As early as
the Jackson administration the United States evinced interest
in acquiring the province. In 1841 a United States naval and
scientific expedition reconnoitered northern California. It was
commanded by Lieutenant Charles Wilkes who realized the
strategic value of San Francisco Bay and predicted that *"the
situation of Upper California will cause its separation from*

Mexico before many years." The Wilkes expedition visited California just as the first of the organized overland parties was bringing real home seekers to the region.

On October 20, 1842, Commodore Thomas Catesby Jones, commanding the United States Pacific Squadron, elevated the Stars and Stripes over the old castillo at Monterey. In error he had assumed his country was at war with Mexico and that Great Britain had seized California. Two days later the American flag was hauled down and the blundering sea dog apologized to Mexican officials. In 1844 Thomas Oliver Larkin opened his office as United States Consul at Monterey. This shrewd entrepeneur eventually became President Polk's confidential agent and stealthily worked for the peaceful annexation of California.

In the decade before the Mexican War, political conditions were unstable in California. Civil strife and insufficient military forces had weakened Mexican control of the territory. On March 4, 1846, Faxon Dean Atherton, a young American businessman at Valparaiso, inquired of Larkin:

"...Why do not the Californians declare their absolute independence from Mexico? There is certainly no great good will existing on either part towards each other, and there is little fear of Mexico doing them much harm, however much they may desire it. Are there not wild Yankees enough in California yet to take management of affairs into their own hands?"

In the meantime, on January 15, 1846, Captain John C. Frémont and his exploring party had arrived at Sutter's Fort in the Sacramento Valley on his second visit to California. When Frémont reached Monterey thirteen days later, he was ordered out of California. At Gavilán or Hawk's Peak, Frémont erected a fortification and defied General José Castro by raising the American flag. Frémont's soldiers observed Castro's clumsy maneuvers down at his San Juan Bautista headquarters through a field glass. Although Castro prepared to assault Frémont's position, no military action materialized. Frémont then retreated and moved north toward Oregon. On the way he alarmed American settlers by spreading rumors of a possible attack by Mexican forces.

The Hawk's Peak affair was a direct cause of the Bear Flag Revolt and the incident was one factor making American settlers suppose that all foreign residents in the province would be expelled. The initial hostile act of the Revolt occurred on June 10, 1846, when a dozen men led by Ezekiel Merritt seized a drove of horses guarded by Lieutenant Francisco Arce of the Mexican Army near Murphy's ranch on the Consumnes River. Meanwhile, Lieutenant Archibald H. Gillespie of the United States Marine Corps, a secret agent and courier, had located Frémont in the Klamath Lake region. Frémont suddenly returned southward and first encamped at the Marysville Buttes and then along Bear Creek.

On the quiet Sunday morning of June 14, 33 American settlers from the Sacramento Valley and Napa Valley descended upon Mexico's northernmost outpost at Sonoma. The insurgents seized the commandant, Colonel Mariano G. Vallejo, his American brother-in-law Jacob P. Leese, Colonel Victor Prudshon, and Captain Salvador Vallejo. The revolt received Frémont's blessings and he ordered the prisoners confined at Sutter's Fort.

At Sonoma William Brown Ide emerged as the third and final leader of the revolutionists and as the only President of California. Ide issued a proclamation creating the California Republic and the Bear Flag, principally designed by William L. Todd (a cousin of Mrs. Abraham Lincoln), was raised over the plaza. The flag had an uneven five-pointed red star. To the right of the star and facing it, Todd scratched a crude grizzly bear. Critics on the scene claimed it looked more like a pig. Beneath the star and bear were printed the words: CALIFORNIA REPUBLIC. On the unbleached cotton cloth a stripe of red flannel was sewn on the lower edge.

The Bear Flaggers engaged in minor military action with Henry L. Ford as chieftan, but the California Republic lasted only 25 days. Commander John B. Montgomery, commanding the *U. S. S. Portsmouth* at Yerba Buena (San Francisco), maintained a neutral position until the naval forces under Commodore John D. Sloat began the actual conquest by occupying Monterey on July 7. Two days later Lieutenant Joseph Warren Revere of the Navy, a grandson of Paul Revere, lowered the Star and Bear and raised the Stars and Stripes at Sonoma.

Meanwhile, Frémont had organized the California Battalion consisting of Bear Flaggers, members of his scientific exploring expedition, and newly-arrived settlers. This unit was officially sanctioned and contributed to the conquest. The Constitutional Convention held at Monterey in 1849 adopted a form of government providing for statehood. Robert Bayard Semple, a Bear Flagger, presided over the convention meeting in Colton Hall. His contributions were largely in the field of education and he proposed a University of California. Ironically, the principal prisoner of the Bears (or Osos), the affable Mariano G. Vallejo, was likewise a delegate at the convention. Actually, Vallejo had been sympathetic toward Larkin's unrealized plan for the peaceful acquisition of California and now he helped to ease the transition to American rule. The influx of Americans brought in by the gold rush caused discontent with military government. Although California remained theoretically under Mexican law, the first legislature meeting at San José assumed California would soon win statehood. Vallejo also represented the Sonoma district as a senator in the first legislature and several decades later he served as director of the California State Board of Agriculture.

The Vallejo name has always been revered in California. The city of Vallejo and a famous street in San Francisco are named in his honor. According to either legend or fact, depending on one's choice, Mare Island was named by Vallejo when his favorite white mare saved herself from a capsized boat by swimming to the island. In appropriate ceremonies held at the Mare Island Navy Yard on December 16, 1966, 112 years after its establishment, the Polaris nuclear submarine, *U. S. S. Mariano G. Vallejo*, was commissioned.

On September 9, 1850, almost five months after the first California legislature adjourned, President Millard Fillmore signed the bill admitting California to the Union as the 31st state. After the Bear flag had been hauled down from the staff on the Sonoma plaza, it was eventually taken to Boston and Washington, D. C. In 1855, Senator John B. Weller obtained the flag from the Navy Department and it was donated to the Society of California Pioneers in San Francisco. The Pioneers carried the flag in the 1855 Admission Day parade in that city.

The flag once a symbol of independence from Mexico became a symbol of loyalty to the Union, but on the eve of the Civil War, advocates of a Pacific Republic and of secession gave the emblem a different connotation. In the event of war, Congressman John C. Burch of California urged his people and their neighbors to "...*raise aloft the flag of the Bear, surrounded with the hydra-pointed cactus of the western wilds and call upon the enlightened nations of the earth to acknowledge our independence, and to protect us, the only 'waif from the wreck of our once noble union, the youthful but vigorous Caesarian Republic of the Pacific.*"

When the war actually came, California remained loyal to the Union. The Bear Flag continued to be displayed on Admission Days. In 1875 the Native Sons of the Golden West was founded. This organization used the Bear flag in its fraternal and patriotic ceremonies. The original flag was destroyed in the San Francisco earthquake and fire of 1906. On February 3, 1911, Governor Hiram W. Johnson signed the bill making the Bear flag the state emblem of California. Through the years flag manufacturers had varied the design of the bear and other features of the flag. On June 2, 1953, Governor Earl Warren signed a measure standardizing the state flag.

A prime source for any study of the Americanization of California is *A Biographical Sketch of the Life of William B. Ide*, by Simeon Ide. This significant biography was first published by Ide's older brother at Claremont, New Hampshire, in 1880. He also issued a shorter version the same year entitled *Who Conquered California?* Both books were reprinted about two years later, but neither had wide distribution since they were only given to friends and relatives. In 1944 Joseph A. Sullivan published the first book in a limited edition of 500 copies printed by the Grabhorn Press. Today all editions are quite scarce and virtually unobtainable on the rare book market.

Simeon Ide himself is the subject of a biography authored by Louis W. Flanders and published by the Tuttle Company (in 1931) at Rutland, Vermont. It relates that Simeon was born in Shrewsbury, Mass., on September 28, 1794. When 15, he was apprenticed in the shop of the Vermont Republican at Windsor, Vermont. He worked in printing until about four years before his death on June 22, 1889, at Roxbury, Mass.

California and Western bibliophiles, historians and librarians have long appreciated the importance of Simeon Ide's book despite its laudatory account of his brother. It is number 45 of the famed Zamorano list of 80 most significant works relating to California history. In discussing the Bear Flag Revolt, the two major nineteenth century California historians, Hubert H. Bancroft and Theodore H. Hittell, cited Simeon Ide's book in their multi-volume studies. Bancroft called the Ide biographical sketch one of the two best authorities on the details of the march of the Bear Flaggers to Sonoma. In his assessment he stated that the book's first part comprised biographical data with original letters contributed by members of the Ide family. He also mentioned that the first part had "*...a most praiseworthy sketch of the life of a prominent pioneer, containing interesting reminiscences of the overland trip by Ide's daughter, Mrs. Healey.*" Bancroft unfairly appraised the second part, a description of the Revolt, as "*...of no value whatever...*", since Simeon Ide was unable to acquire *"accurate information"*. Moreover, Bancroft asserted that Ide's proof readers in California *"...were not well qualified for the task."* For the third part of the book, William Ide's letter to Senator M. M. "Wambough", Bancroft had both praise and criticism, but alluded to it *"...by far the most important part of the work."*

In his chapter on the "Bear Flag Revolution", Hittel listed nine footnotes, eight of which cited the Life of. Ide. Although he probably used other sources, Hittell relied largely upon the biographical sketch. Professor Josiah Royce, the Harvard philosopher, in his *California* (Boston, 1886) mentioned that he first consulted a copy of the biographical sketch in Bancroft's library. Although he was anti-Bear and anti-Ide, Royce added in a footnote, *'...I have since bought a copy of this still uncommon book, which surely deserves a wide circulation"*

Among early twentieth century California historians who consulted Simeon Ide's book as a source were Cardinal Goodwin, Robert G. Cleland and Zoeth S. Eldredge. Only two biographical studies of Ide have since been written. In 1935 a small pamphlet entitled, *William B. Ide: The President of California,* by George Kirov was published by the California Senate. In 1962 an excellent critical biography of 101 pages, *William Brown Ide: Bear Flagger,* was authored by Fred B. Rogers. The recognized authority on the Bear Flag incident is John A. Hussey of the National Park Service, who has authored several scholarly articles on the subject. In 1941 Hussey had completed a superior doctoral thesis, *The United States and the Bear Flag Revolt,* at the University of California under the direction of the expert on the Spanish Borderlands, Herbert Eugene Bolton.

By the terms of the Treaty of Guadalupe Hidalgo of February 2, 1848, Mexico ceded the territory of New Mexico and Upper California to the United States for a payment of $15,000,000.00. Mexico also accepted the boundary line of the Rio Grande, which the Texans had gained after the Battle of San Jacinto. Like the Lone Star flag of the Republic of Texas, the star painted on the Bear flag symbolized the American spirit of Manifest Destiny envisaging continental unity.

Besides written records several California registered historical landmarks remind us today of the life of William B. Ide and the Bear Flag Revolt. These include the Bear Flag Monument and Vallejo Home at Sonoma, the William Ide Adobe near Red Bluff, and the marker at Frémont (Gavilan, Gabilan, or Hawk's Peak.) It is most gratifying that The Rio

Grande Press has reprinted in an exquisite edition and made available again an important classic about the Bear Flag Revolt of 1846.

Benjamin F. Gilbert

Benjamin Franklin Gilbert, Ph. D.
Professor of History
San José State College

San José, California
October, 1967

A

BIOGRAPHICAL SKETCH

OF

THE LIFE OF WILLIAM B. IDE:

WITH

A MINUTE AND INTERESTING ACCOUNT OF ONE OF THE LARG-
EST EMIGRATING COMPANIES, (3000 MILES OVER LAND),
FROM THE EAST TO THE PACIFIC COAST.

AND

WHAT IS CLAIMED AS THE MOST AUTHENTIC AND RELIABLE
ACCOUNT OF "THE VIRTUAL CONQUEST OF CALI-
FORNIA, IN JUNE, 1846, BY THE BEAR
FLAG PARTY," AS GIVEN BY
ITS LEADER,

THE LATE HON. WILLIAM BROWN IDE.

PREFACE.

WHEN the present writer, at the request of the surviving children of the subject of the following memorial pages, commenced the work assigned him, it was not expected that sufficient material suited to its publication, in BOOK-FORM, could be found. Indeed, the original arrangement with his employers contemplated his compiling and putting in type some fifty pages—then strike off from his proof-press a few copies, and send such proof-slips, only, to them. Under this arrangement he proceeded with the work until, some 70 or 80 pages of it were in type, and impressions from it were thus sent; when, for various reasons, his labors, (mechanical and otherwise) on it were suspended for the greater part of a year. The principal cause of this suspension, however, was, that at that stage of his progress the WAMBOUGH LETTER *then* first came to light, the contents of which put a new phase on the manner of further proceedings. Whether or no it was " written for the press", is unknown, as even its existence was before unknown to any of the living members of its writer's family or their kindred. Its perusal prompted them to make liberal subscriptions towards the expense of a small edition of this book.

The contents of this Letter unravels and explains to them the mystery : *why*, or *how* it has happened, that the devoted, self-sacrificing, patriotic labors of Judge IDE remained so long unknown to them and the reading public generally. Yet so it is. Thousands of our best citizens go down to their last resting-place "unheralded and unsung", who, in their humble sphere of labor, have become real "benefactors of their race", by living sober, honest and industrious lives. Therefore, say we, in the words of WEBSTER's favorite poet:

> " Let not AMBITION mock their useful toil—
> Their homely joys and destiny obscure ;
> Nor GRANDEUR hear, with a disdainful smile,
> The short and simple annals of the poor."

CONTENTS.

A BIOGRAPHICAL SKETCH OF THE LIFE OF WM. B. IDE.

———•———

CHAPTER I.

WILLIAM BROWN IDE was born in the town of Rutland, Worcester Co., Mass., March 28, 1796. His ancestry, as far back as tradition has reliably traced it on his father's side, emigrated to this country soon after the landing of the *Mag-Flower* at Plymouth—about the year 1620. The theory has been handed down in one branch of this Ide-family to the present day, that about the year 1630, two brothers, *Josiah* and *Daniel Ide*, came to this country from England, settled in Rehoboth, Mass., and that the subject of this memoir is a descendant of one of those brothers. A son of one of them, (*Daniel*, it is stated), was engaged as an officer in the noted *King Phillip* war, and took from that Indian chief a small tin cup, which has been handed down as an heir-loom in the several succeeding generations of his family to the year 1874 ; when Mrs. EUNICE IDE, widow of the late Daniel Ide of Croydon, N. H., deposited it, accompanied with an account of its history, in the archives of the New Hampshire Historical Society.

The present writer refers to the subject of lineage or descent, in this connection, more particularly on account of the fact, that we have grounds for claiming those two enterprising emigrants above named (who, about 240 years ago, when New England was, comparatively, a wilderness, planted themselves as farmers on the then productive soil of the ' old Bay State') as the progenitors of the entire race of the name of *Ide* in this country. There is reason to believe that no one of this name, now inhabiting this ' land of the Free and home of the Brave', can produce a well authenticated line of descent from *any other ancestry*, since the landing of the " pilgrims" in the " May-Flower" in 1620, than from one or the other of these two brothers.*

---

* During the past 12 or 15 years, (the Editor is informed), a genealogically inclined member of this Ide-family has made it a point of inquiry, by letter, of all persons bearing this name, whose address he was able to obtain : " To what part of this country do you trace the first landing of your

We have wandered somewhat from the subject in hand, presuming that if these memoirs
should fall into the hands of any considerable
number of this "race" or progeny of those two
" emigrants," it might be interesting to those
of them who are much given to genealogical
research: (and who, of the present generation,
will rise up and say to any of his *kindred*, however distant his relationship, " *I am not*" *?*)—
But to proceed with the genealogy of WILLIAM
B. IDE :

His grandfather, DANIEL IDE, is understood,
by a careful study of chronological incidents,
to be a descendant of one of the "two broth-

ancestry, on your father's side ?" or in terms of that import.
The answers to this inquiry—numbering some dozen or so—
refer to Massachusetts or Rhode Island, and the greater part
to Providence or Rehoboth. And furthermore : it is pretty
evident that the race has not been a very prolific one—for
the same genealogical interviewer says that in the fall of
1874 he found but two persons of the name in the New York
city Directory—and, in 1877, but six in the Boston Directory ; and one of these whom he called on said he was "the
head-man" of the other five: and this " Interviewer" infers
from these statistics, and from his long and extensive acquaintance with business-men in different parts of the country, that "all persons of this name, now living in the United
States, are descendants of the two emigrants, Josiah and
Daniel Ide."

ers" before referred to. He spent his days in
Rehoboth—had three sons and two daughters.
His first son's name was Simeon, his second,
William, and his third, Lemuel. The two first
died early : Simeon married Hannah Kollock,
by whom he had one daughter, Abigail K.,
born April 19, 1789 ; and one son, Daniel, born
Dec. 19, 1791—both of whom died unmarried ;
their father in 1793, their mother in 1792.

LEMUEL IDE, the father of William B., was
born in Rehoboth, R. I., July 22, 1770—died
at Newfane, Vt., Sept. 18, 1825. He was bred
to the joiner and carpenter's trade, which occupation, in connection with that of farming
on a small scale, he followed for a livelihood
during his after life. He resided a short time
in Shrewsbury, Mass., after commencing house-
keeping, soon after his marriage in 1793. In
'95 he removed to Rutland, Mass. ; and from
there to Clarendon, Vt., in '98, where his twin
daughters, Sarah and Mary F. where born, and
where his eldest sister, Mary, who married Zi-
ba French, Esq., tavern-keeper, and lived with
him there some forty years—and, after his decease, with her children, to the advanced age
of about 85.—From Clarendon, in '99, he removed to Reading, Vt. ; left his wife and three

of their children with her brother Zenas Stone, (his second son, Wm. B., then in his 4th year, having been, at least temporarily, *adopted* by the Rev. ISAAC BEALS, the first settled minister in C., with whom he lived till about 1805.) Having heard of his brother William's death at his residence in one of the Southern States, (S. C., we think) Mr. Ide proceeded there by water conveyance to look after and take care of the small estate left by him, and was gone about one year. Soon after his return he took a small tenement of two rooms of Isaac Baldwin, near the south line of Reading, in the town of Cavendish, Vt., and applying himself to his trade, he began to lay by a part of his earnings ; and, in 1803–4, being assisted by a friend, he bought a 20-acre lot, having a mere *hovel* for a *house* upon it. Having now before him the prospect of being able to provide for the support of his family, his son Wm. B. was returned from the kind care and protection of the Rev. Mr. BEALS, to that of his parents, and remained with them till " of age." His father, however, continued to rove from place to place, despite the apothegm that " A rolling stone gathers no moss"—owning, as he did in after life, one after another, three different farms

in Reading, two in New Ipswich, N. H., and
a few acres of land, with a gristmill thereon,
in Newfane, Vt.—He possessed an active, in-
quiring mind—was much given to reading and
the discussion of the political party issues of
that day ; and, in 1809, was elected by the
Republican party to represent the town of
Reading in the Legislature of Vermont ; and
lacked but one vote of a re-election the following year. He was not an " open professor
of religion" ; but his " life and conversation"
gave satisfactory evidence ·to his " professing"
friends, that he *was*· a " believer" in the es-
sentials of practical religion. As indicative
of a prominent trait of his *moral* character,
his son William B. caused the inscription :

" An Honest Man 's the noblest work of GOD,"

to be engraved on his tomb-stone.

To continue on in this genealogical line :
The writer is in possession of data going no father back, on William B. Ide's mother's paternal side, than the birth-day of his great-grand-
father, Lieut. ISAAC STONE, which was on the
3d of September, 1697, in Framingham, Mass.
He married ELIZABETH BROWN* of Sudbury,

---

* The initial letter (B), in Wm. B. Ide's name, was in hon-
or of this great-grandmother.

July 24, 1722—settled in Shrewsbury, Mass., in 1727, and was a member of the *first* board of selectmen of that town. He died April 22, 1776, aged 78 years, 8 months. His widow lived to the great age of 96, and died in 1794 ; the same year that one of her great-grandsons now (1880) living, (a brother of Wm. B.) was born—thus showing, in this instance, the lives of two individuals extending through five and a half generations, or the average age of mankind, as computed by statisticians of the present day.

Mr. IDE'S grandfather, JASPER STONE, was born in Shrewsbury, April 30, 1728. He married GRACE GODDARD, daughter of Dea. Benjamin Goddard, April 17, 1755. He owned and lived on a farm of about 250 acres, in the south-westwardly part of that town, on which one of the first two-story framed dwelling-houses built in that town now stands in good order—which farm is now owned and occupied by a grandson of him who bought and cleared it over a hundred and twenty years ago, and lived on it all the days of his wedded life. He died Oct. 20, 1802, aged 74 years and 6 mos. —his widow, Oct. 31, 1815, aged 80.

We have but little more to add in this an-

cestral line.   The mother of William B. Ide,
Sarah, daughter of Jasper and Grace Stone,
was born Oct. 16, 1767,—married Nov. 24,
1793,—died at the residence of her oldest son,
in Claremont, N. H., January 4, 1859, aged 91
years, 2 mos., 19 days.   Mrs. Ide was a pattern
of industry and economy, in the management
of her domestic affairs.   Her early days were
spent happily, and in comparative ease under
the paternal roof ; yet she was not exempt from
the common lot of the daughters of farmers
of those primitive times.   Household duties—
the hum of the spinning-wheels, and the rat-
tle of " the weaver's shuttle," afforded the
kind of *instrumental* music that was the most
familiar, if not the most charming, to her ear.
But all along through the lapse of twenty subsequent years, the rearing of seven children (one
dying in its infancy) she had an unusual share
of a mother's cares, anxieties and labors to con-
front her, till her children were all comfortably
settled in the married state.   She spent the
last thirty-three-or-four years of her useful life
among her dutiful children, in comparative
ease and comfort—and, at the close of a long
and well-spent life, departed in the enjoyment
of a well-grounded hope of a happy re-union

with them in the New Jerusalem—whither two of her daughters, and one of her sons, besides the subject of this memoir, had " gone before." Her only surviving daughter informs me, that in her 91st year, she read her Bible through twice, without the use of glasses—was for some forty years an exemplary and pious member of the Baptist church.

The writer has thought the preceding sketch in relation to the birth, residence, etc., of such portion of Mr. IDE's ancestry as he could find the material for, would be interesting and instructive,—if not to the present generation, yet to the generations that will succeed it.— His ancestry on both parental sides were of the humbler walks of life—dependant on their daily labors for their "daily bread." On his mother's side, so far back as we have gone in these researches, they were a benevolent and pious people, " zealous in every good word and work."

CHAPTER II.

SOME FEW INCIDENTS OF MR. IDE'S SOJOURN IN THE STATES
OF VERMONT, KENTUCKY, OHIO AND ILLINOIS.

WILLIMA B. IDE worked at the carpenter
and joiner's trade with his father a greater part
of the time till of age.   His "schooling" privileges were limited to the common schools of
those days, which were seldom kept in the several districts where he lived more than two
months, each season, summer and winter.   In
1819 he built a dwelling-house for his brother
SIMEON, in Windsor, Vt. ; and afterwards followed building operations in Winchendon and
Keene, N. H., and Newfane and Woodstock,
Vt., to the year 1833.

At an accidental interview with President
HAYES' uncle Burchard of Fayetteville, Newfane, in 1876, the old gentleman, who is quite
deaf, inquired of the writer about " one William B. Ide"—said he knew him well some 50
years ago—that he built the house in which he
(Mr. B.) then lived : and he assured me that
Mr. Ide was a good and thorough workman—

that although his house had stood the test of
the Vermont climate, exposed to rapid changes
of wet and dry, heat and cold, for so long a
time, it was then "about as good as new."

April 17, 1820, Mr. IDE and Miss SUSAN G.
HASKELL were married by her uncle Grout, at
his house in Northborough, Mass., and not by
the Rev. Joseph Sumner, D. D., pastor of the
first Congregational church in Shrewsbury for
about sixty years, as stated in "Ward's History of Shrewsbury," (from which the writer has
gathered several other "items," in his progress
thus far), and the fact that "Their mothers
were daughters of (their grandfather), Deacon
Jasper Stone."

Although he had had full employment at his
trade in Vermont, yet Mr. IDE's adventurous
turn of mind, (which he came honestly by)
made him a "victim" of the then prevailing
"Western Fever." His first objective point
was Canton, in Kentucky ; whither, in June,
1833, he directed his steps—and where, with
his young family, (a wife and six children,) he
remained about three months ; then removed
to Madison, Montgomery Co., eight miles from
Dayton, Ohio, in 1834—and, in 1839, he removed to Jacksonville, Illinois.

During several months residence at Madison his health did not permit his working at his trade, except occasionally in the warmer seasons; and he spent most of the winter months as a teacher in the district schools. And we will here give an extract from one of his letters to his mother, then living with her eldest son at Windsor, Vt., dated "Madison, Ohio, Feb. 23, 1835," which will show something of the troubles attending the pioneers of the new settlements of our country:

"And now, my dear Mother, I will, in answer to your request to SUSAN, (for she seldom gets time to write), proceed to give you some account of our little ones: and I will begin with the eldest. James M. is, as you know, pretty well advanced in his 13th year; and it is time to begin to expect some small development of *mind*. He is still very small of stature—not above the size of most boys of 9 or 10 years old.

"When I first arrived in Ohio, and commenced teaching, James was sick; and I was scarcely able to walk. I could not look after and take care of my children at school—was frequently under the necessity of being carried home. So the first quarter James attended only about 25 days. As I was about attending my second quarter, James had the misfortune to inflict a severe wound upon the ancle of his left leg. The accident occurred as follows: I had just put a handle to, and ground very thin and sharp, an axe for my own use, and laid it

on a high shelf—saying to Susan, at the same time, that
I was going to a raising about a mile off, and that the
boys were not to meddle with this axe, as I had made
it very sharp.   Scarcely had I left the house, when
James came in, and began to climb up the logs of the
house to get the axe.   His mother told him he must not
have it; but James answered: ' Why, marm ? father
allows *me* to use it.'   So, like a *good, easy* mother, she
said no more, and James went out into the orchard to
chop some dead peach trees.

"Directly Susan heard some one hollering; but as
the girls and William were playing about the house,
and making much noise, she thought no harm; when,
a little while after, she discovered that James had cut
his ancle, and was bleeding very fast—the axe having
entered nearly half of the blade, severing some of the
leaders of the toes, and opening one of the arteries.—
His mother finding him in this situation, held the wound
together, while William ran after me.   Understanding
about the case by William, I sent a man for a surgeon,
and then hastened home.   But recollecting that the
man had seven miles to go, and that the road was ex-
tremely bad at that time—and the wound continuing
to bleed, it was evident he could not survive the loss of
blood that must be occasioned by waiting for the surgeon.   *   *   *   I went immediately about dressing it.
I tied up the blood-vessels, then sewed the parts together.   James fainted, and afterwards became very sick;
but soon began to recover.

"In the evening the said man returned without the
doctor.   In about 8 or 10 days James began to sit up
on his couch—and by the first of June (2 months after)

was able to hobble to school; since which time he has
been very steadily. He is a very excellent reader—
understands the English very well—has studied his ge-
ography once through—has gone through Adams' New
Arithmetic, and is now engaged in defining some of the
more intricate words in the English language.

"William had about the like opportunity, but has not
improved so well. He is some larger than James, and
stout. He is not much troubled by *care* of any kind.

Mary is a good girl; helps her mother a good deal;
reads and spells well; studies grammar and makes her
own clothes, pretty much: is as tall as James, and generally stands at the head of the first class, of late; since
each scholar has to *define,* as well as spell the word.

"Sarah is the baby, and is therefore her *father's* dear
child; and, *therefore,* I will say but little about her—
only that she reads with *Mary,* and thinks she can do
any thing as well as *she* does!"

The foregoing extracts from one of the numerous letters of WILLIAM B. IDE to his " Beloved Mother", (as he uniformly addressed her)
which are in the writer's possession, are introduced here, as evidence of his wonderful sagacity and presence of mind in a trying emergency; and we shall have occasion, in our succeeding pages, to notice many more noteworthy instances of this rare inate endowment. And it
will show that parents may *learn* their children, at the tender age of eight or nine years,
how to " *help their mother a good deal,*" and

to "*make their own clothes, pretty much*"— while, at the same time, they "generally stand at the head of the first class."

We give extracts from another of his letters, dated "Madison, O., Sept. 13, 1835," to show the filial affection with which he ever regarded his parents.

"I have a little plan of operations which I will communicate to you. If it succeeds, it will unite again the largest half of my Father's family, in or near one village.—I have now in my trunk my Father's letter of advice, written Feb. 20, 1817, [39 days before William became of age], which I have often read with renewed interest, since I have lived in the great valley of the Mississippi. Though it may be true that I have not been able to find a country exactly, in all things, to answer the " picture of my youthful fancy," yet I have by far " bettered myself;" and my Father's injunction was, (after having done so) " next to seek to better my friends of my Father's house." I have sought so to do. Here is a wide field for industry and usefulness; and although you, dear Mother, may be too old for much labor, yet your presence will cheer the hearts and enliven the countenances of those that can labor. Think it not too much: I have commenced this letter expressly to persuade you to come and live with me. I have a plenty. We are not now in Vermont, eating flour at eight dollars per barrel, and corn at one dollar a bushel. Yet the price of labor is not diminished—nor am I beset, on either hand, by duns and unpaid accounts—by

notes over-due, while I have little or no cash to spare
I do not now anticipate the errand of every stranger
who approaches me to be the collection of some note
he has bought against me. But now, when I see an un-
expected neighbor or stranger coming, I begin to anticipate—he comes to ask a favor, not to claim justice—
he comes to borrow money, or to pay what he owes—
to solicit conditions, not to enforce them.

"Yet, blessed as I am in worldly matters, I do not
feel entirely independent. No! the few streaks of ad-
versity that have come over me since I saw you, dear
Mother, I trust have had their due effect. I do not now
argue against the cause of CHRIST, or preach Universal-
ism. No: I have seen something of the value of
Christian submission and of Christian example and influence among men. * * * But I have little or no
Christian fortitude to boast of. I feel that my obligations are great; and had it not been for the miss-spent
opportunities of my youth, and for that unwillingness
of mine to rely on the Spirit of CHRIST for aid, I might
have been greatly useful in the sphere of my acquaintance to the cause of humanity and truth. The past is
gone!"

While living in Ohio and Illinois, from the
year 1834 to '44, while his health would permit, Mr. IDE worked at his trade a considerable part of the spring, summer and fall months,
—when not engaged in farming operations—
and taught in the district schools a portion of
the winter months.

His only surviving daughter, Mrs. SARAH E. HEALY, represents his farm in Madison, Ohio, as "a very good one—having good buildings, being well fenced, and under a good state of cultivation : he paid a part down for it, and the balance in less than two years, which we made off the farm—Father and brothers (as well as the rest of the family who were old enough) all working ; for we did not hire any help, and were soon out of debt. This was a comfortable and pleasant home, with kind and intelligent neighbors.

" In the fall of 1838 Father sold that farm, with the intention of removing to Missouri. In October we started on our journey thither, with two wagons comfortably fitted up. The weather was changeable—sometimes cold and rainy, and the roads very bad. As nearly as I can remember, we spent about four weeks traveling to Jacksonville, Ill. We spent the winter there—father working at his trade. In February, 1839, he moved onto the farm near Springfield, Ill."

Mrs. Healy, in her note to the writer from which the above is taken, says her Father held no public offices in Ohio or Illinois, " but took great interest in politics ; and, while in Madison, O., he wrote a great many articles of agreement for his neighbors, and was often consulted by them on occasions of disputes occurring between them, about rights to land and division-lines, and other missunderstandings. Even our Justice of the Peace consulted him a good deal"—thus acting, as a genial and mutual friend, without fee or reward, as a "peacemaker" among them.

The year 1845 was a more eventful one than any that had preceded it in his checkered life hitherto. During his stay in Kentucky, Ohio and Illinois he had not added largely to the means he took with him on leaving New England. His active spirit did not brook the tedious process of farming which he had resorted to in those States, to make provision for the support of his family in his declining years. He had not realized the fond hopes inspired by the glowing newspaper accounts of "*the West.*" And he had heard of a still more promising field of enterprise in the far off—still farther off "land of promise"—and thither he concluded to direct his steps. And, notwithstanding the hardships, difficulties and loss of property attending the adventure, we have the authority of his daughter for stating, that if he could

have foreseen them all, it would not have de-
tered him from making it : for, says Mrs. H.,
in a note to the writer : " My Father was not
sorry, but proud of being among the first to
open the way here."*

In the winter of '44-5, MR. IDE made ample
preparation for his advent into the Pacific sol-
itudes, by the purchase of a large and well-as-
sorted herd of cattle,—a competent outfit (as
he supposed) of provisions and other necessaries, for a six-months tour ; with his wife and
five children, and the necessary assistants, to
accompany him—Oregon being then his objective point.

* Mrs. HEALY now resides in Santa Cruz, Cal.

CHAPTER III.

MRS. HEALY'S ACCOUNT OF THEIR JOURNEY FROM ILLINOIS,
THROUGH MISSOURI, KANSAS, NEBRASKA, DECOTA, IDAHO,
UTAH AND NEVADA, (AS NOW ORGANIZED), TO THE SIER-
ERRA NEVADA MOUNTAINS.

THE writer is indebted to a brother of Mr.
IDE for many of the incidents of his life narrated, thus far, in this memoir. He will now
avail himself of the kind assistance of Mrs.
HEALY, to whom he applied for a detailed account of their journey from Illinois to California, in 1845. At that date Mrs. H. was in her
18th year. She depends on her memory chiefly
for the minute circumstances she relates ; and
I believe it is generally understood that at the
age of fifty years and upwards we remember
the pominent, exciting events of youth—say,
between our 6th and 18th year—more distinctly than we do those that occured at a later
period of our lives. We give the greater part
of Mrs. H.'s narrative in her own words :
"In 1838 my Father sold his farm in Ohio,
and moved to Jacksonville, Ill. We lived there
but one winter. In the spring of 1839 he mov-

ed onto his farm eight miles east of Springfield, where we resided until 1844. In the fall
of that year he sold his farm, and removed
his family into uncle Harrison's house, where
we lived till April 1, 1845. On that day we
bid our good friends farewell. It was a sad
day to us. All our old neighbors came to help
us pack our things into our three wagons, and
to see us off. My Father selected the timber
for two of these wagons, and had them made
to order during the winter. He also made the
beds, bows and covers at our home—Mother
and I sewing the canvas covering; which, being fastened to the bows and side-boards of
the wagons, were painted a light slate-color,
the same as the bed or body of the wagon.

"Our wagons were very neat looking, and
attracted a good deal of attention while passing through Illinois and Missouri. Many questions were asked as to our destination, &c.

"We had a sale the morning we started, and
sold off the greater part of our furniture. We
packed our cooking utensils, tin cups, tin plates
—with provisions to last us six months. Mother, my little brothers—Daniel, aged 10, and
Lemuel, aged 8, and Thomas Crafton, (a little
boy that had heen given to my Mother), all

rode in a wagon. I rode on horseback 3 days,
to help drive the cattle; riding on a side-saddle.
The drove of cattle numbered 165, including
28 working oxen. We camped the first night
10 miles from our old home—cooked our sup-
per by a camp-fire.   Mother and I slept in a
wagon all the way to California.   Some of the
men slept in the tent, when not too tired to
pitch it.   Brother William came with us and
drove an ox team from Fort Hall to Sutter's
Fort, and drove cattle the rest of the journey.
Our number, all told, young and old, was thirteen—five of these were young men, who drove
the teams " for their board and passage."

    " The journey to Independence, Mo., was
accomplished in four weeks, without any severe
accident, but was attended with great care and
anxiety to my dear parents.   I remember my
brother James, (then in his 24th year) was
away from us buying cows, and was gone so
long, that it caused them great anxiety.   He
had been taken suddenly with bleeding from
the nose or lungs, among strangers, and his
health was so much impaired, that he could
not for some time afterwards help take care of
the stock, or of himself.   We were thankful
that his life was spared.

" We camped one week within one mile of
Independence, Mo., to lay in ammunition, guns
and pistols—clothing for the men, and many
little things needful on so long a journey.—
Father made an iron to brand his cows with
his name (IDE) on the right-side horn.   This
was hard work for him, but very necessary.

" On the 10th of May we left Independence
and traveled to the 'Big Camp', where we spent
a week or two,"—organizing, it would seem, a
large company of emigrants to the far West,
(in accordance with their previously concerted
plan) consisting of 100 wagons, and the necessary team-cattle, horses and other appliances.
They chose a Mr. Meek, a Mountaineer, Pilot.
This large company, Mrs. Healy thinks, was
sub-divided into "three bands", who chose
a "captain over the three"—whose name she
does not remember ; but recollects he rode
ahead of the entire train—had a fine team of
grey horses, which was driven by a Mr. Buck-
ley.   She remembers the names of others in
the train, viz : Capt. James Taylor and Capt.
—— Smith.   She says " The companies took
turns traveling in advance, so that each might
have the privilege of being out of the dust
one week out of every three.

"A company or firm styled 'J. Smith, Risley & Taylor,' owned and drove a large herd of cattle to Oregon. My Father started to go to Oregon, and 'OREGON' was painted in large black letters on the back curtain of our hindmost wagon.

"The cattle of this large emigrant company was so numerous that it was difficult to find grass for them ; and it was a great deal of work to control them—also *dangerous*. After several weeks it was given up, and a 'cattleguard' organized. My Father was captain of this 'guard', and chief herdsman. Any one losing an ox or cow came to him at once, and he would send a man or go himself in search of the lost,—after supplying an ox, if an ox of a team were missing—so that the train could move on ; for it was moving so *slow*, it was necessary for us to *keep moving*.

"At one time when Father remained behind to look after the missing cattle, the report came to the company, that he was last seen surrounded by Indians. The train halted quite a while : but Mother and I did not know why; all being careful not to cause *us* alarm. A number of men went back, who met him coming in, driving the missing cattle. They said

Father saw an Indian partly hid in grass and willows, with arrow on bow, ready to shoot him : on which he raised his gun and took aim at the Indian, who immediately took to his heels and ran. No doubt, they said, if Father had been frightened, and had started to run, he would have been killed ; for there were several Indians seen in the bushes near him. This oc-cured on or near the banks of the Humblold River, I think.

"We traveled in one of the three companies having a camp-guard—a captain and sergeant on guard every night—until within a few days travel of Fort Hall. Then there was a general stampede, to see who would get to the Fort first. We found a good camping ground there, and also Indians to trade horses with. One of-fered a very pretty poney for two calico dress-es. Here was a company of mountaineer trap-pers, enroute for California, who told us of a good route, and plenty of good grass.

"While there Father changed his plan—con-cluded to go to California : but first, before definitely settling the question, put it to vote of his company, and they voted for California instead of Oregon.

"A party of young men concluded to '*pack*

through;' that is, to go on horseback—pack
themselves and their baggage on horses. This
party consisted of Messrs. Knight, R. C. Keyes,
Jacob R. Snyder, —— Lewis, William Black-
burn, George McDougal, and several others,
whose names I have forgotten.

" A few days travel, west from Fort Hall,
brought us to where we bade our Oregon friends
good-by. I was sorry to part with those with
whom we had become acquainted. It reduced
our company so much, that we all felt lonely
for some time. I believe I can remember the
names of nearly all the men of our *small* party who had families. These were Messrs. E.
Skinner, J. Elliot, Rolett, Keeny, M. Griffith,
Grigsby, Scott, Bonner, Potter, Seeres, An-
derson, Thomas, Meeres, Davis, Tustin and
Buffin. All these men took their families with
them. There may have been one or two more
who had no children with them.

" The names of those without families I re-
member, as follows : William Cooper, Wm.
Todd, Scott, B. Grant, Beal, Old Harry, Wm.
Swasey and Wilmot. Our Pilot's name was
' Old Greenwood';* and his son John, (whose

* " This old man", says Mrs. HEALY, "died in California,
in the mines, somewhere near Orville. I heard a report that

mother was a Crow Indian). They were mountain men, and dressed the same as Indians.

"After we started for California, the Pilot
said there was no longer any danger from the
Indians, and our company began to scatter. I
remember one night in particular, my Father,
with one other family, camped alone, with no
other guard than a faithful watch-dog we were
so fortunate as to bring with us from our old
home in Sangumon county, Ill. This dog would
not allow an Indian to come near the camp.—
None of our company were killed by the Indians ; but John Greenwood, son of the Pilot,
shot down an Indian by the road-side, and afterwards boasted of it.

"Thus far there were no very steep mountains climbed. The course we traveled was
through passes between high mountains, or up
gradual ascents on long spurrs, until after
passing the 40-miles descent, and crossing the
Truckee River *thirty-two times*, we came to

he insisted on lying out of doors, with his rifle by his side,
and would not allow even a tent over his body to obscure
the sky—threatening to shoot the man who should attempt
to put a shelter over him. And thus he died, out of doors,
more than 18 years since. I was more afraid of these two
men than of the wild Indians."

Truckee Lake : then, after traveling along the
Lake—some of the way being obliged to drive
our wagon on the edge of the Lake ; some of
the time the water coming almost up to our
feet—keeping the women in constant dread of
being drowned. It was a fearful time for the
timid female passengers, both young and old.
At night we camped at the foot of the rocky
mountain—the Sierra Nevada ; and were told
by the Pilot that we would have to take our
wagons to pieces, and haul them up with ropes.
Father proposed to build a bridge, or a sort of
inclined railroad up the steep ascent, and over
the rocks ; but few of his companions would
listen to any such scheme.   So he went to
work with the men and fixed the road."

[Here we substitute for the daughter's account of this most difficult of the many trying
emergencies with which Mr. IDE and his associates were confronted, during their six or sev-
en months pilgrimage to the "promised land,"
what the writer recollects to have been told
about it by Mr. IDE, on his first visit to his relatives in N. E., after his settlement in California.]

CHAPTER IV.

THEIR TEDIOUS "ASCENT OVER THE NEVADA MOUNTAIN—DE-
SCENT INTO THE AMERICAN RIVER VALLEY, AND ENCAMP-
MENT NEAR FORT SUTTER.

ABOUT the year 1849 we had an interview
with Mr. IDE, in which he gave us an account
of his "trip over-land" to California, in 1845.
He did not go minutely into detail, but dwelt
more particularly on the manner in which he
ascended the Nevada Mountain ; as that performance was the most laborious and difficult
of the many difficulties they had to encounter.
And not the least of these difficulties was the
task of convincing the men with him that his
plan of operations to accomplish the hard task
then in prospect was practicable. Their guide
had told them the only way was, to "take the
wagons to pieces, and haul them up with
ropes !" Our Yankee adventurer thought he
would find and try a better way. He took a
survey of the premises, on foot—climbing up
the rugged "cliffs of the rocks" till he reached the plane above, and finally concluded there
was a "better way."

Mr. IDE found on the line of the ascent several abrupt pitches, between which there were comparative level spaces, for several rods dis-tace, where the team might stand to draw up at least an empty wagon. Accordingly, he went to work, with as many of the men as he could induce, by mild means, to assist him—removing rocks, trees, &c., and grading a path 6 or 7 feet wide, up the several steep pitches and levels to the summit. The next thing for them to do, was to get a team of 5 or 6 yoke of cattle up onto the first inclined grade or se-mi level. This was a tedious process. The first pitch was longer and more abrupt than any of the others. I think Mr. IDE told me they had to take one ox at a time, and by the help of men, with ropes assist him up the first steep grade. After having, by this process, their ox-team of 5 or 6 yoke in order, on the first "level," (as we call it) they then, by the use of ropes and chains, attach a wagon to it, haul it up one "hitch," then block the wheels, "back" the team, take another hitch and another start forward,—and they thus continue the operation till the wagon is 'on the first "inclined grade." It was then, by a similar, but less tedious process, drawn up over the re-

THE LIFE OF WILLIAM B. IDE.

maining steppes or " pitches," to the level plain
above—and the same operation wa§ repeated
with all their wagons. And at the close of
the second day after their arrival at the foot of
Sierra Nevada, these then well educated moun-
taineers found their entire retinue of wagons,
" goods and chattels" safely landed at the sum-
mit-level. Mr. IDE told me these were the two
hardest days' labor he experienced, for himself,
men, women and children (and cattle, even), of
the train, during the entire journey. Nothing
short of *Yankee pluck* could have conceived
and have accomplished such an undertaking.

We will add Mrs. HEALY's version of a little
more she remembers about this enterprise :

" It took us a long time to go about 2 miles
over our rough, new-made road up the mountain, over the rough rocks, in some places, and
so smooth in others, that the oxen would slip
and fall on their knees ; the blood from their
feet and knees staining the rocks they passed
over. Mother and I walked, (we were so sorry for the poor, faithful oxen), all those two
miles—all our clothing being packed on the
horses' backs. It was a trying time—the men
swearing at their teams, and beating them
most cruelly, all along that rugged way.

"Not long after this we met a pack-train on
their way to some fort. They told us that the
Spaniards would take us all prisoners as soon
as we should arrive in California, and that all
the Americans who then were there were ordered to leave, or they would be imprisoned.

"Some of our company wanted to stop and
build a fort, and spend the winter there; but
on further consideration it was thought better
to risk the Spaniards, than to be shut up in the
midst of those high mountains to starve. So
we hastened on our way, losing no time to
meet our fate, be it what it might.

"We camped one night on a level place near
a lake of very clear water; also very deep.
During the night we were startled by a loud
report that shook the ground under us like a
heavy clap of thunder. We were terribly
frightened. It 'proved to be an explosion of
gun-powder—a keg or can of it in one of the
the wagons, which it set on fire. At the time
it was supposed to have been accidentally set
on fire; but afterwards circumstances led to
the conclusion, that the man having charge of
the wagon set it on fire, with the object in view
of getting possession of a sum of money in a
trunk, the owner of which having gone to Cali-

fornia with the company that 'packed' from
Fort Hall.

"In driving down into ' Steep Hollow,' the
men cut down small trees to tie to the hind
end of each wagon, to keep it from turning over or slewing, and also to hold it back. In at-
tempting to ride my poney down, the saddle
came off over her head. She was so gentle as
to stop for me to alight, and lead her the rest
of the way down.

"We camped one night in ' Steep Hollow.'
Our best milch-cow died the next morning.
We did all we could to doctor her. We supposed she was poisoned by eating laurel leaves
—grass being so scarce.

"Traveling though the Sierra Nevadas, up
hill and down ; fording streams in the small
valleys, with muddy bottoms, and small rivers,
with large boulder rocks at the bottom ; so
large as to almost upset the wagon ; driving
over rocky roads—all this, though it might be
considered *healthy* exercise, was somewhat fa-
tigueing : and our Pilot wanted to stop a day
or two to rest ; but Father did not think it
best to, and drove on.

"The next morning we continued our march
without a pilot ; and, after traveling all day,

we camped, as usual, for the night. Soon after
getting quietly at rest, our Pilot came up, and,
swearing as he came, said he was not responsible for our 'driving into a Cañon *that we
could not get out of!*' My Father seemed perfectly cool—said scarcely a word, for he knew
that he was right. While Greenwood was
scolding, I saw the stump of a small tree that
was cut down the year before, which showèd
that we were camped on a road made last year
—so all that needless alarm was soon ended.

" Somewhere near the summit we came to a
place where a company of ten or twelve wagons had camped the year before, and emptied
their feather beds. They left their wagons and
' packed' their oxen into the valleys. We
could see the tracks of these wagons very plainly—there having been no rain since the melt-
ing of the snow last spring. These were the
first wagons that ever crossed the ' Plains,' on
their way to California, but were not brought
into California till 1845. Our Emigrants, on
coming, to *this* Plain, all made a rush for the
long sought for California; ambitious to be *first*
—not much waiting one for another ; the best
teams leaving the rest ; every one looking out
for himself, only. Some went to one part of

the country, and some to another. I have since met but few of our first company, except those who passed our house on their way to Oregon.

"The rest of the way we traveled very slow; our cattle—the small remnant of the flock we started from Illinois with being poor, and nearly worn out—having lost so many oxen as to be obliged to work cows in their place. While on the way, near the Humbold, the water was very bad. Some of our best oxen became poor and unfit for work, and were left on the sandy desert, some 40 miles this way of it, to shirk for themselves; and they probably died, or were 'cared for' by the Indians. An ox would lie down in his yoke, and could not be got up; so we would unyoke and leave him. Some of them were able to walk, after the yoke was taken off: these we drove on as long as they were able to go, hoping they would hold out till we came to good water. Our cattle, all told, numbered only 65, when we moved onto our Rancho, in April, 1846.

"On the 25th day of October, 1845, my Father drove down into the American River valley, and in a few days more we camped near Sutter's Fort, where Sacramento City is now."

Thus we have given Mrs. HEALY's graphic

and interesting account of their seven months
journey from Illinois, through the States and
Territories now seen and described on a *modern*
made map of the United States, as *Missouri,
Kansas, Nebraska, Decota, Idaho, Utah and
Nevada,* "to where Sacramento City is now"
—an air-line distance of about 2350 miles, but
a distance of not less than 3,000 miles, on the
path traveled by MR. IDE's company.

When we consider the state of the roads—
the fact that a great part of the way was an un-
inhabited plain, or an unbroken wilderness, inhabited by wild beasts and Indians ; and consider, also, the obstacles to be overcome by such
a retinue—composed, as it was, of an unwieldy
herd of cattle ; of women and children unac-
customed to traversing deserts, fording rivers
and scaling mountains—in view of all these
impediments that *were* overcome, it would seem
that by hardly less than the interposition of a
miracle, as in the case of the Israelites on their
way to the " promised land," could they have
surmounted them.   Mrs. HEALY's account of
some of the (to her) most exciting incidents
of the tour are none the less interesting to the
sensible reader, from having been given in an
unstudied, plain, every-day style of writing.   It

must be borne in mind that she is not writing a sensational made-up story, but is treating of incidents and facts that were too deeply impressed on the mind, at that early period of her life, to be easily eradicated from her memory—and therefore her account is reliable.

We have, by "the mind's eye," witnessed many scenes of hardship and suffering by these pioneer emigrants ; but from what we have in store to say further about them, it will be seen that, so far as relates to Mr. IDE and family, they had yet many hardships to encounter. By a few more extracts from Mrs. HEALY'S narrative it appears that, although they had been providentially preserved to reach the end of their journey, further toil, anxiety and hardship awaited them. They had not yet realized the promised boon of "A land flowing with milk and honey"—the "Eldorado" which has, in later years, attracted thousands upon thousands of enterprising, well-to-do citizens of the New England States to the Pacific coast.

"While encamped near Sutter's Fort, where Sacramento City is now," (Mrs. H. continues,) "Father met a Mr. Peter Lassen, who owned a large tract of land 130 miles up the Sacramento valley, on Deer Creek, who told him that he

was the very man that he wanted to build him
a sawmill.   Lassen having the water-power,
and Father a circular saw and some mill-irons
which he had brought across the Plains, he told
Father to go right up with his family to his
Rancho, and tell Mr. Sill to clean out one of
his tenements, and that he (Lassen) would be
home soon, and show him the mill-site and
set him to work.   In just one week after we
had moved into this small house of one room,
Mr. Lassen came home, and brought another
family with him, (one of his own countrymen,
a German) ;   and the first thing he said to
Father was, that he wanted his house !

"This was about the middle of November,
1845.   We packed every thing into our wagons ;   and, getting our cattle together, started
up the river and forded it.   After going about
seven miles, we came to a camp of one family,
(a Mr. Tusting) who had bargained to take care
of a Mr. Chard's cattle, and live on his Rancho
—had camped near Sacramento River, on H. R.
Thome's Rancho, in order to have the company of Mr. Thome's man who had charge of his
(Mr. T's) cattle.   We camped near them, they
being very anxious to have us remain with
them all winter   As the rainy season had al-

ready commenced, the weather was stormy.
Father, with two other men, built a log-cabin.
All of us lived in it until April, 1846. During
the winter, which was a very wet one, we were
surrounded with high water-floods—our cattle
swimming from one bank to another—Indians
yelling night and day, while the river was at
its height—we living on beef, butter and milk,
with but little bread and no vegetables. Perhaps 100 lbs. of flour was all we had during the
winter and spring, or until the wheat grew.
A little boiled wheat was a treat to us. These
privations, (not to mention many others), made
us somewhat homesick.

"We could get but little wheat to sow,
which was bought of Capt. Sutter. We could
not buy flour at any price : it was not in the
country. There were eight in our family, including a Mr. Tustin, his wife and child.—
Three young men—a Mr. Boker, having charge
of Mr. Thome's cattle and horses—a Mr. Belden, an Eastern gentleman, and a Mr. Pitts,
who were weather-bound, and were of course
some company for us, all lived in a log-cabin
several months. They made themselves a canoe, and the two last named men put into it a
supply of meat, their fire-arms, ammunition,

&c., left us, and made their journey by water
to some point down the river where they could
embark on a larger craft. * * * One of
these men (Mr. Josiah Belden) owned the farm
now known as the ' IDE RANCHO.' Mr. Belden gave father one half of it for living on and
taking care of his (Mr. B's) cattle three years.
After the discovery of gold, Mr. B. sold his
half to my Father, my husband and my brother
JAMES ; each paying him $2,000—Mr. B's
cattle being included. * * *

"In April, 1846, we moved from the first
cabin ever built in Tehama Co. into our partly
finished cabin on Mr. B's farm. . We had not
been there long before a young man, Mr. L. H.
Ford, came to tell Father that Gen. Don Castro was on his way from Monterey to drive all
the Americans from the country. Father left
home the same day,—I think about the last of
April or first of May, 1846, and went, with
other American settlers, to Fremont's camp.
F. told them he could not assist in attacking
the Spaniards, except in self-defence. Then
the settlers organized, and chose Capt. Merritt their commander. They hastened on to
Sonoma. The Captain appointed two of his
men to go into Gov. Vallejo's mansion and take

him prisoner, while the rest of the company
were guarding the building outside, mounted
on their horses,"—[Here Mrs. H. refers the
writer to other sources of information relating
to the capture of the Spanish Fortress by the
" Bear Flag" party, etc., and proceeds to say:

" How sad for Mother and I to see Father
and Mr. Henry Ford ride off on such an expedition ! Would they ever return ? Should we
ever see them again? Fright from the Indians,
distress and grief from hearing rumors of Father's and William's death by the hands of the
cruel Spaniards, and weeks passing before we
could hear or know to the contrary. No post-
offices or mails; no neighbors but wild Indians!
not hearing from them, direct, for months !—
Thus all that long summer passed !

" Finally, sometime in November, after an
absence of between six and seven months, Father and William came home. Oh, the joyful
day ! I wonder that I cannot recall the exact
day of the month."

Mrs. H. then adds to her account of their
" over the Plains" excursion, a few more items
of interest :

" We had no deaths in our train ; in the
large company, I mean. In it there were two

births, detaining it but two days.   One lady
(a Mrs. Rolett) was so feeble when we first saw
her at Missouri line, as to be carried on a bed,
and lifted in and out the wagon like a helpless
infant; and at our journey's end she was a well
woman.

   " We began to lose cattle the first week after
leaving Illinois, and kept on losing all the way
—some dying from the want of grass and want
of good water ; others, and perhaps the greater number, being lost and killed by the Indians.
Palmer was the name of the large company's
Captain.   He went to Oregon—had no family
with him.   There were a few families who did
not wait to organize with the large company,
but drove on and kept in advance all the way.

   " To me the journey was a ' pleasure-trip'—
so many beautiful wild flowers, such wild scenery, mountains, rocks and streams—something
new at every turn, or at least every day.   I was
with my dear parents then.   To them it was
quite different.   They had care and toil all the
way.   My Father was broken of his rest and
sleep a great deal—taking charge of the cattle
early and late ; yet his health was good all
the way."

CHAPTER V.

WHO MADE THE "BEAR FLAG :" BY W. M. BOGGS, ESQ.—SOME
ACCOUNT OF THE PARTY WHO TOOK UP ARMS IN DEFENCE
AND PROTECTION OF THE EARLY PIONEERS' RIGHTS.

WE have now come to that period in the life
of MR. IDE, when man's faculties for usefulness
to himself, his family and his fellow-men are
generally most fully developed. On his arrival
and first encampment in California, he was in
his fiftieth year : and, according to his daughter's recollection, soon after his arrival there
he was confronted with the solution of an important problem, regarding the rights and privileges of himself and his fellow-emigrants who
had so recently taken up their abode in this
(then) " desolate wilderness." He had built a
cabin for the temporary protection of his family, until he could provide more comfortable
quarters for them. In so doing, with the view
of making this new country his future abode,
he supposed he had conformed to all the legal
conditions entitling him to all the privileges,
rights and immunities of a citizen of his newly adopted country. The question to be settled

was—whether he should be forcibly ejected from his humble abode, and driven back again to ' the States'; or whether he would unite with his fellow-emigrants in resisting the threatened " war of extermination", as put forth in a Proclamation of the then reputed Governor of the country. It took but a moment's reflection for him to decide the question.

There have been many different accounts published of the proceedings of the citizens (principally emigrants from the East), who banded themselves for the protection of their lives and property, in 1846. These accounts varying in some important particulars, we shall rely mainly on the statements of those who were eye-witnesses of the transactions they refer to. Of course the events cannot be narrated in the consecutive order in which they occurred —and, in some cases, repetitions will occur of accounts of the *same* transactions, from *different* sources.

Soon after the writer concluded to comply with the request of the only surviving daughter of WM. B. IDE, that he would collect the material for this memoir, he addressed a note to one of the party who (a newspaper article informed him), had had a hand in getting up

the renowned "*Bear Flag*": to which note he
received a letter in reply from W. M. Boggs,
Esq., dated "Napa City, Cal., Jan. 18, 1878,"
from which we propose to make liberal extracts.
Mr. B. explains by saying: "Your letter to
the late Peter Storm, dated Jan. 7, '78, was
handed me by a friend of Mr. S., with the request that I would answer it. Mr. Storm died
recently at Calistoga, Napa county, and was
interred by a delegation of Pioneers of Napa.

"I will undertake to answer some of the in-
quiries of your letter ; as I was, perhaps, as
well acqainted with Wm. B. Ide as any of the
pioneers of 1846. I became acquainted with
him at Sonoma, in 1846 or '47. But first I
will answer as to ' who made the *Bear Flag*.'

"A party of Americans had organized themselves in Napa Valley for the purpose of capturing the garrison of Sonoma, (or, *Puebalo y
Sonoma*). The place was occupied by Mexican
citizens, and was the residence of Gen. Vallejo,
who was commandant General of the northerń
district of California. His brother, Don Sal-
vado Vallejo, who was a Captain in the Mexican service—Col. Victor Prudshon, (a French-
man), but who became a Mexican citizen ;
Jacob P. Leese, an American, but who had

married Gen. Vallejo's sister, Dena Rosalia
Vallejo.

" The aforesaid party of Americans,(of which
Mr. WM. B. IDE was a member), afterwards
known as " The Bear Party," proceeded to Sonoma and captured the place by surprising the
General and his brother officers in bed at break
of day. This party was headed by Capt. Merritt, an old bear-hunter. The prisoners were
sent under an escort to Sutter's Fort, to be
held as hostages by Col. Fremont, until released on parole. Fremont had been recalled, and
was at Sutter's Fort, awaiting further orders
from the U. S. authorities ; but in the mean
time indirectly coöperated with the Independent or Bear party—holding the prisoners for
some weeks at Sutter's Fort. The Californians, in the mean time, were rallying their forces
to drive the handful of ' American marauders,'
as they termed the Bear party, out of the country. They having possession of the barracks
at Sonoma, held the place, and proceeded to organize an Independent Government, by electing WILLIAM B. IDE governor and commander-in-chief of ' the Independent forces,' as they
were styled, and JOHN H. NASH Chief Justice
(commonly known as the Alcalde, under the

Mexican government).—It was thought by
some, that they should adopt a Flag to represent their Government ; and most of them being hunters and adventurers, the idea was suggested by one Capt. FORD, that a *Grizzly Bear*
should be the motto.

"A young man named William Ford, who
had been held in their Fort, as a prisoner, by
the Californians, and re-captured in the first
fight with them at Camillo's Rancho, near the
present city of Petaluma ; William Todd, (a
Norwegian), of Illinois, assisted by old PETER
STORM, painted the ' Bear Flag'. It was simply a piece of unbleached, domestic-made cotton cloth, about a yard and a half long by one
yard wide.   A rude figure of a bear, standing
on his hind legs, was sketched and painted by
Todd and Storm, as above stated, in the presence of a number of the Bear party."

Mr. BOGGS kindly adds : "A number of the
Bear party still live in this vicinity, and I am
personally acquainted with many of them. My
nearest neighbor, Mr. WM. HARGRAVE, is one
of them ; and he is the person who gave me
your letter to answer—knowing that I was acquainted with the facts.

"I arrived in California in 1846—in time to

take part in the Mexican war ; which I did by
serving in a battalion of Mounted Riflemen,
commanded by Capt. MADDOX, a marine officer
under Commodore Stockton. I left my family
—that is, my wife and father, Ex-Gov. L. W.
BOGGS of Missouri—at Petaluma Rancho,
where my eldest son, Gaudaloupe V. Boggs,
was born ; the same boy you mention in your
letter as the first American born in California
—which I think is a mistake. He is probably
the first American white child, *born under the
American Flag*, on this coast. I was in the
U. S. service at the time ; and on my return,
after my discharge at Monterey, I found my
wife and boy at Petaluma Rancho—the property of Gen. Vallejo, who had kindly tendered
my father and family the use of the house, and
generously furnished beef and other necessaries
in the way of living. The seven months journey across the Plains and over the Mountains,
at that time, had nearly exhausted our supplies. The ill-fated Donner party was a part
of my train most of the way across: I say a
part of *my* train, because I was elected Captain of the emigrant train of 1846, at Ash-
Hollow, on the Platt River, and conducted my
party safely over the Plains and Mountains

into California: and had the Donners remained
with us, they would have escaped the suffering
and starvation that they experienced in their
snow-bound camp in the Sierra Nevada Mountains. I knew them all. *   *   *

"Mr. IDE had kept a journal, and wrote a
large volume, in book-form, of these proceedings,* and I saw and read a portion of it at
his Rancho, in May, 1847, when on my way
to the mines. He thought Fremont had not
treated him right in the interchange of governments. I never learned whether his writings
have been preserved or not ; but think they
were lost in the great gold excitement.†

"The 'Society of California Pioneers' has
collected many interesting facts connected with
California's early history : but such facts as a
personal acquaintance with such men as Wil-

* The "Proceedings" of the "Bear Flag party" are here
referred to.

† It had escaped the recollection of the surviving members
of Mr. IDE's family, until this notice of these writings in this
kind letter of MR. BOGGS, was written them, that such writings were in their possession. After diligent search, since
that notice came to their hands, they were found among the
effects of Mrs. HEALY's brother JAMES M., who died a few
months before. We expect to find in that 'book-form' manuscript much valuable material for this work.

liam B. Ide, Capt. Grenill, P. Swift, Capt. Ford, Capt. John Grigsby, and a few others who were prime movers, and the leading spirits who struck out boldly at the commencement of the Revolution that gave California to the United States, almost free of cost, so far as local operations were concerned—such facts, I say, can only be obtained by or through those who were active participants in them, or were intimately acquainted with those brave men —the most of whom are now no more."

In a subsequent letter to the writer, Mr. BOGGS says: "In the work of forming the Independent, or ' Bear Flag' party, MR. IDE took a prominent part. You may rely on his statements to you as being more correct than those of any of the newspaper correspondents, who gather from different sources, and add their own conclusions besides. Scarcely any two of them give the same version of affairs. What I know about our history is from personal experience and personal acquaintance with nearly every man engaged in the war of 1846-7, on this coast—both land and naval officers, volunteers and regulars, marines and sailors : having served and associated with many of them since —more especially with the leading men ; many

of whom were my old neighbors for many years
since.

"My lamented Father arriving here in time
to participate in the closing of the Mexican
war by appointment of the Military Governor,
Col. Mason of the U. S. Army, aided in establishing law and order, and in carrying out the
laws of both Mexico and the United States,
pending the hostilities, and during the settlement of them according to the treaty of peace;
which position he filled to the entire satisfaction of all concerned, for a considerable period
of time ; and for which service rendered his
government his bill remains, unpaid, in Washington. A more just claim, perhaps, has never
been presented to Congress. But, for want
of funds to fee agents, the claim has been, up
to this time, ignored."

Mr. BOGGS concludes this second letter by
saying : " I hope you will succeed in obtaining
the information concerning the events alluded
to in your letter to Mr. Storm—authenticat-
ing, as no doubt it will, the statements to you
by a brother of the lamented WM. B. IDE concerning this part of his history, for which no
man was better qualified to give a correct version than himself. My Father often spoke of

him as being a man of superior intelligence ; a
very competent and useful citizen—a *patriotic*
co-worker in establishing law and order where
none before existed. Such men as he and my
Father rarely receive justice at the hands of
their country. Those who render IT the most
important services, are often the least com-
pensated."

CHAPTER VI.

THE "BEAR FLAG GOVERNMENT" ORGANIZED.—SOME ACCOUNT
OF PROCEEDINGS UNDER IT.—THE RAID UPON GEN. CAS-
TRO'S CAMP.—NARROW ESCAPE OF FREMONT'S PARTY.

In 1849, during Mr. Ide's residence several
months with one of his brothers, he gave said
brother a verbal account of his six or seven
months services in the Bear Flag enterprise,
and, (as he understood the case), as a U. S.
soldier under the command of Col. Fremont.
We give this brother's statement : and it will
be borne in mind by the reader, that this brother relies entirely on his memory for what he
told him ; and that the incidents of this narrative were related to him some 28 years ago—
at a period of his life when a detail of such interesting events makes an abiding impression
upon the memory. But should the volumin-
ous manuscipt Journal of Mr. Ide, referred to
by Mr. Boggs, on page 57, come to light before
this memoir goes to press, it will be corrected,
wherein its statements may materially conflict
with those of that journal, as it may seem nec-

essary to insure accuracy, in giving an account
of what transpired under the "administration
of Governor IDE."

" My brother Wm. B. told me that he left
his family about the first of May, 1846, and
rode around among the early emigrants from
the States, to arouse them to action in self-defence.   He had seen the Proclamation of Gov.
Don Castro, warning those emigrants to leave
the country in a given time, or they would be
driven into the mountains, or made prisoners
of; or they would be shot, in case of resistance.
This, he said, 'stirred them up to the quick.'
They very soon rallied a company of about
one hundred mounted men, armed as best they
could be, with hunting guns, rifles and pistols.
They rendezvoused at or near Sutter's Fort,
and organized by choosing a Captain Merrit
as their commander.   They then proceeded to
Sonoma, the headquarters of Gov. Castro, who
had issued the aforesaid threatening proclamation, and of Gen. M. G. VALLEJO.   They surprised the Garrison at day-break, captured Gen.
Vallejo, his brother Don S. Vallejo, Jacob P.
Leese, Col. Victor Prudhon and two others,
took them prisoners ; and Capt. Grigsby, with
a small guard, escorted them to Sutter's Fort."

And here the Editor will suspend the brother's narrative for a moment, to make room for a few items of interest obligingly furnished him by Mr. Boggs, who informs me that the individuals captured as above stated were officers of the Mexican Government, and that

" Gen. Mariano Gaudaloup Vallejo was the highest military officer in the northern department of Upper California, in the Mexican government—was the first native Californian to embrace the cause of the United States, under its flag. Don Castro was the Governor, and retreated before the Bear party captured Sonoma. It was Capt. Grigsby, with only a guard of five or six men, who took the prisoners from Sonoma to Sutter's Fort ; a distance of about 100 miles."

Mr. Boggs adds : " Gen. Vallejo's family was not molested at all, but were assured by the Bear party that he and his friends should only be held as hostages for the future good behaviour of the Californians ; who had, without the sanction of their superiors, caught and barbarously murdered two young Americans, near the Santa Rosa Rancho, sometime previous to the capture of Sonoma by the Bear party." These young men, (Mr. B. says), " were lassoed, dragged alive, their tongues cut out, and other portions of their bodies mutillated while fastened to trees. The Americans, (not the Bear party), to their shame be it recorded, by way of *retalliation* for this shocking barbarism, killed three peaceable Californians at San Raphael, who had not taken up arms against them, neither had they taken any part in the massacre of the two young Americans. This was done, in would seem, under the eye of Col. Fremont, who was then at the Mission of San Raphael, not far from Putaluma. The celebrated Kit Carson, Fremont's guide, killed the first one. He discovered and reported them to Fremont, his superior officer, as prisoners his squad had taken, and asked him what he should do with them ? F.'s reply to Carson was, that he 'had no use for prisoners ; but do your duty.' Kit returned, and, in company with one or two others of Fremont's command, killed an old Mexican and his two sons. "This circumstance (says Mr. B.), was related to me by Carson himself, in my house at Sonoma, where he visited me. I knew Kit Carson in the Rocky Mountains, and he and my Brother were intimate friends at Beut's Fort, on the Arkansas River, where they were traders with the various tribes of Indians on the Plains ; their traffic being in buffalo robes and other peltries.

"Carson was a bold and daring man, when an emergency required, and gentle as a lamb, when engaged in peaceful pursuits. I told him I did not approve of that act of retalliation ;— that he should have pursued the guilty ones, who had escaped across the Bay, as no punishment within the rules of war would have been too severe for *them*. But Kit Carson had been trained to Indian warfare, and its customs were deeply impressed on his mind at an early age.

"These were the type of men who were engaged in making the first move towards acquiring a Territory for the Union, that has since added hundreds of millions to its wealth : and now that a few of them are left, broken in constitution and health, ask a pittance from the best government the world ever saw, in the way of a pension—I mean, a pension to the few destitute survivors of the orphans and widows of those engaged in the Mexican war—it seems a fitting time to inquire whether or no the old adage, 'Republics are ungrateful', will not apply to 'Uncle Samuel'."

Mr. B. elsewhere says : "Capt. Merrit remained at Sonoma with the remainder of the

Bear party, until they were disbanded. Fremont afterwards placed Capt. Grigsby in command at Sonoma.   Merrit was lost sight of.
He was merely an 'old Hunter'; very brave
and resolute, but somewhat rude."—[We now
resume the "brother's" narrative:

"At the time of the assault on the Fort, I
think my brother told me that he had the command of their party.   The case was this : not
long after the first organization of it, or while
on their way to Sonoma, it was noticed that
their Captain, from some cause, had lost the
full confidence of his men, and they elected my
brother to take his place.   But whether it was
before, or after, the surrender of the Fort, I do
not distinctly remember.

"After getting somewhat quietly established
in the Fort—putting its cannon and small arms
(of which they found a pretty good supply) in
order for service, in case of annoyance from the
enemy, they began to consider what steps it
was next best to take for self-preservation.   As
then situated, brother said they would be considered and treated as rebels and outlaws, if
overpowered and taken prisoners by Don Castro and his men.   It was finally concluded that
'While among the Romans, they must do as

the Romans do'—that they must inaugurate
an Independent Government. The authorities
they were under arms to combat derived their
governmental status by the Mexican Pronunci-
amento process ; and they decided to adopt the
same process for organizing a new civil government for the Californians. They accordingly
elected WILLIAM B. IDE their Governor, and
JOHN H. NASH, Chief Justice, or Alcalde, to
conform themselves to the Mexican laws and
usages for the time being.

" It will be remembered, that up to the day
of the uprising of the emigrants in self-defence,
they knew nothing of the war operations between the United States and Mexico. They
were, in Yankee pharse, ' fighting on their own
hook.' But my brother told me he had no
other object in view, in accepting the office of
Governor, than that of doing all in his power
to protect the emigrants, and establish their
Indpeudence of Mexico.

" The account my brother William gave me
of their ' war-like' proceedings, after getting
up their *National* Flag, and issuing his ' Pro-
nunciamento' proclamation, and while they so
bravely 'held the Fort,' has much of it escaped
my memory, except two or three prominent in-

cidents, which I will endeavor to relate substantially as he gave them to me.

"I have never seen a copy of this proclamation ; but I understood brother to say that it
briefly recited the grounds for their revolutionary movement—among them the threatening
missal from Don Castro, and the right of self-
preservation—the fact that they had been invited by the home Mexican authorities to come
and take up land and settle among them : and
closing with the promise of protection to all
law-abiding citizens of California, who would
remain peaceably at home.

"My brother recited to me some of his military operations—new, and somewhat exciting
to himself and the greater part of his men who
had never before seen actual service, 'in the
camp or upon the tented field' : one or two of
which I will relate.

"He had not been long in command, before
word came to him through one of his scouts,
that the enemy under Don Castro was encamped at a small settlement, distant about twenty
miles from Sonoma. He selected a squad of
twenty of his '*sharpest* shooters', had them
mounted on his fleetest horses, and supplied
with the best rifles and guns in the Fort, put

them in charge of a trusty officer, with orders
to proceed leisurely to the enemy's camp ; and
when within easy gun-shot distance of it, to
dismount, give an Indian war-whoop to attract
the enemy's attention; and, as they made their
appearance, each one of the party, in turn, to
take deliberate aim, fire a single charge, re-
mount his horse, and return with all speed to
the Fort. The order having been faithfully
executed by the squad, brother said he afterwards ascertained that a number of the Don's
men were made to ' bite the dust.'

" Not long after this rather unique military
exploit of the Bear Party, one of their men
picked up, on the street, a letter addressed to
one of the citizens of Sonoma, notifying him
that Don Castro's party was preparing to make
a raid upon the Fort very soon. This notice
coming to the Governor in an apparently authentic shape, he set about making preparation
to give the Spaniards a warm reception. Fremont, with a small company of his surveying party and a few other emigrants, was at
that time located at Sutter's Fort, and brother was not expecting assistance from him.

" In the mean time every thing in the Fort
was put in order. The cannon and small arms

were loaded with cannister, balls, or buck-shot, as it was thought would render them, respectively, of most service. Scouts were sent in different directions to bring back to the Fort early notice of the approach towards it of any hostile force ; and, with these and other precautionary measures, the officers and men of the Bear Flag party patiently awaited on their arms a short time, to see what would next turn up. Precisely how long they waited, I dont recollect that my brother told me : but he said that quite late one evening, one of his scouts came hurridly up to the Fort on horseback, and announced the enemy's approach within a short distance ; it might be half a mile or more : when the cannon were drawn out and put in position in front of the Fort, matches lighted ; the men inside of it formed in 'battle array', with loaded arms in hand, and all things ready for action.

"Thus prepared, (brother told me), he gave orders to his men not to fire until, by a given signal, he ordered them to fire : he then went some ten or twenty rods towards the coming foe, and he soon heard a voice from among them call out—'*See!* *their torches are lighted!* *they 're going to fire upon us ! !*' He knew

the voice—it was KIT CARSON's, and instantly threw up his arms as the signal for them
not to fire; saying to his men, at the top of his
voice : ' *Dont fire! It is Fremont !*' Thus,
(said my brother) Kit Karson, who I knew was
with Fremont, probably saved us from a pretty
bad disaster : which, had it happened, would
have resulted from Fremont's failure to give us
seasonable notice of his coming. His excuse
for not doing so was, that he sent a man ahead
who, being a foreigner, did not understand his
order. And, as showing that Fremont took in
readily the perilous situation of his squad, he
hastily ' switched himself off on a side track',
out of harm's way, even if we had fired upon
his party."

CHAPTER VII.

FORMAL, IF NOT LEGAL TRANSFER AND CHANGE OF GOVERN-
MENT—MR. IDE'S TOUR UNDER FREMONT, DOWN THE PA-
CIFIC COAST.—HIS CONTRACT FOR A PASSAGE HOME.

WE omit his brother's statement of the reasons why, and the manner how, the ' Bear Flag'
was inaugurated—Mr. BOGGS having furnished
us with that item : (see ante pages 56-7), and
continue his account of what he remembers in
relation to Mr. IDE's further movements.

"Soon after the commencement of hostilities between the United States and Mexico,
and the arrival of Commodore Stockton around
on the Pacific coast, in pursuanc of orders
from his Government to receive the transfer
of the Californias, by the then nominal Govern-
or, to the United States, my brother told me
that ceremony was *formally*, if not *legally* performed on board the Commodore's ship, in the
presence of its officers and men, and a number
of the respectable citizens of the place near
whieh his ship lay at anchor.

"Soon after this ceremony was over, there

was a collation on board the ship prepared in
honor of the occasion : and brother said 'it
was the happiest day of his life to be relieved
from the responsible position of Governor, and
at the same time to feel assured that the day
was not far distant, when California would become one of the States of the Union.' And,
although he died at just about the meridian of
man's life, fitting him for usefulness in the people's service, he lived to see that 'day.'

"This transfer having been made, Commodore Stockton, having been authorized by the
U. S. government to do so, gave Col. Fremont
command of a small force, to drive the hostile
Mexicans from the territory. Although this
turn of affairs relieved brother from much care
and anxiety, it did not satisfy him that there
was no further need of his services in the case.
It devolved on Fremont to drive Castro and
his adherents out of the territory, and to organize a 'small force' for that purpose. To do
this the Bear Flag Company, which had seen
' some service,' would be an important acquisition. Aware of this, he tried to enlist them into his service ; but a large number declined, unless their late Commander would go with them.
Though his private affairs, and the care of his

family urgently required his presence at home,
still, in view of these appeals from his brave
comrades who had also left their homes to serve
their country and for the protection of their
own firesides, he thought it his duty to continue still in its service ; as, by so doing, he would
secure to Col. Fremont his needed assistance
in driving Gen. Castro and his horde down the
Pacific coast : in view of this state of the case
he thought it his duty to go with them.

"And here I may be permitted to inquire,
—as I did of brother, when he related his experience under Fremont during the 3 or 4 months
novel campaign—*if* he was not a little im-
provident (as the sequel will show), in not having an explicit understanding with his commander, as to his position in the company of
men he had been of so essential service in procuring for the expedition, who had for a brief
period been under him as their commander.
He said that, during their entire tramp of several months, down the westwardly coast of
Lower California, he occupied the post, and
was subjected to all the hardships of a common
soldier—at times being on foot for miles, while
nearly all his comrades were mounted, and while
an officer rode a horse of his, which accompani-

ed him from Illinois. His reason for submitting
to this indignity was, that he consented to the
sacrifice of personal interest and comfort, in
consenting to go with his men, to assist his
commander in driving the enemy out of the
country, by the best way and means he could ;
and if his superiors thought he would be most
useful to them as a private, it was his duty to
serve in that capacity : although he did expect
when he enlisted, to occupy a different position
in the service. This is the sum and substance
of my brother's reply to my inquiry.

"But I have not yet come to the *finale* of
the *peculiar experience* of my brother during
this long and tedious excursion. The most
novel and interesting part of what I have to
add in relation to it, I obtained though a dis-
interested party, (so far as blood-relationship is
concerned.) He merely told me that when he
was 'mustered out', he found himself without
money, some four or five hundred miles down
the coast away from home, and that he took
passage aboard a ship that carried him within
about 75 miles of it ; where he arrived, after
an absence of more than six months. When
discharged from this U. S. service, he *was* not
only ' without money', but also without decent

clothing, and without *credit,* 'into the bargain.'
He applied to the Captain of a vessel (I think
my informant told me it was that on which
Commodore Stockton was aboard of) for a passage up to San Francisco ; saying he had no
money with him to pay his passage ; but that
he had a plenty at home. The Captain eyed
his would-be-customer's ragged and uncouth
garb with a rather suspicious look, and said it
was his custom to recieve his passage-money in
advance. Mr. IDE then proposed to '*work* his
passage.' 'Can you saw wood ?' the Captain
asked. 'Yes, Captain, I have sawed lots of
it in my day'. 'Well, step aboard, and the
Steward will set you to work', said the Captain.
So he then took leave of a few of his 'Bear
Flag' associates, and went aboard the vessel,
not much encumbered with baggago, but cheered with the prospect of soon embracing the dear
ones he had so abruptly left in his hastily and
rudely constructed log-cabin, soon after his six
or seven months' journey across the Plains and
over the Mountains : cheered, also, with tbe
conscions rectitude of his intention to serve his
fellow-citizens by the best way and means in
his power, and nowise disheartened in view of
the prospect before him, of a few more days'

endurance of toil and privation. He cared little for the honors and emoluments of office, or
the pomp and pride of high station ; for he believed, with the Poet, that

"Honor and Fame from no condition rise :
Act well your part—there all the honor lies."

"It is true that sawing wood aboard ship
was new business to him ; and it was also true,
as he told the Captain, that he had 'sawed lots
of it in his day', while engaged in the employment to which he had been bred in early life.
But before the ship had got under way, Commodore Stockton, (then around on that coast
with the U. S. ship Princeton, who had called
to pay his respects to the Captain), while walking arm-in-arm with him on deck, saw my
brother at his new vocation, and said :

"Captain, do you know who that old man
there, (pointing to Mr. IDE), sawing wood for
you, is ?" "No ; I did n't ask his name," replied the Captain. "Well, that is Governor
IDE, of the Bear Flag party." "Can that be
so ? do you know him ?" asked the Captain.
"Yes, I know him," was the reply. Whereupon the Captain called his steward and said
to him : "Here, Steward, go tell that man

sawing wood, yonder, that the Captain wants
to see him at his office."

"The above incident and coloquy came to
my knowledge through a different channel, as
I have before remarked. It was told to a friend
of mine by the said Captain, to whom the Commodore introduced Mr. IDE : 'and on his said
introduction, he (Mr. I.), was made welcome,
not only to his passage, but to as good fare
and accommodations as the ship afforded.'

"At that time this Captain was on his way
to San Francisco, in the merchant service. In
1855 he had retired from a sea-faring life with
'a competency,' (as sea-faring captains sometimes do), and settled in a town near Boston,
where my said friend had an interview with
him in '55, during which the Captain related
the above incidents,—adding: that 'during
the passage he had frequent interviews with
Wm. B. IDE, and had formed a very favorable
opinion of him.'   And my informant added,
that this Captain, about that time, furnished
an article for the ' Boston Journal,' in which
he gave a short account of the Bear Flag enterprise, and dwelt particularly on what he
considered the important service Mr. IDE had
rendered his country, in the part he took in

' the conquest of California' at so trifling expense to it of blood and treasure.

" My brother was a plain, unpretending,
matter-of-fact kind of man—not much given
to outside show and parade. This peculiarity
of habit and turn of mind sometimes subjected
him to *neglect*—or what, in 'high life', might
be regarded and resented as *insult;* but, conscious of honesty and integrity of purpose in
whatever he undertook, such slights did not
annoy him ; they passed by him unheeded, as
' the idle wind, which availeth naught.' This
trait of character was strikingly illustrated by
his forbearance of resentment towards Col. Fremont. In the course of his conversations with
me, in alluding to his official and subsequent
intercourse with him, the hardest words he ever
used in relation to his (F's) treatment of him
were, that he thought he.' *had not treated him
right;'* but never, in my hearing, made use of
words that indicated feelings of resentment or
ill-will towards him, on account of what he
considered his unfair treatment.

We have now concluded the brother of Mr.
IDE'S account furnished us at the commencement of this undertaking on our part : and,
will here add some further reminisences of his

daughter, which have come to hand since her previous articles were in type.

During Mr. IDE's long absence from his family, while in the U. S. service in 1846, many trying and exciting scenes and privations were witnessed and endured by Mrs. Ide and her children. Mrs. Healy gives us slight sketches of some of them. It will be remembered that soon after their arrival from "across the Plains and over the Mountains," and before engaging in the Bear Flag enterprise, Mr. IDE built a log-cabin, and Mrs. Healy says :

" While there, in our little sunny home surrounded by Indians, we were accosted by an Oregon Indian Chief, who inquired of us by an interpreter, if we belonged to Capt. Sutter? and *I* replied : ' No ; we belong to our Father.' He then asked how many men Sutter had—how many horses ? how many cattle ?, etc., and I then answered all his questions as well as I could. Then the Interpreter took down, carefully sighted and minutely examined each of the four or five guns and carbines which hung upon wooden pegs driven into the logs composing the *ceiling* of our ' drawing-room'. While they were doing this, the suspense and anxiety of my Mother and myself may be im-

agined, but cannot be described ; but we remained silent and listless, till the examina-
tion was over ; " when, after a little conversation in their own language, between the Chief
and his men, they all mounted their ponies, and
started off into the woods, singing as they went.
Their tune rang in my ears, O how long ! They
were soon out of sight ; for they rode in a gallop, raising a cloud of dust. But we were not
greatly relieved of our fears. My oldest brothers, James and William, were away. I mounted my horse to go for James, who was at where
Tehama is now, distant about seven miles from
our cabin. The sun had set, and in the twi-
light I looked back to see Mother—I thought
perhaps for the last time—as she ran out and
motioned to me to return. I did so, and found
it was unnecessary for me to take that long
ride in the night, all alone ; for, said Mother,
' Mr. Meadows is on the opposite side of the
river, and perhaps *he* will go.' So my young
brothers, Daniel and Lemuel, crossed the river
in their canoe, and came back with Mr. Meadows, who told us that these Indians would not
hurt us—that a lady who lived near him had
recently come from Oregon, where these Indians
lived ; that she understood *Jorgon,* a dialect

spoken by them and the Hudson Bay Company. She said they came from Oregon to get satisfaction from Capt. Sutter for the death of the Chief's son, who was shot the year previous while trading at Sutter's Fort. The Chief was determined to have one of Sutter's men to shoot: and, in case he would not give up a man, he must have 100 horses, or 200 or 300 cattle. This Chief of the Walla Walla tribe came prepared to enforce his claim.

" Mr. Meadows staid all night at ' our *house,*' and in the morning went down the river about 7 miles, and from there a messenger was sent post-haste to Sutter's Fort, to warn them of the coming of an unfriendly visitor." Whether the irrate son of the forest got his man, or his horses, or his cattle, by way of "satisfaction" for the death of his son, Mrs. H. does not inform us ;* but continues: " This was in the

* Mr. Boggs, on returning the proof-slip of this article, says: " I can corroborate the story of Mrs. Healy about the Indians. When I arrived at Sutter's Fort, in 1846, there was a small band of the Walla Walla Indians there, who came over from Oregon to demand satisfaction of the whites for killing one of their tribe, by an American named Grove Cook. I knew Cook—an old mountaineer, and brother in-law of the celebrated Bill Sublette, from St. Louis, Mo., of Trapper fame out West. Cook lost two horses, while en-camped near this band of Indians. They were bold and in-solent—were well mounted and armed—were good horse-

summer of 1846, while my Father and brother
William were in the war : but William was
not with, and had not seen his Father since
November, 1845. Being just about that time
of age, he went to work for Capt. Sutter awhile,
and from there to the Santa Cruz Mountain to
make Redwood-shingles---was there when Gen.
Castro tried to take him prisoner. To escape

men and expert hunters. I met one of the band on the
west side of the Sacramento River, after I had crossed over
with my wagons and family. I had gone ahead, as usual, to
look out for good camping; and, near sun-sent, I espied a
large badger lying in the road. Having a good rifle, I dis-
mounted and put a ball through the neck of the animal—
killing it. Just as I was turning it over to examine the cu-
rious looking creature, a Walla Walla Indian warrior rode up
and asked me to give him the badger. I did so; and he
expressed real satisfaction, and galloped away on the plain,
with his badger strapped behind his saddle. These animals,
I afterwards learned, were hard to find, and the Indians priz-
ed them for their beautiful striped sknis, and for their oil.

"I learned that Capt. Sutter protected Grove Cook from
these Indians, and compromised with them in goods or other valuables. They soon returned to Oregon satisfied, and
Cook was allowed to go free. He settled near San Josè, Cal.,
and at one time was interested in the Grant of land on which
the celebrated New Alnoden Quick Silver mines are located.

"I knew Sublette & Cook, when a boy, at Independence,
Mo.—when that place was the frontier town of ' the West'.
He was of the firm of 'Sublette & Campbell', American Fur
Traders on the Upper Missouri. Sublette accompanied Sir
William Stuart, an English nobleman, as guide to the Rocky
Mountains, in 1842 or 3."

being so taken, he had to leave his work, and
secrete himself in the woods, alone, living on
raw venison ; as he dared not make a fire, lest
the smoke should show the place of his con-
cealment. Thus he lived about a week, when
his partner in the shingle business (who was a
foreigner) came to him, and advised him to go
and surrender to Castro ; saying, it would be
safer for him to do so than to be taken—as he
might, otherwise, be shot by Castro's men, who
were hunting for him. So, William went and
gave himself up a prisoner of war. Castro
gave him a comfortable room, and set a guard
over him : telling him he should be treated like
a gentleman. He asked him by an interpreter
many questions about his Father—how many
sons he had ; where he was, &c., &c. In a few
days he told William he was at liberty to go ;
but advised him to stay under his body-guard,
lest he should be shot by his (C's) men. He
did so, for some time, and until Castro and his
men all mounted their horses in great haste,
and suddenly left Santa Clara ' for good.'

" Brother William being thus set at liberty,
went out with a company to fight the Indians
in the San Joaquin Valley. I cannot tell how
long he served. He then knew no more about

his Father's movements than did Don Castro, nor so much.

"Now, during this time, Mother and I had heard that William had been a prisoner—had been released ; and, while walking away, had been lassoed by a Spaniard, and dragged to death : and that Father was a prisoner, and likely to share the same fate.   Mr. Meadows told us this sad news, and we mourned, night and day, many long weeks over it, before it turned out to be a false report—as we had no means of ascertaining the truth.

"When Father came home from the War, late in November, 1846, William came with him.   He had earned two good horses, and Father rode home on one of them ; leaving his own faithful horse, which he brought with him from Illinois, in a pasture to recruit : a U. S. officer had rode him, and, for want of proper care, had made his back so sore, that Father could not bear to put a saddle on him.   Through this means he lost this valuable animal: for, while thus necessarily recruiting in the pasture he was stolen, and never recovered.   On loaning the use of this horse to ' Uncle Samuel', the ' U. S.' brand was put on the top of Father's ' *W. I.*'; and afterwards the horse was claim-

ed as U. S.'s property ; but Father proved it
to be his.

"My brother James," Mrs. Healy continues, "was away several months, saving the
wheat Father had sown at Tehama. The un-
settled state of the country made him think it
necessary to *cache** a portion of the wheat, so
that he might have some to sow another year.
So he alone at night, after all the Indians were
asleep, dug a deep hole in the ground, which
he covered with straw during the day-time ;
and, in the night-time he put 12 or 15 bushels
of wheat into this hole, covered it with earth
enough to be safe, in case the stack of straw
he put over it should be burned by the Indians.
No one but James knew the place of this de-
posit. I mention this to show you to what
shifts the early settlers here were driven, for
want of the necessary places to store their produce, and almost every thing else, and also, how
hard my brother worked, day and night —how
thoughtful he was of our necessities and com-

---

* " A Rocky Mountain Hunter's phrase, meaning to *con-
ceal* or *hide*, in pits or caves, goods or valuables—such as
the hunter or traveler cannot carry with him. Such is a
cache, in hunter's parlance, on the Plains and in the Mountains,"—as a friend informs the Editor.

fort. He was a faithful and dear good brother."

Mrs. H. here gives another item about the Indians, in addition to what she said on pages 30 and 81. " A week or so after the Walla Walla company left our place, a company of Nesperces came one day to visit us—two chiefs with their wives, who were Delaware Indian squaws. Mother gave them a dinner. It was quite amusing to the children to see them eat. I presume it was the first table that they ever sat down to ; and their 'manners' were rather odd—one of the chiefs fanning his squaws with a large eagle's wing, frequenly, during their repast. They were dressed in buckskins cloth, profusely ornamented with beads and porcupine quills—also with buckskin strings inserted in each seam of their garments."

CHAPTER VIII.

NATIONS, like individuals, in the course of
their history, pass through certain great crises
or epochs, which have an important bearing on
their future character.   These epochs are not
regular, but intermittent ; and are often the
result of, what looks like accident ; though
doubtless, as in the phenomena of vegetation,
they have their hidden laws of growth and development.   Hence, on perusing the history
of a people you will find periods of expansion
which have their origin, to some extent, in the
restless, impulsive life of society, and the thirst
for acquisition.

An epoch of this character largely affecting
the industries, the wealth and the commerce
of the American people, occurred in the year
1848, on the discovery of gold in California.
Previous to that time emigration to the Far
West had been going on, but confined to comparatively small limits ; not assuming a gen-

eral character stimulating large bodies of men.
But the marvellous stories spread abroad by
the accidental dicovery of gold on the American Fork, as it was called, of the Sacramento
River, caused the wildest excitement throughout the country.   People everywhere, of all
classes and conditions of society—artizans, ag-
riculturalists, mechanics, merchants, doctors,
lawyers, and even ministers of religion,—were
suddenly arroused by dreams of untold wealth.
Vessels, crowded with enthusiastic adventurers, sailed from every port in the United States
for the newly discovered Eldorado ; and hundreds who registered their names for the voyage
full of hopeful and cheerful anticipations of
the future, went forth only to encounter hardship, disappointment, disease and death.

The course of history takes us back to the
local conflicts of the two or three years preceding this period of excitement, which was no
doubt hastened in its development by the occurrence of events which form the topic of discussion in this and in several of our succeeding
chapters.   And, for the better understanding
of what is to follow, it may be well for us to
take a hasty glance at the civil and political
condition of California, at the time when these

events occurred. It is well known, that from its first settlement by Spanish adventurers from Mexico, no well-ordered system of national or provincial government had been established. Aristocratic "Dons," originally from Spain, formed a self-constructed oligarchy, by which the few emigrant and native laboring population were oppressed. This lordly race owned, or laid claim to, almost the entire domain of arable land—parcelled out as it was to them in 3-miles-square sections, known among the inhabitants, then and now, as *ranchos.* The laboring people there were in a condition but little better than that of the serfs of Russia, or the slaves of Virginia, in by-gone times. Common schools and the higher institutions of learning, and houses of public worship (unless there were here and there found at a Romanist "*Mission*",) were unknown to them.

One of the peculiar grievances to which the emigrants from the States were subjected, was the inhuman and arbitrary exaction by their "*Alcaldes*," or sole civil magistrates, of a capita tax from said emigrants, on taking up their residence among them : and a correspondent of high standing in California, who took a conspicuous part in the troubles of '45, writes the

Editor, that Gen. Castro's threatened raid upon them was to compel the payment of this tax,

Hence it will be seen that a state of anarchy
and misrule confronted them at every step, and
that they could do no less than rise as they
did, for self-preservation, and attempt a " Revolution," by which they could " establish law
and order where none had existed before."

In the historical course of events, it is now
in order to invitte the reader's attention to " the
large manuscript volume" seen and partially
examined by Mr. Boggs—referred to on page
57. This was probably written during the winter of '46–7 ; as, during the " gold excitement"
of '47–8, Mr. Ide's time was too much occupied at " the diggings" to admit of his attention to such matters. *When* it was written is
immaterial. After it had lain over 30 years in
obscurity—until nearly all the preceding pages
of this work were in type—and after the recent decease of his eldest son, James M. Ide,
it was found among his (J. M.'s) effects, in a
good state of preservation, and a correct copy
of it has been placed in the hand of the Edit-
or, and nearly all of it will be found in the succeeding pages.

We have a reasonable guaranty, in the repu-

tation of its writer for honest integrity in all
his dealings, of its truthfulness of statement :
and it is confidently believed that those of his
personal acquaintance who are still alive, and
who may be favored with its perusal, will do
his memory the justice to disabuse it of any
sinister or unworthy motive, in taking the part
he and his compeers deemed it necessary to
take in their "Revolutionary" movements of
'46. We entertain the opinion, furthermore,
that when the general reader, unbiased by
class, sect, or pre-national prejudice or attach-
ment, shall have thoroughly perused this document, and will take into consideration the situation of the country—the state of anarchy
then existing—he will cheerfully admit, that
however *unmilitary*, in the eye of gentlemen
skilled in warlike movements, their *modus op-
erandi* for the accomplishment of the object
in view—he will admit, I repeat, that *they did
accomplish it.* And we beg leave to make a
further suggestion—viz : that it might have
been a problem of difficult solution, for the
wisest adept in military science, or even in
"*path-finding*", to inaugurate a different line
of proceeding, by which that heterogeneous
population of Spanish, Mexican, Indian and

Yankee origin could, in less than one month's time, by the well-directed labors of a handful of men under the direction of an experienced *military* leader, even, have been brought from a state of bitter antagonism, into that of peaceful subjection to the United States' authority —and that, too, at so trifling a "sacrifice of blood and treasure."

Suppose, for instance, there had been no *organized* resistance to Castro—that, as would naturally in that case have been the result, had not Mr. IDE, or some one else, promptly moved "among the emigrants," and got up the celebrated, *justly* "celebrated, BEAR FLAG PARTY" *organization,* setting at defiance the exterminating Proclamation of Gen. José Castro ; and that there had been a cowardly shrinking from self-defence—a "fleeing to the mountains for safety" by some, and a sort of gorilla, hand-to-hand warfare between pioneers and Castro's scouts by others, until they knew of the war between Mexico and the United States; what would then have been the condition of the contending parties ?

That such a state of warfare between the natives and emigrants then existed, we respectfully refer the reader to ante-pages 65 and 66

for ample proof—where Mr. Boggs tells us of
the barbarous murder of two young Americans;
and that Americans, (not of the Bear Flag party), by way of *retaliation*, killed three peaceful Californians, " who had not taken up arms
against them, neither had they taken part in
the massacre of the two young Americans."
And what is added seems unaccountable : this
act of " retaliation" was performed by Kit
Carson, with Capt. Fremont's approval.

Had Gen. Castro remained a month or two
longer than he did, in the undisturbed possession of his fort, arms and military supplies, is
it to be doubted that he would not have used
them somewhat *successfully* in his threatened
exterminating process ? and thus have aroused the retaliatory energies of the U. S. government ; so that, when the actual state of war
between it and Mexico arrived, much " blood
and treasure" would have been expended on
both sides in California, before the return of
peace.   Had there been the Bear Flag movement, or an organized opposition to Castro, and
no formal state of war between the U. S. and
Mexico, is there any reason to doubt the event-
ual erection of an Independent Republic on the
Pacific Coast ?   That war existed between

the two nations was not known in California, until, by comparatively peaceful measures, this province had been prepared, without the "loss of blood or treasure", to become an "Independent Nation". The "Bear Flag Proclamation", (every word of which, Mr. IDE remarks in his Letter to SENATOR WAMBOUGH, was penned by him on the 15th of June, 1846, between the hours of 1 and 4, A. M.) was the *entering wedge,* so to speak, that separated a down-trodden people from allegiance to an oppressive oligarchy under which they had groaned from time immemorial. It annunciated principles of government new and attractive. It contained no vindictive or coercive threat ; but, on the contrary, was persuasive and conciliatory. It approached the people as brethren, rather than as enemies. It was sought for, circulated among and read by them so earnestly, that copies of it could not be written fast enough to supply the demand. Its circulation in Castro's camp, it is stated, had the effect to withdraw from it one half (300) of his followers, and convert and transform them into peacable ctizens, under the new order of things.

After due consideration of these and other circumstances connected with " the conquest of

California", it is submitted to an honest, dispassionate and appreciative posterity to pass upon the validity of William B. Ide's claim to the merit of *upright intention*, at least, in doing what he did do, towards the " Conquest of California", and the *" wisdom* or *unwisdom"* of the measures he adopted to accomplish that object. If he had been an aspirant for fame and high place in governmental affairs, would he have quietly yielded to the adroit manœuvreing and contriving of his "successor, in that General Assembly" he refers to, at the close of his narrative?—by which a "change of Administration" was effected, and "We, who are out of office, may have a chance to get in."

It is deeply regreted that his narrative of those proceedings ends so abruptly. Mrs. Healy thinks her Father gathered the main facts and dates it treats of from a memorandum he kept of events as they occurred, which he carried in his pocket. This memorandum-book, (she says), her brother JAMES was robbed of, —together with a sum of money—on his way to Utah, several years before his decease, and does not doubt that it contained an account of his experience in Fremont's expedition "down the coast", in July, August, September, Octo-

ber and November, 1846 : allusion to which by
one of his brothers will have been noticed in
our preceding pages. And this suggests the
idea, that inasmuch as that that "brother's"
statement of what Mr. Ide told him about the
occurrences under the "Bear Flag Government", during its brief existence, does not *essentially differ* from the version of the same
transactions in his SENATOR WAMBOUGH LET-
TER, we may conclude that said brother's account of said "expedition" is substantially correct. Therefore we may give credence, also,
to his statement that Commodore STOCKTON,
as an authorized officer of his government,
formally received the transfer of the Californias to the United States, aboard his ship, by
the only governmental authority he then found
there ; and, in recognition of Mr. Ide's authority as Governor and Commander-in-chief, the
Commodore gave him the compliment of a reception, collation, etc., as before stated. And
we cite this circumstance as evidence that his
services in the cause of order and good government were duly appreciated by that noble officer.

The Compiler of this memorial sketch of an
unpretending citizen and early pioneer of Cal-

ifornia has deemed it due his memory, that his "Letter to Senator Wambough," giving a minute account of the "Bear Flag enterprise," should be placed before the American people, that they may be able to decide the question, whether he, or Capt. Fremont, originated and conducted this 'enterprise' to its successful issue.   We believe the generally received opinion is, that the credit of it is due to Fremont.

This theory we recollect to have heard very unreservedly advanced by a distinguished public speaker, the Hon. JAMES WILSON, an ex-member of Congress from New Hampshire. He had just returned to resume his residence in his native town, (Keene, N. H.), after an absence of four or five years during the war of the great rebellion, *in California*, where he no doubt imbibed his views on this question.   He gave, in several towns in N. H., very interesting lectures on California—geographical, mineralogical and historical—soon after his return; and, while on the latter named branch of his subject, he stated distinctly before a large audience among whom this writer was an interested listener, that John C. Fremont was the originator and leader of the "Bear Flag Party", and conqueror of California.

After having attentively read the circumstantial statement of the moral, industrial and
political aspect of affairs, and the account of
that short-lived " embrio Republic", from the
pen of Mr. IDE—written, as it undoubtedly
was, within a year of its " rise and fall"—the
unprejudiced and candid reader will find little
ground on which to base said lecturer's theory,
except on the presumption that Mr. IDE intentionally misrepresents the whole concern.   And
we leave it to the dispassionate judgment of
posterity to settle the question, as to *which* of
the two most conspicuous " *Heroes*", the unpretending mechanic, or the renowned " Pathfinder", did the country the most valuable service in the "Conquest of California" ?

CHAPTER IX.

MR. IDE'S EXPLANATION OF THE SITUATION OF AFFAIRS IN
CALIFORNIA, ON HIS ARRIVAL THERE IN 1845.

TO THE HON. SENATOR WAMBOUGH:

DEAR SIR:

BEING ever willing to contribute to the pleasure of those with whom I am associated, I am persuaded, although somewhat reluctantly, to comply with your request, by furnishing a detailed account of what is called the "Bear Flag Enterprise" or Revolution—embracing a copy or rehearsal of what was then written, or may still be among my papers; and in such manner as truly to represent any matter or circumstance that may have led to its origin, unexampled success, sudden overthrow, and—— total eclipse.

It will be with much diffidence that I engage in giving an account of the past; which at best can serve but little other good than to awaken curiosity in the mind of some, with scarce the hope of its gratification; while in

the mind of others it will not fail to renew the
memory of those scenes, and sharpen regret,
that time has blunted and robbed of power to
sting : but if duty require, I will sacrifice the
happiness I choose and enjoy in hidden retirement ; and, regardless of consequences, frankly relate occurrences that may lead to a just
estimate of the motives and designs of those
concerned as actors ; being aware that if in
aught I am mistaken, the means of correction
are at hand.

Then permit me, Sir, to call in requisition
your general knowledge of the situation of the
two parties in their relation to each other, who
were immediately concerned in, and affected by
the *" Independent Bear Flag Nation"*—for in
fact it was nothing short of National Independence to which it aspired—I say the two
parties, native Mexican citizens and natives of
other countries—including, more particularly,
recent American emigrants.

Being, on one side, excited to jealousy by
the then recent events in relation to Texas,
and a manifest disposition of certain American
gentlemen to re-enact the like scheme in California ; and by a determined resolution on the
part of the other side, to assert and maintain

the unalienable right of all men to the enjoyment of life, liberty and personal security, and
to attain the right of honorable acqusition, use
and enjoyment of the comforts of life ;—there
were, apparently, two parties ; *but, in truth
and in verity they were one people.* They were
made enemies by their prejudices and jealousies ; but it was as apparent as the face of day
that they could be bound in the bonds of mutual friendship by their common interest and
common consent and fellowship.

Let us appeal to your own heart, dear Sir :
Is it not the interest of *all men,* everywhere,
to be protected by an honorable, just and liberal government ?

And again : Do not all men desire for themselves exemption from oppression, and the liberty of justly acquiring, enjoying, possessing,
appropriating and bestowing the honest avails
of their labor, according to their own pleasure ?
If so, then men are made enemies by oppression, injustice, jealousies or ignorance. But
those who love true Liberty, and abide by the
unchanging law of justice, will subdue enemies
without protracted violence.

The above granted, it will be more easy, (or
less painful), to proceed through the tame and

lifeless narrative of simple matters of fact necessary to the formation of an opinion in relation to a matter, now no longer of the smallest
moment, only as the everlasting, self-evident
principles of self-government were concerned,
whereby universal peace can only prevail; although the rehearsal can awaken to recollection
and measurable endurance, the cares and sleepless solicitude, the far distant hope that prom-
ises peace and glory to a Nation as extended
as the race of man, because built amid the
foundations of that liberty that delighteth itself in the *Balance of Truth.*

I would, Dear Sir, that another pen than
mine might gratify the curiosity, and subserve
the interest that has been awakened : but thus
to desire is but to shrink from the task your
favorable consideration has imposed upon me.

Then be pleased to bear in mind, that prior
to the year 1846 the peace, prosperity and quiet of the good citizens of California had been
deranged by eight successive Military Revolu-
tions, which had devastated almost entirely the
whole country, from San Diego to its northern
extremity.

It will be unnecessary to describe in particular this general ruin. It was everywhere ap-

parent—presenting itself sorrowfully, and forc-
ing its consideration upon the minds of all who
were capable of perceiving the extent of that
cruelty—of that depraved spirit of injustice,
tyranny and theft, which had tempted a portion
of its most enterprising citizens to abandon the
path of common honesty—to listen to the sug-
gestions of the deceptive policy of foreign artifice, and to seek wealth and distinction by
seizing, diverting and changing the fatherly
care of government to an engine of rapacious
piracy.

Thus, on an occasion like the one I am called on to describe, it was easy to imagine that
all good, honest and intelligent citizens of California were tired of this state of continued violence, injustice and misrule.

But, dear Sir, before we bring ourselves to
the consideration of the events which gave
birth, unexpectedly, to the "Independent Bear
Flag Nation", it will be well that we consider
the situation, origin and character of the few
that were destined to be crushed and annihilat-
ed by the fears and jealousies of an apparently
well appointed, overwhelming military despotism.——Then, Sir, let us remember, that the
then recently arrived American emigrants were

no *Cuban volunteers!* They were not enlisted
from the lounges of dissipation, nor drilled in
the school of political intrigue and dishonesty.
They came not to *provoke the Mexican authorities to "strike the first blow", in a war
sought for the acquirement of that fair and
shining land to which they journeyed.* They
came not equipped and provided with military
stores. In short, they came not as enemies ;
but AS FRIENDS COME THEY, with hearts burning with love of liberty—of that liberty that
is founded on the immutable principle of equal
justice ; that gives an equivalent for what it
receives.

They were not, like your modern gold-hunters and squatters, prepared for *"fight or flight" ;*
but bearing with them their wives, their children, their flocks and herds—their home, their
all at stake ; prompted by no groveling desire
to obtain something for nothing—to rob, to
plunder those they might find possessed of
wealth, happiness and peace.

They were collected and banded together,
not by any preconcerted scheme of any kind,
but by individual enterprise,—by long cherished love of that pure, unadulterated freedom,
known only to the just and the brave ; to those

who, for the sake of peace, plant their foot and build their habitation beyond the reach of political oppression, where nature smiles in holiest loveliness—where there is naught to entice those vile miscreants who prey upon the rights of others.

Then, kind Sir, please imagine the disappointment of those brave men, who, having conquered the difficulties of the untrodden, pathless Sierra Nevada ; after having maintained their peace, unstained even by the blood of the untaught savage ; and having with toil, privation and watchfulness, known only to those who have endured similar privations—who, having pierced the trackless wilderness, had arrived within sight of the ever shining vales they had thus sought ; when, by the intervention of a self-constituted government, heated to madness by jealousies excited by designing emissaries, we were forbidden the usual hospitalities of the country, and *" ordered to return"!*

It is in vain to trouble you further to consider the situation of the newly arrived emigrants, when you remember that 13,000,000 of dollars had been offered and refused for the possession of the Bay of San Francisco, and

that the acquisition of the same had been un-
successfully sought by negotiation for more
than fourteen years.

But there was another class of citizens
concerned, who were principally of American
origin, and constituted about one-tenth of the
citizen population of California.   They had,
in many instances, intermarried and become
associated with the native citizens, and enjoyed
their common advantages.   Indeed, a portion
of them had become the merchants and finan-
ciers of the country ; and thus failed not, in
the genuine spirit of Yankeedom, to direct and
profit by those political impositions, change of
administration, and continued increase of tariff duties, by which, during ten years of increasing distress and ruin, the main body of the
people were made *miserably poor.*

But of this class the mass had fallen among
the oppressed ; and it appeared to be the pleasure of the more successful, to set the whole
community at variance—to increase public expenditure and tariff duties, which constituted
their principal stock in trade.   Whatever
scheme the merchants proposed became the rule
of action ; for it was claimed they *"paid all
the people's taxes" !*

You cannot fail to remember the preconcerted seizure and ironing of every American, except T. O. Larkin and a very few others—the
plot to scuttle the vessel and throw them all,
while in irons, into the Bay of San Diego—the
failure of· the plot by the humane interposition of the better disposed portion of the native citizens—their subsequent five months' imprisonment at Mexico ; and, withal, that those
favored merchants, (at least their leader), improved this favorable opportunity to collect
inflated demands against these prisoners. It
is quite impossible to trace, in written characters, the reflections that crowd the mind, in
view of their hypocritical and murderous acts.

While the aforementioned causes, and numerous others of like character, were producing
their legitimate fruits—fruits which were proprolific of seeds of new dissensions—Captain
Fremont came among us ; who, after having
provoked the assumed authorities of the country, left us to experience the wrath and retaliatory vengeance his acts had engendered.

Immediately after, (about the first day of
April, 1846,) Gen. José Castro, naturally humane and generous, caused to be issued and
posted up at Sonoma and various other places—

the temporary residences of the newly arrived emigrants—a proclamation, ordering " All foreigners, whose residence in the country was less than one year, to leave the country, and their property and beasts of burden, without taking arms," on pain of death.

It may well be supposed that this proclamation produced no little consternation among the recent emigrants.   But the prudence and sagacity of some of the resident (American) citizens prevented much alarm, by proposing to the authorities to call the said emigrants together, and to instruct them orally.   This was agreed to, and the citizen Americans were visited, and persuaded their new neighbors to dress themselves decently in California fashion, as far as possible, without loaned articles of clothing, and to attend respectfully and submissively the meeting.   Thus cautiously was a meeting and separation effected at Sonoma, without producing a general rupture.   But notwithstanding every effort, a large party of young men and two or three women, to escape the much expected scene of blood, left the country for Oregon.

Next came Lieut. Gillespie, who failed not to give cautionary advice in relation to a state of

preparedness, on the part of all of U. States
origin, but dissuaded from any kind of organization ; no, not even in the externals of an
" Agricultural Society"; " for such", he said,
" is the watchful jealousy of the Spaniards towards the last emigration, that the slightest
attempt at organization in any shape, or by
any name, would be but the signal for the massacre of the whole of the last emigration."
He made known that he should, as soon as
possible, recall Capt. Fremont ; and suggested
that his camp would be the means of temporary protection : or, if matters came to the
worst, to effect a retreat to the States.

CHAPTER X.

FIRST UPRISING OF THE EMIGRANTS.—CAPT. FREMONT'S PLAN
OF "NEUTRAL CONQUEST".—INTERVIEW WITH THE CAP-
TAIN AND COMMENTS THEREON.

ANOTHER month rolled on, and Capt. Fremont came not; for the snows were not yet
fully melted in the mountain gulches of the
Sierra Nevada.   The Oregon company were
long gone.   Forces were every day increasing
under Gen. José Castro at San Juan Baptista.
Six hundred armed men were known to be
foaming out vengeance against a few foreigners.   Everybody spoke of and felt the impend-
ing danger—admitted that organization and
resistance was desirable ; but all agreed that
it was impracticable.   A want of confidence in
the ability of any man among us to conduct
such an enterprise was everywhere apparent
and fully expressed, and a—a " certain fearful
looking-for of judgment and fiery indignation,
that would devour the adversary", should we
fail of success, bound and paralized the energy of that portion of our *friends* who were so
miserable as to possess more wealth than they

could *swallow at a meal.* " What was to be
done ? Were they to risk their lives, and the
lives of their wives and children in the fath-
omless snows of the Sierra Nevada ?" Oh,
no, Sir, no. This was impossible : the snows
were melted. It was the 6th of June, and all
eyes were turned to watch the approach of
Fremont ——He came !—the glorious era !—
memorable day !—when it was determined, as
we were informed nearly a year after by Col.
Benton's letter to Congress, to " *Overthrow the
government, and conquer California at once !*"
But pardon me, my dear Wambough, for thus
darting away to the consummation of such a
scheme, without describing the *modus operan-
di* whereby this was to *have been,* before coming to the subsequent plan of operation by
which it *was* accomplished.

I am requested to give such papers, among
my cast-off memoranda, as may be in point :
then read : "Notice is hereby given, that a
large body of armed Spaniards on horseback,
amounting to 250 men, have been seen on their
way to the Sacramento valley, destroying the
crops, burning the houses, and driving off the
cattle. Capt Freemont invites every freeman
in the valley to come to his camp at the Butts,

immediately; and he hopes to stay the enemy, and put a stop to his"—— (Here the sheet was folded and worn in-two, and no more is found). This document was not signed by Capt. Fremont, nor by any person in his legal company ; else it would have been legal evidence of unwarrantable interference in the difficulties brewing in the country, which *he uniformly and unequivocally declared he should refrain from.* This letter came to hand by an Indian " agent", on the 8th of June, between the hours of 10 and 11, A. M.

You may be assured there was no hour of deliberation—not a moment; the horse bounded back to the cabin ; the rifle, pistols and ammunition were, by every inmate of the house, produced at the door ; one brief sentence gave the parting advice to the fond wife and listening, excited and wondering children, while the blanket was being lashed to the saddle. Every house in the valley was visited ; but not one was found willing to leave his *goods,* not his *wife,* (for there were only two within the valley)—and we hastened to the camp of Capt. Fremont, where we arrived at break of day on the 10th, and, by dint of apparent acquiescence, learned "THE PLAN OF

CONQUEST"; which was quite simple and easy
of accomplishment—and here it is : First, select a dozen men who *have nothing to lose,* but
everything to gain. Second, encourage them to
commit depredations against Gen. Castro, the
usurper, and thus supply the camp with horses
necessary for a trip to the States. Third, to
make prisoners of some of the principal men,
and thus provoke Castro to *strike the first blow*
in a war with the United States. This done,
finish the conquest by uniting the forces, and
" marching back to the States."

The foregoing constituted the whole of the
" first edition" of Capt. Fremont's *plan of neutral conquest* of California.

And here I would beg a moment's indulgence, that I may the more fully show the true
position of the " Bear Flag nation", so far as
relates to any influence Capt. Fremont may
have had in its origin or organization.

I do not wish to impugn his motives or conduct, but have no doubt he acted honestly
in accordance with what he conceived to be
the will of his superiors. Nevertheless, we
must speak the whole truth, and say that the
aforementioned plan was fully presented to us,
with the advantages it would bring ; to wit :

THE LIFE OF WILLIAM B. IDE.

a war between Mexico and the U. S., and the
conquest and union of California with them.

Capt. Fremont, while we were alone in his
markee, on the evening of the 10th, rehearsed
the above plan, humanely providing that none
who had anything to sacrafice should be implicated therein ; and asked the opinion of his
auditor, who said in reply, that "it would be
a long time ere he would consent to, or join
with, any set or company of irresponsible persons, who first commit an outrage, and then
dishonorably leave the country and others to
settle the difficulty, or endure its consequences." Capt. F. remonstrated against this reply ; and especially against the reflection of
dishonor cast on himself—went on to show that
the emigrants had received great indignities
from Castro, and would be justified in any
measure they might adopt for their safety—
went on to say, that if the emigrants waited
to receive the first blow, all hope in resistance
would be in vain ; and cited, in support of his
argument, the seizure of all Americans that
had taken place, as herein before mentioned.

I then informed him that no personal reproach was intended ; that he, (Fremont), as
an accredited American officer, was supposed

to act in obedience to his instructions from his
superiors ; but that we, although beyond the
protecting shield of the U. States' flag, still
cherished the memory of the AMERICAN NAME,
the honor of which was yet dearer to us by far
than any rewards of falsehood and treachery
dishonorably won.   Whereupon Capt. F. became exasperated.   Rising hastily he said : "*I
will not suffer such language in my Camp; it
is disorganizing !*" and went immediately out.

Thus ended all intercourse, on our part, with
Capt. Fremont, until the 25th of June, when,
in due course of events, his next salutations
will be given.   A few minutes after his departure Mr. King came into the markee, and
politely invited us to another tent, and very
soon commenced asking : " Suppose the men
succeed in taking the horses, what will you in
that case propose to be done?"   The reply was,
" When the breach is once made that involves
us all in its consequences, it is useless to consider the propriety of the measure.   We are
too few for division. *In for it, the whole man!*
Widen the breach, that none can stand outside
thereof. *Down on Sonoma!   Never flee the
country*, nor give it up while there is an arm
to fight, or a voice to cry aloud for Independ-

ence. But let truth and honor guide our
course. The United States may have cause of
war against Mexico ; but that is nothing to
us. We have cause of war and blood—such
as it is impossible for the United States to
have received." "Good !" cried Mr. King,
and ran out to repeat the sentiment. "Good !
Hurrah for Independence !" cried the whole
camp ; and several persons, among whom was
KIT CARSON, begged of Capt. Fremont their
discharge from the service of the exploring expedition, that they might be at liberty to join
us. This was peremptorily refused. Fremont,
in my hearing, expressly declared that he was
not at liberty to afford us the least aid or as-
sistance; nor would he suffer any of his men
to do so; that he would not consent to dis-
charge any of them, as he had hired them ex-
pressly for, and needed their assistance on his
journey over land to the States; that he had
not asked the assistance of the emigrants for
his protection; that he was able, of his own
party, to fight and whip Castro, if he chose,
but that he should not do so, unless first as-
saulted by him; and that positively he should
wait only for a supply of provisions,—two
weeks at farthest, when he would, without fur-

*ther reference to what might take place here,
be on his march for the States."*

Scarcely were these statements made, ere it
was reported and acclaimed : " The horses are
coming !"—and on they came ! All was animation in the camp. Capt. Merritt (for it was
understood it was he who was to be the leader
of this little band of heroes), made report that
he had followed his *instructions,* as given by
the " *advice"* of Capt. Fremont, and had surprised the guards and captured the *whole* band
of 250 horses—had offered to give back the
arms of the guard ; and, for " fair play", to
fight the battle over again, at 50 or 100 yards
distance. This favor being refused, he had generously given each man his arms and two horses ; and boldly directed the released prisoners
to tell Gen. Castro " if he wanted his horses,
to come and take them."

This conduct was highly applauded by Capt.
Fremont, (who, a moment before, would not
and dare not, on his honor, offer us the least
protection or assistance). The said horses were
acknowledged to be the rightful property of
the twelve men who so valiantly had captured
them, and were delivered over to the care of
Capt. Fremont for safe keeping, while their

new owners might acquire new spoils in the direction of Sonoma.

It was 12 at night, and all possible haste was made to be off, as it was known that the men who had been imprudently released would, in all probability, separate and spread intelligence of the rising of the emigrants, and of the taking of government horses, in every direction ; and it was more than probable, that the garrison at Sonoma might be *alarmed,* rather than *surprised.*

CHAPTR XI.

THE PARTY LARGELY RE-ENFORCED BY NEW RECRUITS—THEIR
MISTAKEN NOTIONS EXPLAINED.—WHAT HAPPENED ON
THEIR ARRIVAL AT SONOMA.—MR. IDE MADE COMMAND-
ER-IN-CHIEF, " BY ACCLAMATION", AND TAKES THE FORT,
INSTANTER.—THEIR INCIPIENT MOVEMENTS UNDER THE
" INDEPENDENT BEAR FLAG GOVERNMENT".

JUST about sunrise on the 11th of June, '46,
thirteen mounted men, armed with rifles and
pistols, crossed the Sacramento River, a little
below, or at the mouth of Feather River.
Much time was spent in procuring fresh horses,
and no accessions were made to our forces that
day. We supped at Gordon's, on Coche Creek,
who gave us a bullock ; but was too deeply interested in our enterprise to join our party just
then. At night we groped our way over the
mountain pass, and ere the sun had become *oppressive,* we were safely at the Rancho of Major Barnard. He, also, allowed us to klll and
eat a fat bullock, but like the other dear friends,
was too fond of the goods of this life, seriously
to think of dying in defence of others.

Here or hereabouts were a considerable num-

ber of newly arrived emigrants, and the day
was spent in obtaining recruits. Much time
was spent in procuring as many as swelled our
number to *thirty-two;* and on the 13th, at 11,
P. M., sleep and drowsiness were on the point
of delaying, if not defeating our enterprise.
We were 36.miles from Sonoma. The sleepless energy of some arroused their companions
by representing the danger of delay, and half
an hour's debate turned the scale in favor of
immediate action, and all *put* for Sonoma for
dear life, as fast as our jaded horses could carry us, so, if possible, to arrive there by a rough
path away from the traveled road, before the
day-light gave notice of our approach.

And now, dear Sir, as it will be some little
time before we get there, I will improve the
time to state the views of the party as to the
object of their intended visit.

It will be borne in mind that none of this
party, save myself, were present when the sentiment of INDEPENDENCE was so heartily cheered in the camp under the Nevada mountains ;
nor was it reasonable to suppose that any of
them were informed by any of Capt. Fremont's
men, that his plan was to provoke an attack
on Castro's camp, *before he left for the States,*

to take along with him the offenders, to save
them from certain destruction. It was known
that Capt. F. possessed the unbounded confidence of those twelve men, and also that most
of them desired to avail themselves of the opportunity for a safe return to the States, in the
service of the United States, at $ 60 per month
for the trip. The subject of *Independence* was
only talked of as an event that might occur ;
and no one of them seemed to understand that
the taking of Sonoma formed any part of our
errand there.

And, moreover, Capt. Fremont, who is allowed to be proverbially cautious and prudent,
gave his directions—or rather " advice",—in
such manner as to avoid legal testimony in any
matter of interference in California politics,
(which he invariably and solemnly disavowed)
that it was impossible to prove, authoritative-
ly from him responsibility for any line of conduct by our party ; but every one, (especially
those of the " twelve"), seemed, as if by intu-
ition, to undertand that our only business was
to capture and convey to Fremont's camp Gen.
M. G. Vallejo, Don Salvadore Vallejo, Col.
Prudshon and Capt. Jacob P. Leese, if practicable, and if not, to drive off another band of

horses, or commit any other act of violence, in its nature calculated to provoke pursuit and attack in the proper quarter.

Fully impressed with the importance of this mission of benevolence and good will towards the sleeping and unsuspecting gentlemen to whom we were about to pay our respects, we took timely precaution to swear certain of our number against the commission of violence against either of those gentlemen. This step was considered proper, as we were aware there were certain *breathings of vengeance* against some of them, in the minds of a few of our party.

It was known that Doct. Semple, who was an active and conspicuous leading man of the host, was in favor of Independence, *instanter;* but we knew of none willing to *push* the measure. Under these circumstances it was thought prudent not to broach the subject generally, until some crisis should call the principle into immediate action.

Thus circumstanced, we arrived at Sonoma; and, after reconnoitering the place, and notifying our friends of our object in seizing the aforesaid gentlemen, and having secured the captain of the guard whom we found a little

way out of town, we surrounded the house of
Gen. M. G. Vallejo just at daybreak, on the
14th. William Merritt. Doct. Semple and
Mr. Knight, (who took wise care to have it
understood on all hands that he was forced into the scrape as an interpreter), entered the
house to secure their prisoners.

Jacob P. Leese, an American by birth, and
brother-in-law of Gen. Vallejo, who lived near
by, was soon there, to soothe the fears, and otherwise as far as possible assist his friends.
Doct Salvadore was also found there, and Col.
Prudshon was also soon arrested and brought
there. After the first surprise had a little subsided, as no immediate violence was offered,
the General's generous *spirits* gave proof of
his usual hospitality—as the richest wines and
brandies sparkled in the glasses, and those who
had thus unceremoniously met soon became
merry companions ; more especially—the weary visitors.

While matters were going on thus happily
in the house, the main force sat patiently
guarding it without. They appeared to understand that they had performed all the duty
required of them, and only waited, that the
said prisoners might be prepared and brought

forth for their journey, and——waited still.
The sun was climbing up the heavens an
hour or more, and yet no man, nor voice, nor
sound of violence came from the house to tell
us of events within : patience was ill, and lingered ill. " Let us have a captain," said one—a
captain, said all. Capt. Grigsby was elected,
and went immediately into the house.   The
men still sat upon their horses—patience grew
faint ; an hour became an age.   "Oh ! go into the house, *Ide,* and come out again and let
us know what is going on there !"   No sooner
said than done.   There sat Doct. S., just modifying a long string of articles of capitulation.
There sat Merritt—his head fallen : there sat
Knight, no longer able to interpret ; and there
sat the new made Captain, as mute as the seat
he sat upon.   The bottles had well nigh vanquished the captors.   The Articles of Capitulation were seized hastily, read and thrown
down again, and the men outside were soon informed of their contents.   Pardon us, dear Doctor—we will not make an exposition.   It is
sufficient to say, that by the rule of opposition,
they gave motion and energy to the waiting
mass, and all that was necessary was to direct
the torrent and guide the storm.

No one hitherto in authority had thought of seizing the fortress, or disarming its guard. Capt. Grigsby was hastily called, and the men demanded of him that the prisoners should be immediately conveyed to the Sacramento valley. Capt. G. inquired, " What are the orders of Capt. Fremont in relation to these men ?" Each man looked on his fellow, yet none spake. " But have you not got Capt. Fremont's name in black and white to authorize you in this you have done ?" cried the enraged Captain— and immediately we* demanded, that if there were any one present who had orders from him, either written or verbal, he declare the same. All declared, one after another, that they had no such orders. Thereupon the Captain was briefly but particulary informed, that the people whom he knew had received from Gen. Castro, and others in authority, the most insolent indignities—had been, on pain of death, ordered to leave the country ; and that they had

---

* The modest writer of this Letter, it will be observed, invariably uses the pronoun *we*, instead of *I*, in referring to what he had said or done; and the Editor has not felt himself at liberty to change his phraseology in these cases, as it may be necessary for the reader to do, mentally, in order to a correct understanding of what he *said* or *did.*

resolved to take the redress of grievances into
their own hands ; that we could not claim the
protection of any government on earth, and
were alone responsible for our conduct ; that—
(Here the Captain's "fears of doing wrong"
overcame his patriotism, and he interrupted
the speaker by saying, " *Gentlemen, I have
been deceived; I cannot go with you; I resign
and back out of the scrape.* I can take my
family to the mountains as cheap as any of
you"—and Doct. S. at that moment led him
into the house.   Disorder and confusion prevailed.   One swore he would not stay to guard
prisoners—another swore we would all have our
throats cut—another called for fresh horses,
and all were on the move—every man for himself ; when the speaker [Mr. Ide] resumed his
effort, raising his voice louder and more loud,
as the men receded from the place, saying :
" We need no horses ; we want no horses.
Saddle no horse for me. I can go to the Spaniards, and make FREEMEN of them.   I will
give myself to them.   I will lay my bones
here, before I will take upon myself the igno-
miny of commencing an honorable work, and
then flee like cowards, like thieves, when no
enemy is in sight.   In vain will you say you

had honorable motives ! Who will believe it ?
*Flee this day, and the longest life cannot wear
off your disgrace!* Choose ye ! choose ye this
day, what you will be ! We are robbers, or
or we *must be conquerors!*"—and the speaker
in despair turned his back upon his receding
companions.

THE LAST WORD—NOW THE BATTLE !

With new hope they rallied around the desponding speaker—made him their Commander, their Chief ; and his next words commanded the taking of the Fort. Joy lighted up
every mind, and in a moment all was secured :
18 prisoners, 9 brass cannon, 250 stands of
arms, and tons of copper, shot, and other public property, of the value of 10 or 1200 dollars, was seized and held in trust for the public benefit.

Arrangements were immediately made for
putting the garrison in a complete state of defence. Tools suitable for fortification, and for
supplying a well of water within our walls ;
and a liberal stock of provisions were procured
on contract—pledging the public property now
in possession for future payment. But that
portion of our forces who still adhered to the

" neutral conquest" plan, with the four gentlemen, the aforementioned prisoners at Sutter's
Fort, were allowed to remain under the protection of Capt. Fremont, where every comfort was
granted them that their situation allowed.

Thus and so was the " Independent Bear
Flag Republic" inaugurated.   Other circumstances might be given ; but not to change its
character.   What dear friend of Capt. Fremont will hereafter claim that the taking of
Sonoma, or the hoisting the Independent Flag,
or any other act that grew out of the same,
constituted any part of his plan for the conquest of California ?   If any of those twelve
men who took the horses had have had any
idea that Fremont desired the seizure of the
garrison, think you they would have sat on
their horses more than two hours, within pistol shot of the Fort, and never thought of taking pssession of it ? Or think you that if Capt.
F. had designed the capture and hoisting the
Independent Flag, he would not have so instructed his three champions, who were the
leaders of this force, up to the very moment
of the recalling the scattering soldiers, and the
appointment of the Commander by the people,
who ordered the taking of the Garrison ?

CHAPTER XII.

THE COMMANDER'S ADDRESS TO HIS MEN.—HIS REASONS FOR
ISSUING A PROCLAMATION—ITS TEXT IN FULL—NOTICE
OF ITS PUBICATION ADDRESSED TO COMMODORE STOCKTON
AS A U. S. OFFICER, THEN DAILY EXPECTEED ON THAT
COAST.

NEXT, (if you will be pleased to exercise patience enough), we will consider the circumstances tending to its unexampled success, as
we trace, step by step, its history to its first
acquaintance with Capt. Fremont, and thence
to its finale.

After the return of the three leaders of the
party of the primitive plan of neutral conquest, and seven others had " left us alone in
our glory," the said " Bear Flag"—made of
plain cotton cloth, and ornamented with the
red flannel of a shirt from the back of one of
the men, and christened by the words " California Republic," in red-paint letters on both
sides—was raised upon the standard where had
floated on the breezes the Mexican flag aforetime.   It was on the 14th of June, '46.   Our

number was *twenty-four*, all told. The mechanism of the flag was performed by WM.
TODD of Illinois. The grizzly bear was chos-
en as an emblem of strength and unyielding
resistance. The men were divided into two
companies of 10 men each. The 1st artillery
was busily engaged in putting the cannon in
order, which were charged doubly with grape
and cannister. The 1st rifle company was busied in cleaning, repairing and loading the
small arms. The Commander, after setting a
guard, and posting a sentinel on one of the
highest buildings to watch the approach of any
one who might have the curiosity to inspect
operations, directed his leisure to the establishment of rules of discipline and order, and of
a system of finance, whereby all the defenceless families might be brought within the lines
of our garrison and supported. Ten thousand
pounds of flour were purchased on the credit
of the Government, and deposited within the
garrison ; an account was opened for the supply of beef, on terms agreed upon : and a few
barrels of salt constituted our main supplies.
Whiskey was altogether a contraband article.*

* MR. IDE was a life-long " Te-totaler" and " Temperance
Advocate," of the straightest sect.—ED.

After the first round of duties were performed, as many as could be spared off guard were
called together, and the situation fully explain-
to the men by the Commander of the garrison.
It was fully represented that our success, nay
our very life, depended on the magnanimity
and justice of our course of conduct, coupled
with sleepless vigilance and care.

(But ere this we had gathered as many of
the surrounding citizens as possible, and placed them between four strong walls : they were
more than twice our number.) The Commander chose from these stangers the most intelligent—by the aid of an interpreter went on to
explain the cause of our coming together ; our
determination to offer equal justice to all good
citizens ; that we had not called them there
to rob them of their liberty, or to deprive them
of any portion of their property, nor to disturb their social relations one with another—
nor yet to desecrate their religion. He went
on to explain the common rights of all men,
and showed them that those rights had been
shamefully denied them by those heretofore in
authority ; that the Missions had been robbed,
and the general prosperity of the country destroyed ; that we had been driven to take

up arms in defence of life and the common rights of man ; and that we had pledged our lives to the overthrow of injustice, and the establishment of such government as should give freedom to commerce, and that should collect its revenues of those who, by their improper conduct, make governments necessary for the protection of all good citizens.

He went on further to say, that although he had, for the moment, deprived them of that liberty which is the right and the privilege of all good and just men, it was only that they might become acquainted with his unalterable purpose : and, that having made them thus acquainted, "without waiting to know whether you approve or disapprove—whether you are disposed to regard us as friends or enemies —we will restore you the liberty of which we have deprived you, after we have convinced you"—(and here he assumed all the fierce, determined energy of manner that such an emergency was calculated to inspire)—"that as enemies we will kill and destroy you ! but as friends we will share with you all the blessings of liberty, and all the privileges that we ourselves can hope to enjoy." "Now, dear Sirs", he continued to say, "go and prepare your-

selves for the battle ! We are few, but we are
firm and true. We have not come to hold
forth deceitful appearances. Go. You are
free as the air of heaven. Receive us as friends,
and assist us to give liberty to your country
and countrymen ; or, meet us like brave men,
according to your own time and pleasure."

Although the address was not the twentieth
part interpreted, yet the importance of success
in the measure, to persons circumstanced as we
were, gave expression that would have been understood by every nationality and tongue under
heaven ; and the *Spaniard*, even, embraced
the Commander as he pronounced the name of
WASHINGTON. There was a glow of feeling
beaming from his eye, that defied all hypocra-
cy, as he said, " Suffer my companions to re-
remain until we complete a treaty of peace
and friendship, and then go and come as friends
—only that we be not required to take arms
against our brethren."

By the unanimous vote of the garrison all
the powers of the four departments of government were conferred, for the time being, upon
him who was first put in command of the fort;
yet *Democracy* was the ruling principle that
settled every measure—*Vox Populi*, our rule.

On the evening of the 14th, after every precaution for security for the night coming had
been taken, the subject of issuing a Proclamation was discussed ; and, notwithstanding ar-
guments were used tending to show that we
were bound by a proper respect for the rights
and interests of all honest and good citizens of
California, to represent ourselves as to our doings and purposes, yet a very large proportion
of our men were against making any public
representation of our situation and intentions,
until our numbers should have been increased
to something like a force adequate to the undertaking. But how were our forces to be aug-
mented, and who would come to the assistance
of those who were only represented as robbers
and rebels ? Would our enemies be pleased to
represent us truly, and in such a character as
would induce others to incur the like responsibilities? Or, would Capt. Fremont volunteer for us such kindly assistance, after having
pledged his honor and the honor of his country to remain neutral ?—and, besides, he had
declared his intention to leave the country
within two weeks, and that in our own hearing. Were we to believe that Capt. Fremont
would hold out, publicly, false pretentions ?

Those who would have entertained such an opinion, without cause, of an officer of a government they delight to honor, must have been virtually destitute of any just sense of honor themselves. But all would not do. It was contended by some, notwithstanding all his pretentions to the contrary, that he would yet consent to become our leader. So it was urged that no proclamation should be made until Capt. Fremont, Doct. Mearch, or some other person of distinction, could be persuaded to join us.

So, here we were ; by our flag proclaimed " The California Republic" ! twenty-four self-consecrated victims to the god of *Equal Rights* —unknown by any mortal being, except ten men who had dissented from our plan of operations, and fled to the protection of Fremont's camp, (except 30 or 40 Spaniards, who had, from a brief acquaintance, sworn fidelity to our cause), exposed not only to the wrath of 600 armed men, whom we were compelled, in order to avoid the just imputation of violence and crime, to defy in open fight, but to the unmingled scorn and contempt of all honorable men, whether Mexicans or Americans, if we failed to represent our true character, and the cir-

cumstances which compelled us to assume such
an unusual position.   Was it prudent to delay
a just representation to the public ear? to that
community which had equal rights with ourselves to a representation in any system of government we might establish ?   Was it prudent
thus to delay what it immediately concerned
everybody to know, until the happening of an
event which might never occur ?   Who or
what circumstance was to call to our aid that
august personage capable of duly and honorably representing to the public favor our benevolent designs ?

Under these circumstances, and impressed
with these views, it was believed that any representation was preferable to none ; and our
Commander [invested with "all the powers of
the four departments of the government", it
will be remembered], JACKSON-like, "assumed
the responsibility" of performing his duty, "as
he understood" his obligations to all concerned, and drew up, on the morning of the 15th,*

* This was the morning of the EIGHTH DAY, since he had,
"between the hours of 10 and 11, A. M.," left his family to
arouse the emigrants to action in sel-defence ; but they fled
to Oregon.   The two days thus spent, and then four or five
more days and sleepless nights, in organizing the "new Government", (his relatives believe) was a strain upon his phyic-
al powers of endurance, materially shortening his useful days.

between the hours of 1 and 4 o'clock, the following

"PROCLAMATION,

"TO ALL PERSONS, INHABITANTS OF THE COUNTY OF SONOMA AND COUNTRY AROUND, RÉQUESTING THEM TO REMAIN AT PEACE; TO PERSUE THEIR RIGHTFUL OCCUPATIONS,— WITHOUT FEAR OF MOLESTATION.

" The Commander-in-chief at Sonoma gives his inviolable pledge to all persons in California, not found bearing arms, or instigating others to take up arms against him, that they shall not be disturbed in their persons, property, religion, or social relations to each other, by men under his command.

" He hereby most solemnly declares the object of his movement to be,—first, to defend our women and children, and his brave companions in arms, who were first invited to this country by a promise of lands on which to settle themselves and families ; who were promised a Republican government ; who, when having arrived in California, were denied even the privilege of buying or renting lands of their friends ; who, instead of being allowed a participation in, or of being protected by a Republican government, were oppressed by a military despotism ; who were even threatened by proclamation of one of the principal officers of the aforesaid oppressive government, with extermination, if they would not depart out of the country, leaving all their property— their arms and their beasts of burden ; and who were thus to be despoiled of the means of defence or of flight—and were to have been driven through deserts inhabited by hostile savages to certain death.

" To overthrow a government which has robbed and destroyed the Missions, and appro-priated the properties thereof to the individu-al aggrandizement of its favorites ; which has violated good faith, by its treachery in the be-stowment of public lands ; which has shame-fully oppressed and ruined the laboring and producing inhabitants of California, by their enormous exactions of tariff on goods import-ed into the country :—this is the purpose of the brave men who are associated under his command.

" He also declares his object, in the second place, to be,—and he hereby invites all good and patriotic citizens in California to assist him—to establish and perpetuate a liberal, a just and honorable Government, which shall secure to all, civil, religious and personal liberty ; which shall insure the security of life and property ; which shall detect and punish crime and injustice ; which shall encourage industry, virtue and literature ; and which shall foster agriculture, manufactures and mechanism, by guaranteeing freedom to commerce.

"He further proclaims that he relies upon the justice of his cause—upon the favor of Heaven—upon the wisdom and good sense of the people of California, and upon the bravery of those who are bound and associated with him by the principle of self-preservation, by their love of Liberty and by their hatred of Tyranny—for his hope of success.

"And he further premises that a Government, to be prosperous and ameleiorating in its tendency, must originate among its people : its officers should be its servants, and its glory its COMMON REWARD !"

" (Signed)   WILLIAM B. IDE,
                                        Commander.
"Head-Quarters at Sonoma, }
     June 15th, A. D. 1846." }

A letter was also written, during the night, addresssd to Commodore STOCKTON, who was daily expected to be at the Bay, informing him—and intended, by the earliest possible

means, to inform the world in general, so far
as it was interested, and the Government of
the United States, through its officers, in particular—that we had been compelled in self-
defence to appeal to arms ; that we had possessed ourselves of the fortress of Sonoma—
had set up a Flag of Independence, and were
determined, whether victorious or otherwise,
to approve ourselves not unworthy the sympa-
thy, at least, of those who labor for the glory
of the American name.

And let me remark, dear Sir, that this letter (a copy of which I still have, and have no
doubt of the present existence of the original)
did not, in the remotest manner, ask for or intimate that we desired assistance ; but it was
intended to notify, in due season, the officers
and Government of the U. S., that we had,
agreeably to the universal and immutable right
of all men, claimed the right of self-government for the good citizens of all California ;
that we had solemnly, by an appeal to the last
resort, abjured all connection with the government of Mexico, its protection and liabilities ;
—that although other nations might have just
claims upon Mexico, they could have no claim
upon the sovereignty of the people of Califor-

nia ;—that we had recorded our establishment, and notified our seizure and possession.   And farther : lest the well known desire, on the part of the United States' Government, to possess itself of the Bay of San Francisco should tempt the officers of said Government to commit an unwarrantable and inglorious interference in our affairs, *in violation of the one principle that hath given peace to the world,* we had, in a timely manner, incorporated in this same *"notice"*, most sincerely and unequivocally, that we would embrace the earliest *honorable* opportunity to unite this fair land with the land of our birth.

It was honestly and implicitly believed on our part, that the U. S. officers, whom we were proud to believe were men of deathless honor, would rejoice to acknowledge our right to Independence, and so far become our friends as to conquer any inward aspiring after individual renown as conquerors of California, and still continue to adhere tenaciously to that just sense of national honor which prompted the *Reply to the above mentioned Notice.*

CHAPTER XIII.

ARTICLES OF AGREEMENT AND TREATY STIPULATIONS ARRANG-
ED.—SYMPTOMS OF DISCONTENT AMONG THE MEN OF THE
GARRISON—A CHANGE OF " COMMANDER" TALKED OF.—
THE LETTER TO COMMODORE STOCKTON FORWARDED BY
WILLIAM TODD—CAPT. J. MONTGOMERY, OF THE U. S. SHIP
PORTSMOUTH, RETURNS BY LIEUT. MISSROON A FRIENDLY
LETTER—CAUSING THE COMMANDER, HOWEVER, NOT A
LITTLE DISQUIETUDE.

But it is proper to return to the history of
events, in the order in which they transpired.

Every moment that could be prudently spared from the duty of overseeing the guards, at
very short intervals, (as most of the men had
been deprived of sleep, and some of us for five
days and nights in succession), was devoted to
writing—as we had no clerks or printing establishment.   The remainder of the night was
spent in drawing up such articles of agreement
and treaty stipulations, as were most likely to
enlist the good will of all good citizens of California, without respect to the circumstance of
any peculiar origin of its inhabitants.

These treaty stipulations were based on the

independent right, self-existent in every individual, to cast off at pleasure any former obligation to governments, that experience might
demonstrate as unproductive of the best good
of the governed ; and to remain isolated, if
consistent with their circumstances and pleasure : or, if necessary to secure protection and
peace in the enjoyment of that just Liberty
which is, ever was and ever will be the immutable birth-right of all men, to associate themselves voluntarily for the present necessity, under such regulations as may best guarantee the
protection sought.   *   *   *

But not to stop to make our last appeal in
behalf of equal Liberty, we will simply inform
you that, in addition to the preceding statement, the stipulations provided, First : That
no individual division of the public property
should be allowed, but that such should be sacredly held as security for the faithful payment
of the just value of such articles of provisions
as necessity demanded for the common support
of such as should, without pecuniary consideration or hope of other reward than the con-
sciousness of having freely given their devoted
services to the cause of Independence, and the
the establishment of such government as the

good sense and wisdom of the people of California might desire. Secondly : That Commerce should be free—that no impost should be levied or collected—that frauds and crimes only should be taxed, and that without license! Thirdly : That, the supreme direction of the affairs of Paternal government should be entrusted to those alone, whose generous philanthropy and patriotic regard for the welfare of their children, in common with the rest of their fellow-countrymen, and the race of men in general, would enable them willingly and cheerfully to do so, without enlisting the corrupting influence of the love of money. That no governor, president, legislator, member of assembly, council-man, or Senator, (if you please), should ever be enticed to corruption, fraud and dishonor, by the love of money. Fourthly : That all involuntary taxation of the virtuous, industrious, self-governing freemen of California, or any other people whom we would account worthy of our fellowship, should never be allowed or practiced—that whenever taxation shall be necessary, (except as punishment for the infraction of the moral principle of honesty, justice and equal rights) it shall be between contracting parties equally free to choose or refuse. Fifthly : No persons shall ever be compelled, contrary to their free will, to bear arms, or otherwise to serve the cause of Liberty : for that would prove that its people were unworthy of its blessings ; or, that those blessings were no longer worth enjoying. And, lastly : All good friends, (Spaniards and native Californians), who had taken a solemn oath that they were pleased to support our Independent principles and Flag, were on their part, according to their request, excused from bearing arms against any of their brethren who might not understand, or believe in the sincerity of our professions, or our determined resolution to make a virtue of the stern necessity which had compelled us to assume responsibilities so unusual and unlooked-for ; and voluntarily promised that they would write to their friends and acquaintances throughout all the country, and inform them as to the nature of our intentions, and persuade them not to resist us ; and they further voluntarily agreed to furnish us with any supplies of provisions, or other articles we might stand in need of for the public service, on the conditions we had proposed ;—and, further, it was stipulated and agreed that receipts should in every case be given, signed by the Commander of the garrison ; and that no gift, not even the smallest trifle, should be accepted by any of the soldiers, individually or collectively, lest it should be infered that, in some event, extortion, through fear of violence, should have been practiced.

It was not without the greatest difficulty that these stipulations could be interpreted to the understanding of the first Alcalde of the District of Sonoma ; and still more difficult to make him see how and by what magic the wheel or postule of government was to be made to operate without the aid of the love of money. It became necessary to dissect each sentence, and reduce it to its simplist form, ere it could be interpreted into Spanish, and by another interpreter changed back to English again, which was considered necessary in order to any certainty of understanding.

There was another difficulty of no inconsiderable magnitude, which was a want of proper understanding on the part of many of our own men, of the policy or principle of action necessary for success. That portion of our little band of heroes who at first enlisted for plunder and flight to the States, who proposed to tear

down and pillage the house of Gen. M. G. Vallejo (as it was known that he had charge of a
large amount of money in his house) still earnestly contended that a Spaniard had no right
to liberty, and but very little right to the enjoyment of life.

You will not, therefore, dear Sir, be surprised to incredulity, we hope, when you are informed, that after a portion of the men had
exhibited the most surprising vigilance in capturing all the Spaniards, and even some others
whose love of freedom was considered questionable, and thrusting them indiscriminately within the walls of the callaboose ; that after the
Alcalde had been taken from thence by the
Commander—not without the most earnest remonstrance on the part of a large portion of
our " Independent Freemen"—that after they
had witnessed the assurance that the said Alcalde gave of his approbation of our cause ;
after they had refused their consent to the publication to the world of our intentions, lest it
might be the means of hastening our indiscriminate destruction ; when you are informed
that the release of one man was sufficient to
fill them with consternation—to fill their minds
with distrust as to the sagacity and ability of

their leader to conduct an enterprise fraught
with such terrible consequences ;—we add,
when you are also informed that it became
necessary to conduct these friendly negotia-
tions without the camp, and without the full
knowledge of the garrison, you will not be surprised that it was by a great sacrifice of feeling on their part, that the garrison continued
their Commander in office.

But on the other hand it was acknowledged
that no fault could be found with his watchful
care in providing for the maintenance of that
security of "*persons*", now become so apparently necessary ; and, as he was the only man
then present that could command with that
determination and decision necessary to insure
obedience, it was again agreed, that until a
more suitable man could be found, he should
be sustained.

Early in the morning of the 15th of June it
was deemed necessary to send an ambassador
to the Bay, to carry the letter heretofore spok-
en of to Commodore STOCKTON, if he were
then arrived ; and if not, to deliver it to him
who should be highest in command in the U.
S. Navy then present. But as no man might
be found willing to risk his life in going to the

Bay of San Francisco (to Yerba Buena) simply to carry a letter, it became necessary to make other and more important business. It is necessary and right, sometimes, to take advantage even of the fears, as well as of the bravery of those with whom we have to do. That the fears of the men of the garrison, after the first moments of excitement had subsided had prevented, and would continue to prevent desertion, and to bind them close to the loaded cannon, and to the 250 loaded muskets, was easy to understand ; but how to compel an individual, by the same fear, to travel 50 or 60 miles through an enemy's country, was a problem not so readily solved.

The men of the garrison were accordingly summoned to attend, and the circumstances of our situation were recited ;—positions upon the neighboring hills were pointed out, where Gen. Castro might plant his cannon ; and, in case of the want of a sufficient supply of powder, we might be greatly annoyed : and the men of the garrison were informed that a letter had been prepared for Commodore STOCKTON, and a volunteer was necessary to carry it, and take charge of anything that might be sent back in return.

William Todd, whom circumstances afterwards proved to be a brave man, volunteered
to go—who was conducted on his way immediately by the Commander of the garrison, beyond the guard lines, where he received the said
letter and full information in relation to the
existence of the Proclamation and treaty stipulations, which had been partially made known
to the Alcalde before refered to, and the hopes
of the Commander were communicated in relation to the same. He was then charged in
relation to his journey ; and, withal, to be sure
not to ask for anything from the men or officers of the ship where he delivered the letter,
as the letter contained all the business of his
mission ; but simply to take whatever (if anything) was put into his hand, and be sure to
make his way back by another route than the
one he pursued thither.

The balance of the 15th, the 16th and 17th,
was spent in translating and re-translating the
simple elements of the articles of the treaty
of peace and amity, and of the Proclamation,
by so many of the men as could be spared from
the general oversight of the garrison.

The men were divided into 4 night guards
of 6 men each, and into 8 day guards of 3 men

each. One half of the men were at all times, by day, employed in camp duty—the other half guarded and slept ; and the Captain, who was never counted anywhere, served as officer of the day and night. The camp service consisted in cleaning the muskets, providing wood for cooking, bringing in provisions and cooking. Roast beef, fried pan-cakes and cold water served us for rations.

We received no intelligence from abroad the first four days ; and such had been the vigilance with which our camp was guarded, that none were known to approach it near enough to be at all acquainted with our means of defence, and to escape. Every opportunity was embraced to make ourself and our plan of government known and approved by our prisoners ; for which purpose we took occasion to make them understand it was necessary to detain them a few days.

On the evening of the 17th came back Wm. Todd, and with him Lieut. Missroon, of the U. S. ship Portsmouth, bearing a letter from his Capt. J. Montgomery. He was bearer of verbal dispatches, which for prudent reasons were not written, but refered to and authorized by written documents from Captain Montgomery.

It appeared on investigation, that our messenger, after having delivered the letter, and
waiting some time, and nothing was said about
any powder, thought it necessary, notwithstanding his orders not to ask for anything, to
inquire if any powder was to be sent ; and the
letter, which was written to be read before the
garrison, contained the following sentence :—
" Although we have ample means to defend
ourselves from any attack that can be made on
us by Castro, by the use of small arms, we
have not a sufficient quantity of powder to
withstand for any considerable length of time,
an attack by the use of cannon".

Thus, under these unfortunate circumstances, it was easy for our good Capt. Montgomery
to mistake the real design of the letter, (which
it is true was written in haste, but with care),
and which contained no intimation that we desired of him the slightest assistance—no, not
" so much as one charge of powder"—which to
have asked would have been the begging our
own destruction, and inviting that unwarrantable inteference we feared, and which afterwards ingloriously arrested our progress, defeated our plans—caused disobedience of our
orders, and ourself to be bitterly, and, else,

justly reproached by more than a hundred of
our companions who knew us only by our
Proclamation—who had secretly organized under Weaver, Bird and others on the south side
of the Bay—waiting in vain, because of the
disobedience of our orders, for that assistance
which it was abundantly in our power to have
given—whereby Castro's main army would
have been suddenly and wholly defeated.

But to reserve this part of our history for
the leading subject of another division, we will
rehearse from recollection Capt. Montgomery's
answer to our said "Letter of notice", which
he unfortunately not only failed to understand,
but failed, for nearly six months, to deliver to
Commodore STOCKTON.

Capt. Montgomery's letter bore date June
16th—and, after the usual compliments, went
on to say, that he was "here as the legal rep-
resentative of the Government of the United
States of America—having in charge the proper interests and peace of its citizens engaged in commerce," etc., and it was more than
his gallant ship was worth to give us so much
as one charge of powder.   He responded, very
handsomely, to the sentiment that it is right,
on every proper occasion, to resist oppression

by all honorable means ; and that it was the
settled policy of his Government always to acknowledge any authority they might find in
power, without considering the legitimate
rights of the contending parties—said he was
happy to learn by my messenger, that we had,
by Proclamation, secured the proper rights and
peace of the inhabitants of Sonoma and country around, and hoped that the same humane
course of conduct would characterize all our
future operations.

Capt. Montgomery closed his letter by saying he had not time to communicate all he
would say in answer to my letter ; that he was
in expectation of important news from Mexico
or the United States, and refered us to any ex-
planations Lieut. Missroon might make, which
were thereby made a part of his communica-
tions to me.

Lieutenant Missroon, after we were quietly
seated in a room by ourselves, read the said
letter, and went on to explain and say that, as
officers of a Government at peace with Mexico,
to assist, or in any way to interfere in any revolution that might be going on in any country
where they might be present, would justly subject their Government to dishonor, and them-

selves to be disgraced and driven from the service of their country : but that, in the event of war with Mexico, his Captain had instructed him to say that he would supply any amount of ammunition we might be in need of, and would also place the half of his men under my command, and coöperate with his ship against the common enemy. He then asked for a copy of the Proclamation of the 15th. He was informed that we had no clerks to perform our writing, and that one would be handed him at the time of his return. He thanked me, and said he would direct the clerk of the ship to copy and circulate it. He took his leave, and agreed to meet me at sunrise, at my room next morning.

I gave charge of the guards, for the first time, to Capt. Sears and Lieut. Ford : after writing until 11, went quietly to rest for the first time since the 8th of June, and slept until sunrise. These matters are of trivial importance ; but they show how much labor was performed in order to avoid what was conceived to be *a dishonorable act.*

CHAPTER XIV.

THE LIEUTENANT INTERVIEWS THE GARRISON, AND FINDS IT
STILL DISTRUSTFUL.—THE COMMANDER INDULGES A LIT-
TLE DESPONDENCY, FOR A MOMENT.—THE MEN APPROVE
THE PROCLAMATION, AND ALL ARE JUBILANT IN VIEW OF
THE SITUATION.—AN ATTEMPT TO DRAW A FIGHT.—CAS-
TRO'S SECOND PROCLAMATION.—TWO YOUNG MEN INHU-
MANLY MURDERED BY HIS MEN.—THE FIRST AND ONLY
FIGHT WITH THE ENEMY.

A LITTLE after sunrise came Lieut. Missroon,
whose every expression indicated that a sad
change had come over his mind in relation to
the subject of our Independence. He said,
sorrowfully, that he had been talking with the
men of the garrison, and it was thought best
not to put out any proclamation ; and that
something might be done by way of relieving
us from our disagreeable situation—but as he
continued to speak in sad, sorrowful tones, we
tossed the copy of the Proclamation of the 15th
we held in our hand, which by its dangling motion caught his eye, despite his sorrowful abstraction of mind. " What have you got in
your hand, Sir ?" said he—his voice a little

elevated by curiosity. " It is a copy of the
Proclamation, Sir ; and as it is already published, and as the men of the garrison so seriously disapprove thereof, it is very proper that
they should know what it is, that they may
be able to provide a timely remedy for the evils
it may otherwise cause. Will you be so kind
as to take it up to the garrison and read it to
them ?" Lieut. Missroon very gravely reached
out his hand, without saying a word, and took
the copy ; his countenance indicating more of
sadness and pity than before, as he slowly
opened it and began to move his eye along the
lines.

This was a moment of horrid apprehension !
Was it possible that the men of the garrison
were to be taken on board the ship, and all our
labor in proving to the world, that *we scorned
death and danger in any shape, rather than
be shown up to the world as a band of Mountain thieves and robbers ?* With what inde-
scribable anguish did we trace each kindling
emotion in the mind of the Lieutenant, as he
slowly and carefully passed his eye to the end
of it. But this horrible suspense was of short
duration : it required no word of promise, nor
word of any kind—nothing but the language

of *the soul, the life of men,* was capable of removing the apprehensions which had prompted our mind to the endurance of sleepless vigilance,—which was first quieted the evening before, by the assurances of Capt. Montgomery's letter, that the U. S. officers would not interfere,—to be thus horribly renewed !

Hitherto not a single voice (except Montgomery's) had spoken encouragement—not a man of influence came to our assistance. Four days had passed, and the men of our little garrison were only brave when wound up by the *melodious sounds of Liberty aud Independence,* to become cold and desponding again, as soon as the excitement of action was past. If left to ourselves we would at least prove by our blood poured out, and by our written documents sent abroad, that we were " no base band of robbers, bent on mischief."

But, my dear Wambaugh, we had cherished, in our more cheerful moments, a brighter hope than this. We knew with positive assurance, that the whole country was groaning to be delivered from that excessive tariff taxation that had reduced our exports to less than nothing, and had left us to clothe ourselves, our wives and children, in skins or fig-leaves, if we would maintain independence of lordly merchants. We also believed, in all sincerity, that if some man, even an entire stranger, would present us even the hope of a desirable change before the public mind, *that one general crowding to the uplifted standard* would render all "individual" entreaty and persuasion to adopt our cause unnecessary.

It was therefore that we neither importuned nor begged of a single individual, even to lend a listening ear to our plan ! *If the whole mass moved not,* in answer to our appeal, it was more honorable *to die singly and alone,* rather than involve others in our fate.

The men of the garrison were already equally involved with ourself—(only, as, perhaps, the head of their leader might ransom *them*) ; but not one single man had thus involved himself through any persuasion of ours. Other *persons* and other *motives* had tempted them to enter the vortex.——But stop !—We must confess our guilt, as well as plead our innocence ! Truth, like the diamond, is always bright and clear ; and the darkest crimes are deprived of half their turpitude by frank confession, and the other half is more than canceled by unfeigned contrition and forsaking.

One solitary man (and others may have been in his situation) vehemently, in the anguish of his soul, accused us of having deceived him, and of having thus involved him in rebellion. What have we said, what have we done, thus to deceive ? was the anxious inquiry. You were along with them. Guilty, we plead. But *we* were involved in the consequences we could not suppress. If *we* could not " gather up the flood in a basket", *we* might, perchance, run along before it, and, at some favored point, direct its course, and change the evil—the " *partial* evil"—to " *universal* good."

Now we were so simple as to suppose that he, whom chance and necessity had placed in the brief and uncertain command of the enterprise—he who had conceived and unwaveringly sustained it—would encounter the applause, the stupid gaze of all the world, by such an act. It was well known that he was charged with entertaining designs more base, more hostile to the interests and wishes of the good people of California, than even the plundering and robbing the house of Gen. Vallejo ! He had been charged by Capt. Fremont with being a Mormon, and his scheme was denounced as an artifice to betray the whole country into the

hands of the Mormons! and it was known
that most of the garrison believed the *foul
slander!*

It was fully known, also, that the men of
the garrison had the most unbounded confidence in these United States officers, and that
they looked to them for protection ; and it
was also known that, if the plan of Independence could be suddenly presented to the public,
it would enlist the bone and sinew—and it was
fondly hoped—the *minds* of all such as were
capable of understanding the difference in favor of conquest, by extending just and benevolent principles of government, and that of violence, bloodshed and political murder.   And it
was fondly hoped there would at least be found
one of noble and upright intentions, who might
be willing to wear the honors, while we might
still be permitted to perform some part of the
labor necessary to the establishment of a government more humane, more honorable, more
just and more enduring, and less oppressive,
than any government that had hitherto arisen
and fallen here in California.   We had indeed
promised, in behalf of its citizens, *union* with
the land of our birth, at the earliest honorable
opportunity—not by the devastation of blood,

nor by the more ignoble system of purchase, but by the more exalted principle of universal and equal liberty and freedom of choice by the people; which remains to be more fully explained as we proceed in our narrative.

" Hope springs eternal in the human breast ;"

And hope sprang up in our mind, the moment hope seemed to rise in the mind of the Lieutenant ; and hope spake thus : " If he reads it before the garrison, and approves it himself, (and he will read and approve), it will make no difference whether they discover merit in it or not : if he approves they will approve, and we shall find means to circulate it: and when the people begin to flock to the standard, there will be a time for action ; the mass will be in motion, and it will be easy to direct it, if no counter current springs up—if no vile interfer · ence defeat our aim."

—But the Lieutenant has finished the reading. With the smile of joy he says : " I *will* read it to them"! He hastened with a long and bounding step back to the garrison—which said to us, (mentally), " The battle 's won ; we 'll triumph still, *in spite of 'fears of Mormonism' !"*

Not long after the Lieutenant returned and
said : " Every man has approved the Proclamation, and has sworn to sustain its principles !"—and from this moment that instrument became the test by which to approve our
friends and condemn our enemies.   Joy and
animation were enkindled in eveiy heart :
even he who had denounced " the damned Mormon as less deserving of respect than a dog",
ſ niled again, and yielded service with cheerfulness and joy, and furnished incontestable
evidence *that it was best not to have punished
with death so trivial an offence as ' Mormonism.'*

The first business was to send out the Proclamation, and also a Letter written by our
friend, the liberated Alcalde ;   and a trusty
man of known ability was dispatched southward with said copies and letters.   Brooker
penetrated successfully his way as far as Monterey ; gave copies to known and faithful men;
spread the copy of the Alcaldes's Letter even
within Castro's camp, and the Proclamation
was written and re-written, and sent as far as
San de Angelos.

It was a fact worthy of note, that within
three days of the arrival of the Alcalde's Let-

THE LIFE OF WILLIAM B. IDE.

ter and the Proclamation at 'Santa Clara, then
the Head Quarters of Gen. Castro, more than
half of his army deserted. Men were sent in
every direction with the Proclamation, and it
was not until our men were reduced to nearly
one half our original number, that we received
the first accession to our force.

A party, on the 19th in the afternoon, arrived from the neighborhood of Napa Valley
and Cash Creek, and as José Castro had, as
early as the 18th, sent out a proclamation calling on all good Californians to unite, and with
one bold effort, " fall on and kill the Bears of
Sonoma, and then return and kill the whelps
afterwards", it was deemed prudent to collect
all the unprotected families, and support them
within the garrison at the public expense, so
long as the services of the husband or father
were required for the common security.

It was known that a party of 70 or 80 of
Castro's men were " cruising" about our neighborhood, and the danger to unprotected families
was imminent ; and therefore it became necessary to divide our forces in such manner as that
the safety of the garrison should not be endangered.   Accordingly, Capt. Sears, of the " 1st
Artillery", and Lieut. Ford, commander of the

"1st Rifle Company", were left in charge of the
Fort, with about 20 men, in addition to those
expected and known to be making preparations to join us. Selecting the husbands, fathers and relatives of those defenceless families,
the " General in Command" started before the
dawn of day, with an escort of 10 men, for the
aforementioned purpose. Proceeding cautiously along we discovered, a little after sunrise; a
party of about 25 or 27 Spaniards, and made
preparation for a meeting, by improving a path
on the opposite declivity of the hill, so as approach unobservedly ; but our wary opponents
disappeared. This circumstance convinced our
leader that any attempt to get a fight, (just
for a sample of what could be done, so as in
the main to avoid bloodshed), could not be effectual, unless the enemy were allowed to have
an advantage of 'five to one' : and even then a
retreat must be feigned. This conclusion he
formed from the fact, that he knew that not
more than one-third of his small force had
been seen by the enemy. The next day (21st)
the families were returned in safety.

Gen. Castro's proclamation, which breathed
out death and slaughter against even the infant that had a drop of American blood in its

veins, greatly assisted us in getting together our forces. Even those who a few days before were unwilling to leave the care of a few calves, were not only ready to leave their stock and ranchos, but their houses and household stuff, and to bring their families, instead of " taking them to the mountains", by by-paths, and in the night-time, to the protection offered by our garrison.

On the 19th of June Thomas Cowey and George Fowler, two young men of peaceful dispositions were sent to Doct. Bails, a dis- tance of about 20 miles, to obtain a keg of powder which had been purchased. They re- ceived particular instructions as to the manner of proceeding, and of avoiding danger : but having proceeded more than half way very cautiously, and meeting no enemy, they took the main road, and traveled as at other times. They were discovered and captured without re- sistance—having trusted the promise of the enemy, that if they would give up their arms, they should receive no harm. They gave them up, and died like martyrs! They were tied to trees and inhumanly cut in pieces, in a man- ner too horrible to relate. *This was the first blood shed in the Conquest of California*—an

exemplary measure of the consequence awaiting all who might be weak enough to think of
retaining life by the surrender of their arms,
in a conflict with such an enemy. But this
vile act of his gave strength to our nerve, and
sharpness to our flint.

On the 21st our force was hourly increasing.
All our prisoners in the callaboose had signed
the " treaty stipulations", and been discharged ; and it is not yet known that any of those
Spaniards who made treaty with " the Bear-
Flag-Men", ever after violated their engage-
ments.

As our numbers were now somewhat increased, and there were men who had families dependent upon their daily labor for their support, an effort was made to establish some system of monthly pay for the service : but as we
had no other means than the securities of the
public properties, and none of these were in any
manner immediately available, it was foreseen
that any system of monthly pay would serve
but to increase our financial difficulties : it
was resolved that there should not be made
any distinction between one man's services and
another's, and that no one should be allowed
an individual perquisite, except rations for

himself and wife, and children under the age of twelve years.

It was further resolved to recommend and pledge ourselves, that there should be given to each man who had not already that amount of land, at least one square league of choice land, as a bounty for which he was to consider himself always bound to defend his rights, in common with his fellow-countrymen ; or, to acknowledge himself unworthy of citizenship.

And again : it was resolved that the Mission property should be considered public property, except so much of it as had been properly vested in the several churches ; and that all persons who were known to have received any portion of these properties be required to account for the same ; and that every transfer of any of this property, wherein a valuable and complete consideration had not passed to some authorized agent of the Mexican Government, shall be considered void.   It was considered that these means would be quite sufficient to defray expenses.

On the 23d of June we learned that another of our messengers, (William Todd), had been captured by means of the treachery of a guide that had been employed to conduct him to a

settlement on the coast ; and great fears were
entertained that he would also be cut in pieces,
(as the two American young men had been)
by the Spaniards who had Todd in custody—
they being 88 strong.

Now it was certain that the only way to rescue Todd, was to get a fight and whip the enemy, and thus enable him to make his escape
at the same moment that the enemy should
make his escape. At this time we could have
met him, man to man, besides guarding our
Fort ; but to have sent such force after them
would have caused the death of our comrade.
So, as the only means of the thing sure, our
Commander selected, one by one, until there
were 18 men in the row. Capt. Ford, then 1st
Lieut. of, and in command of the 1st company
of Riflemen, was selected to carry into execution the especial Orders of (not " General Fremont", for he knew nothing of the matter), but
of another man who was understood, at this
time, not to be on the most friendly terms im-
aginable with that noble officer.

This little band of 19 men, after having
been made up, as nearly as possible, on the ra-
tio of 1 to 5 men of the garrison, was especially charged as to the importance of understand-

ing and obeying orders. The design in particular was to save the life of Todd ; but the
practical utility and importance of properly
conducting this manœuvre was set forth in un-
mistakable terms. The Lieutenant received
Orders to "conduct his men cautiously along,
without fatiguing the horses, until he should
discover himself to the enemy ; then halt, and
as soon as the enemy began to be in motion,
retreat to the nearest clump of trees, and every
man get down and tie his horse fast. Then
mark out the distance of 100 yards, and let it
be understood by every man where the line of
the circle shall be, that there may be no mistake. Then let no man fire before the enemy
reach the well-known line. Then be careful to
take, each one, your man—but be cautious not
all to fire at once, lest they rush upon and cut
you to pieces before you can re-load. Make
no calculation for mounting your horses, nor for
running away. The Spaniards can outrun you,
therefore *don't fight them by running.* Remember that *this day is to decide the fate of
every one of us!* If you do your duty like
men this day, and we be faithful to ourselves,
and follow up its advantages, you will not be
again called on to engage in fight, until the full

conquest of all California is achieved. But if,
on the other hand, you yield like cowards this
day, *not a man of us can save his life!* And
now, if there is a man among you in whom I
have been mistaken in thus putting your bravery and good conduct to this severe test, let him
speak, and I will fill his place. Will you carry
out these orders at the expense of your life, if
need be ?" " *We will do it!*" said the gallant
Ford. " Have you a man with you that you
cannot trust your life with ? Are you all satisfied ? Is every man ready to go and do his
duty ?——Then go ! and not a man of you
will be harmed"—and they bounded away.

There was felt no little anxiety as to the result ; especially as we thought the life of Todd
was at stake, and his release depended on an
entire rout of the enemy. We had heard that
Gen. Castro had already crossed the Bay,
and as he was allowed, even by his enemies, to
be a wiley adversary, it was fully believed that
the operations of his advance party, whom Lt.
Ford was sent to encounter, were intended to
draw out our forces in a western direction,
while Castro, with his host (for we were not
yet informed of the fact that half of his men
had deserted him), would, in that case, sud-

denly fall upon our defenceless garrison from the east.   Therefore it was, that the " Commander-in-Chief" remained at the garrison, and made all necessary preparations for such a movement by Castro : but (as we soon afterwards learned) he had sufficient occupation for his tact at generalship, to keep down and overcome a formidable party that had organized in support of our Proclamation of the 15th, on the south side of the Bay, under the superintendence of Weaver and Bird.   Capt. Grigsby, who was first elected Captain before the taking of the Fort, and who resigned through fear of being found in a state of " unauthorized rebellion", came back from a visit to Capt. Fremont's camp, and begged of the men to be reinstated ; and was elected captain of the 1st Company of Riflemen ; which office he held until the 5th of July.

On the afternoon of the 24th Lieut. Ford came back, bringing Todd with him, and made report to the Commander, in these words :

"I have done exactly as you ordered.   *We have whipped them, and that without receiving a scratch.*   We took their whole band of horses, but owing to the fact that about one half of the men retreated with all possible

haste, I did not think best to encumber ourselves by taking the whole band. So we only
picked out each one a good horse, and thus
supplied the place of the horses we had killed,
and have come back without bringing the
whole band." "Very well done! I did not
order you to bring the horses : I only told you
that you never mind the killing a few horses,
for you would easily get more. You have done
all that I expected of you. *You have given
tone and character to the Revolution. We
have only to follow up this example and the
work is done.*"

CHAPTER XV.

CAPT. FREEMONT'S FIRSF VISIT—IS A BIT CENSORIOUS—CHANG-
ES FRONT, AND IS A TRIFLE LAUDATORIOUS.—HIS WHERE-
ABOUTS FROM THE 11TH TO THE 25TH OF JUNE.—THE
GENERAL ASPECT OF THEIR AFFAIRS SERIOUSLY CONSIDER-
ED BY THE COMMANDER.—NARROW ESCAPE OF FREMONT
AND PARTY.—THE MURDERERS OF FOWLER AND COWEY
ESCAPE DUE PUNISHMENT, THROUGH FREMONT'S INTER-
FERENCE.

On the 25th of June, at 2, P. M., came Capt.
Fremont with the whole of his forces, amounting to 72 men. Doct. Semple hailed us with
joyful greeting, and frankly confessed that a
few days since he had no confidence in any
man among us capable of conducting the enterprise ; but since the event of the 24th he was
willing to risk his life anywhere that such a
man as Lieut. Ford might lead the way.

Amid the general congratulations of the occasion, Capt. Fremont came up to me, and,
without any other salutation, in a sarcastic and
commanding tone, (looking me steadily in the
face), said, " Who wrote that Proclamation for
you ?" and continuing his " stern gaze" a mo-

ment, and perceiving that not the least notice
was taken of his insolence, he indignantly said,
" H-ah !—your name was to it !" and left me
as abruptly as he came. The inference to my
mind was instantaneous, and to the effect that
however I might refuse to. expose an accom-
plice in that offensive act, if there had beeñ
one, he was determined that *I* should not escape his wrath. But in a very few minutes he
re-appeared, changing his whole line of attack,
and I have every reason to believe that ere this
he had *changed his whole plan for the " Conquest of California"!* But as, in the events
of warfare, plans, and especially indefeasible
purposes, are subject to alterations and change,
no farther notice would have been taken of
these trivial demonstrations, had a tithe of his
professed devotion to the cause of Independence been genuine.

But to proceed, dear Sir. If you will be
patient, I will ˙tell you the whole tale, so far
as it came to my personal knowledge; although
we have somewhat difference of version from
what has been published instead of the truth,
about this matter: and if in aught there is
exaggeration or mistake, as I said before, the
means of correction are at hand. It has been

said that " truth should not at all times be spoken"!   But we consider the path of truth the only path of safety—ah, and of glory, too! But we will not contend for glory, since, like a shadow, it fleeth from its pursuer.

We were about to say, that after a few moments Capt. Fremont came in again, and accosted us in a most civil and graceful manner, this time, (as it became a *gentleman*)—said he was happy to see and understand that the Proclamation was all it could have been ; that every word was as he would have it, so far as it went ; that we had done ourselves immortal honor ; that in style of diction it would compare favorably with the best writers in the States ; and only regreted that we had not made the insult and abuse he* had received a part of our grievances :—and went on to say

---

* The " insult" here alluded to happened in this manner : As Capt. Fremont, with his surveying party, on the 3d of March, 1846, was encamped at Hartwell's Rancho, he received a threatening missive from Gen. Castro, " by the hands of a Mexican officer, who was backed by 80 lancers, well armed," ordering him to " return with your party beyond the limits of this Department"—warning Fremont if he did not immediately comply, Castro would take measures to compel him to quit the country.   This mandate was thus officially communicated to Fremont on the 5th of March, and on the 6th

that he would receive it as a great favor, in case Gen. Castro should write or do any act or thing that might call forth another Manifesto, that we would not forget to do him (Fremont) the justice to set forth the insults he had endured at Castro's hand. To this we agreed, and we separated in mutual friendship; at least as sincere as were his unbounded professions of friendship for the success of our labors for unalloyed INDEPENDENCE !

Seeing that we had succeeded in saving the life of William Todd, and as we had learned that about 80 of Castro's men were on duty, this side the Bay, we determined to send a sufficient force to hunt them down so closely as to prevent their re-embarkation across the Bay. Lieut. Ford was sent in command of this expedition, with orders not to turn to the right

he entrenched himself, with his little band of assistants, on the summit of Hawk's Peak, 30 miles distant from Monterey. This place—2200 feet above the level of the sea—he fortified with fallen trees, &c., and stripped one of them of its limbs and foliage, and suspended on it, 40 feet from its base, the American Flag. Castro raised a force of abount 200 men, and marched them off to dislodge his disobedient visitor; but he took especial care not to go within rifle range of his fortified encampment, and finally abandoned the undertaking.—[*From a California newspaper.*—ED.]

or left from pursuit, so as to suffer them to escape. Capt. Fremont said in our hearing that
he had come down, *not to take any part in the
matter;* only to see the sport, and *explore* about
the Bay : and that he would be pleased that
our party should accompany him—or, that he
would be pleased to accompany our party—
which, we cannot certainly say—but so it was
they all set out together, and so anxious were
all hands to " see the sport", that it was with
difficulty we could persuade 75 men to remain
to guard the Fort.

On the morning of the 26th this " pleasure"
party left—in number amounting to about 134
men.—Large numbers continued to flock to our
standard, and to record their names in support
of Independence—pledging themselves to support the principles of the Proclamation of the
15th of June.

Before entering upon the doings of the said
" pleasure party", it may be well to give an account of all we knew (by report) of Capt. Fremont's operations from the 11th to the 25th of
June.   And here, as we knew nothing by personal observation, you will compare it with
other testimony.

We were informed that Capt. Fremont continued his preparations for his journey to the States until the 17th, when he learned that a party had seized the Fort at Sonoma ; and, as it was not reasonable to suppose that Gen. Castro would pass by so small a force as that at Sonoma, to attack the larger force at Johnson's Rancho, more than 100 miles further off, the only chance to provoke that attack, which was, according to his instructions from the Executive Departmeat, to constitute and be, in effect, a Declaration of War, on the part of Mexico, against the United States, was to move down nearer to the liabilities. So, on the 18th he moved to Sutter's Fort, and informed Capt. Sutter that it was necessary to take possession of his Fort, and if he thought fit to yield peacable possession, it would save the disagreeble necessity of taking it by force. Capt. Sutter gave possession, and Gen. Vallejo and his companions were put under guard there.

Here Capt. Fremont waited for a few days, expecting that the garrison at Sonoma would soon be overthrown, and that the much desired assault upon the United States' Flag would soon be made, to rescue the much loved and esteemed Gen. Vallejo and his friends.

But while preparations for the said attack,

and further provision for his journey across the
Plains were being made, he received a letter
from Lieut. Ford, informing him that the men
of the garrison had no confidence in the ability of Mr. Ide to manage matters at the Fort
at Sonoma ; that they were in great danger of
being betrayed into the hands of the Spaniards ; that such an inference was drawn from
the supposition that the Commander had erred
in his conditions of peace with the neighboring
Spaniards.   (At the time this letter was sent
we had no knowledge thereof, as it was sent by
that weekly messenger that was provided by
the hospitality of the Americans, to convey letters from the families of the said prisoners to
Gen. Vallejo and companions, and from said
prisoners to their families, weekly.)

Intelligence of this was soon communicated
to the Commander, and every effort was made
to convince the men of the garrison that our
interest, as well as moral obligations, forbade
that we should refuse to others the same rights
and liberties that we claimed for ourselves, and
that we must not, if we desire the best good
of the inhabitants of California, think of lay-
ing hold of the right to govern by the iron hand
military force, but by the might of such equit-

able principles as we could plainly show were calculated to unite the masses in one common effort to extend the knowledge and blessings of true Liberty.

Lieut. Ford, (as we were informed by an officer who had seen the said letter) begged Capt. Fremont, by all means, to come down and make his camp in the immediate neighborhood of Sonoma. Whether this letter had pith and pathos sufficient to dissuade Capt. F. from all his public protestations against involving himself, his men or his Government, in any unwarrantable and dishonorable interference in the internal difficulties of the people of a nation then at peace with his Government, (as far as was then known by us), or whether a desire to avail himself of the honor of provoking the Mexican authorities to open the floodgates of that war which fate had destined to be the messenger of *peaceful Liberty* to so much of the Mexican domain as it might be desirable to "annex" to the Union, in order to obtain, or rather to *retain* the balance of political power in favor of " the cherished institutions of the South", we will not presume to affirm ; but will state distinctly, that up to the 25th, and even to the 5th of July, he had adhered strictly to his neutral plan of provocation, according to what was fully understood among the knowing ones to be in accordance with his private instructions : and what course of conduct could be better calculated to exasperate—to induce some unthinking agent of Mexican authority (a subaltern of a friar, perchance), to throw an unlucky shot at one of Capt. Fremont's "neutral and unoffending men", and thus to have struck the chord discordant—that had rung the tocsin of war, involving in its consequences *a hundred thousand lives!*   If he who, by the favor of Heaven and persevering study, has seized the lightnings and directed their course, shall be thought worthy the admiration of his surviving race, in how much higher estimation shall he be held, who may introduce a successful mode of conquest, without the shedding of blood—of extending Liberty to the suffering sons of civil oppression and slavery ?

But pardon me, dear Sir, and I will return to the narration of another series of events as they occured, and which imperceptibly produced our overthrow.

Perhaps you would have considered the 5th of July the zenith of our glory!   Not so, dear

Sir. It is true that numbers came pouring in up to the 5th. This continued increase of numbers was the effect of that quiet influence of motives, designs and principles, silently set in motion, which could not be supposed to cease to act, on the commission of the first error, nor yet on any change of the general plan. But you will recollect that no action was had reflecting the least credit to our enterprise, after the arrival of Capt. Fremont at Sonoma : and if we had been ten days in establishing a reputation for our cause, which was capable of enlisting the whole energy of the country in its support, and which did enlist hundreds who had no knowledge of us, except by the one common appeal made to all alike—to enemies as well as to friends—ten days more were fully sufficient to effect an entire revolution, and to divert and change the current of that general interest which none other had power to awaken.

These prefatory remarks bring us to consider the events and circumstances which changed the character of our enterprise, and presented California to the United States as a trophy of that species of conquest that wallows in the blood of murder, or of that ignoble traffic that makes the price of Liberty the price of blood,

—instead of presenting the same fair land on
terms of honorable compact and agreement,—
such as all the world can participate in without loss or dishonor, by the free, frank expression of voluntary consent and good will of the
parties.

We will now refer to a little incident illustrative of the feeling of all California, at that
time, on this subject. The native Californians
were democratic in feeling, scorning subjugation by conquest; but not ignorant of advantages that might have been secured to all California by an amicable union with the United
States. After taking the garrison at Sonoma,
and after confidence had been established by
the equitable course pursued, the highest official officer of the District of Sonoma, on seeing our flag, said to me :   " Why did you not
raise the United States' flag ?"   I said we had
no right to do so ; that the United States'
Government would justly punish us should we
do so, and return within its jurisdiction : but
that we would raise an Independent Flag, and
become a united and free people ; and then,
by peacful agreement, unite ourselves to the
United States by treaty—and *then*, (and not
till then) we would hoist the United States'

Flag. He heartily replied, " Buena ! then will
my people dance all day ! !" But such a day
of glory to the free institutions of America
was not then at hand.——Yes, we would have
gladly " danced", also, *rejoicing*—" Old men
and maidens, in the dance together", if we
might have been allowed to behold the peaceful triumph of just principle, rather than the
triumph of Buena Vista and Sierra Gorda !

On the evening of the 28th one of our men
intercepted a letter addressed to certain citizens
of Sonoma, giving intelligence, that early on
the morning of the 30th Gen. Castro would invade Sonoma, and put to death every soul
found there, without distinction, except the
" Grande Oso", whom they intended to chain
and convey to the other side of the Bay, for
the amusement of their women and children.
All the Spanish people came and requested of
me permission to leave the town, which was
positively refused. After much unavailing persuasion they ceased to importune ; but a short
time after a request was presented, that all the
women and children, both American and Spanish, might be allowed to congregate in one
house, and that the Spanish men might be allowed to take shelter in the callaboose. To

this we agreed. The women and children were hived in the back apartment of Gen. Vallejo's house ; and as the night came on, all were ready for the expected attack.   The two 18-pounders, double charged with canister shot, guarded the main entrance, and 7 other pieces of artillery were in using order, and so arranged as to be available at short notice at any point whither an attack might be made.   The 250 loaded muskets were divided among the men, and so placed as to be within convenient reach.   The rifles, all fresh capped, were ready—the guards were strictly charged, the matches were always burning at night.

About 4, a. m., or a little earlier, our guards came in and reported having heard the tramping of horses in the distance.   Every man was called to the position intended.   The signal for the fight, the onset, was agreed on.   The 18-pounders were first to answer the report of my rifle—each officer had his orders at what particular distance the enemy should be allowed to approach, before he might engage in the fight.   And as we well knew that if the enemy were to succeed at all, it would be by a sudden charge ; therefore we placed a trusty guard, whose duty it was to reserve each a loaded

musket, only to be used in such an emergency.
Thus prepared, in less than one minute from
the first alarm, all listened for the sound of
the tramping horses—we heard them coming!
—then, low down under the darkened cañon,
we *saw* them coming!! In a moment the
truth flashed across my mind : the Spaniards
were deceiving us! In a moment orders were
given to the captains of the 18-pounders to reserve fire until my rifle should give the word ;
and, to prevent mistake, I hastened to a position a hundred yards in front of the cannon,
and a little to the right oblique, so as to gain
a nearer view. "Come back ; you will lose
your life !" said a dozen voices. "Silence !"
roared Capt. Grigsby ; "I have seen the old
man in a bull pen before to-day !" The blank-
ets of the advancing host flowed in the breeze·
They had advanced to within 200 yards of the
place where I stood. The impatience of the
men at the guns became intense, lest the enemy came too near, so as to lose the effect of the
spreading of the shot. I made a motion to lay
down my rifle. The matches were swinging—
"My God ! they swing the matches !" cried
the well known voice of *Kit Carson*. "Hold
on, hold on ! we shouted—'tis Fremont, 'tis

Fremont !" in a voice heard by every man of both parties, we cried—while Capt. Fremont dashed away to his left to take cover behind an adobe house ; and in a moment after he made one of his most gallant charges on our Fort : it was a noble exploit ; he came in *a full gallop, right in the face and teeth of our two long* 18's !

Thus ended this 'glorious' battle ; and thus were our plans defeated ; and thus escaped those very men who cut in pieces George Fowler and Thomas Cowey, through the disobedience of our orders, else had they have paid the penalty justly due to so inhuman an act. But the officer in charge, on being interrogated the reason why he had not left the Fort to the care of him whose duty and privilege it was to have defended it, until he had punished the murderers of Fowler and Cowey ? said "the advice of Capt. Fremont had induced him to forsake the path of duty." The party were immediately ordered back to the pursuit of the flying murderers of Fowler and Cowey ; and, after a hearty breakfast, they departed and arrived at the Bay in season to witness the embarcation of Castro's men.

It appeared on investigation, that—First, a

letter had been addressed to Sonoma, intended
to fall into the hands of the garrison, in the
hope that I wonld recall the men under Ford
for the protection of the Fort ; but this having failed, the flying Spaniards drew lots among
their number, and three men, prepared with
letters in their boots, put themselves in the
power of their pursuers, threw away their arms
and fell on their knees, begging for quarter :
but the orders were to take no prisoners from
this band of murderers, and the men were shot
and never rose from the ground.   But notwithstanding one of the men declared with his
dying breath, that he expected death—that he
came on purpose to die for the benefit of his
countrymen ;   yet Capt. Fremont was either
deceived by the letters found in their boots, or
he deceived our men, by advising them to forsake the pursuit ;—in either case the strata-
gem took effect, and the murderers escaped.

CHAPTER XVI

CAPT. FREMONT AGAIN IN THE FIELD.—THE COMMANDANT'S
ORDERS DISOBEYED.—THE BEAR FLAG GOVERNMENT "IN
QUIET POSSESSION OF ALL CALIFORNIA."—THE U. S. OFFI-
CERS' PLANS—THE BEAR FLAG GOVERNMENT TO BE MADE
OVER TO THEM.—THE "GENERAL ASSEMBLY AND COUN-
CIL" CONVENE ON THE 5TH OF JULY—VOTE TO WIPE OUT
ALL PREVIOUS DOINGS OF THE BEAR FLAG PARTY, AND
RAISE THE UNITED STATES' FLAG, UNDER CAPTAIN FRE-
MONT'S COMMAND.

ON the 1st day of July came three men from
the opposite side of the Bay, and informed us
that all the Americans and other foreigners
were up and doing to spread our Proclamation,
and that a company of 100 were already collected in its support, and requested us to send
them arms.   A boat was provided, and arrangements made to mount a small piece of
artillery on board the boat, so as to secure the
safe conveyance of a party of 12 men in charge
of 100 muskets ; but before these arrangements were complete, Capt. Fremont returned

to Sonoma, and so advised as to defeat the measure.

It now wanted only two or three days to the 4th of July, and our order for the immediate embarkation of the 12 men with the arms, to the assistance of our friends, at the head of whom was Weaver, Bird and others, could not be enforced, because Capt. Fremont was opposed to it, and the measure was postponed until after the 4th.   The 4th came like other days.

Two hundred and seventy-two men had signed our roll.   We were in quiet, and for the time, in undisturbed possession of all California north and east of the San Joaquin River. We had taken possession of Yerba Buena and spiked the cannon there.   All that was necessary was to have pursued our victory, to have made it complete.

It may have been considered very important to the interests of the United States, to have prevented the crossing of the Bay by our forces, and the consequent union and coöperation with our friends there, who had assembled in support of our Proclamation of the 15th of June, as such an event would have rendered the immediate conquest and success of princi-

ples inevitable ; and that, too, before any safe
plan could be devised for getting up the United
States' Flag.   Although this conquest would
not have in the least retarded the union of California with the States ; yet it would have giv-
en the citizens of California the right of being
consulted as to the TERMS of the union ;   and
what was and is of equal importance to those
who delight to cherish the honor of the Institutions of Liberty—it would have prevented
that foul stain of disgrace that attaches to that
very institution of liberty which we delight to
honor.

As relates to the next consideration of moment—which, indeed, may with truth be said
to have had more influence in determining
events than any other consideration whatever
—it is of inconsiderable importance *who* were
to be the renowned ' Conquerors of California.'
One thing was reduced to a moral as well as a
physical certainty : that if the current of pop-
ularity our cause had acquired, thus suddenly,
were allowed to proceed, it would have been
quite impossible for any force of the United
States authority, then within using distance,
to have kept up with it ; and, consequently,
all that glory which had so manifestly inspired

the hopes of its officers present would have
been lost! To prevent a catastrophe so appalling, it became necessary that the greatest
exertions should be used to hurry up a pretext
for hoisting the U. S. Flag, and, Commodore
Jones-like, take possession of the whole country. Now, dear Sir, at what particular date
this new plan of Conquest was matured, is
more than we know ; but, nevertheless, we are
able to leave it between ten days next preceding the 5th of July, '46. We were now no
longer, in case of war with the United States,
to be considered a free people, and regarded as
allies ; but we were soon to be told that it was
the policy of the United States Government
(officers) to treat those as enemies, whom they
might find in an enemy's country !

But before it was prudent to throw such an
insult square in our face, it was necessary to
place one of their number in command of our
military forces ; and not only so, but it was
also *imperatively necessary* to rely much on
our love of country, and devotion to the best
interests of the people with whom we were associated, else had they learned more of the nature and consequence of such an unwarrantable
and uncalled for abuse.

If it is still necessary to state, in concise language, this *second* edition of the plan for the
conquest of California, 'revised and corrected'
by the joint labors of Lieuts. Gillespie, Missroon
and others, we will give it without fear of con-
tradiction. First, secure the command of the
Independent forces of the Bear Flag Republic.
Secondly, hoist the U. S. Flag, and follow up
to the entire conquest. Thirdly, if no war between Mexico and the United States ensue, sell
out all the military stores of the U. S. to the
Government of California, and obtain California by treaty with the new Government. But
in the event of a war, to seize and acquire the
whole by the right of conquest. And it was
admitted by all that the Government of the
United States would, as a matter of course,
cashier whoever might consent thus to violate
its honor, by becoming the leader of the said
Independents. Yet as a solace for his dishon-
or, (to use the language of our informant, who
was one of said U. S. officers), "he will be in
town with a pocket full of rocks."

Further to explain how, and in what manner, this plan was made successful, I will now
copy from my Journal written at the time, and
as I have hinted before : " Capt. Fremont op-

posed the sending men and arms across the Bay
—advised us not to believe every report—that
as one of our informants was an Englishman, it
might be a plan to entrap us : it was not best
to push our success too rapidly, as we would
endanger the safety of Sonoma. Only delay a
day or two—you may receive more information." Further on it is added : "From the
foregoing advice and other inducements connected therewith, it became impossible to convince our men of the danger which threatened
our unarmed associates on the other side of the
Bay : and delay ensued which caused their entire dispersion : while four of their number
were made prisoners—three of whom suffered
extreme cruelty ; but the fourth, who was my
second son, was released with the gift of a horse
and a passport, with the following expression of
Gen. Castro : ' I will not punish you ; I have
released you to convince your Father that I,
too, know how to perform a generous act.—
When I meet you on the battle-field, I will
ask you for your passport.' "

You will recollect that that portion of the
men who were opposed to making themselves
responsible for their own acts, at the time it
was determined to take possession of the Gar-

rison of Sonoma, departed to join Capt. Fremont. These men were again returned to Sonoma, and seeing all the good citizens of California were fast falling into the same fatal error which had well nigh involved themselves in rebellion—from motives of prudence, and by the advice of certain naval officers, resolved to effect by artifice what could not have been done by a fair expression of the voice of the whole. They argued that if Capt. Fremont could be placed in command of our forces, it would amount to an alliance with the United States ; or at least that he would be cashiered, and would remain with us. They seemed fully to understand, that if Capt. Fremont could be placed in command, we should at once come under the protection of the United States : while it is more than supposable, that our very attentive friends of the U. S. marine authority, in connection with their " Civil Engineers", had quite another object in the manœuvre—which may be more fully understood from the narration of what follows :

Early on the 5th of July Capt. Fremont requested the " bear men", as the " Independents" were designated, to assemble ' *without arms*', within a large room at Don Salvadore's house, adjoining which was a smaller room capable of convening the Captain's Company—who assembled there, *under arms,* to the number of 72 of his men, and 8 or 10 gentlemen officers from the U. S. ships then in the Bay. The number of the Independents, in contradistinction, was about 280 men, without arms—a citizens' assembly, convened to deliberate on some proposition expected to be made by Capt. Fremont.

The business was before the Independent citizens, as a matter of course : but the Council was composed of their friends, and an armed sentinel, from Capt. Fremont's guards, kept the door between the private Council-room and the hall of the *Representatives* of the People.

This large assembly might properly be assimilated with the Legislative Assembly of Vermont, in its first organization (the more efficient arm of the government), while the assemblage of armed friends might prefigure the Governor and Council of Vermont ; yet they do not enjoy the *veto* power, but simply the power of *suspension.*

Capt. Fremont, accompanied by Lieut. Gillispie and two or three others—officers in the U. S. Navy—presented himself before the 'gen-

eral assembly', and opened the business of the
session by declaring—(not his determination to
conquer California, to be sure ; for he said he
should not, in any manner, intermeddle in the
affairs of California politics)—but his already
d-e-c-i-d-e-d resolution to conquer Gen. José
Castro, whom he violently denounced as an
usurper in the California government.   He
went on to say that his meditated expedition
against him could not be considered a violation
of the amicable relations existing between the
United States and Mexico.   He continued to
say : " I shall proceed to take Castro, and take
him with me to the States, whether you coöperate with me or not" :   and, in justification,
refered to the manner in which he had been
insulted by Gen. Castro.

After having sufficiently guarded himself
against any future imputation of unwarrantable interference, on his part, in those matters
which exclusively belonged to the citizens of
California, he said, that as *we* (connecting *his*
party with the assembly of citizens), have one
common enemy, he would state the conditions
on which he whould agree to make common
cause with us.

The advantages he proposed to confer on us

were : First, his unwavering support of our
Independence, and of the principles and purposes set forth by our Proclamation of the
15th of June. Secondly, he offered us every
facility his well supplied camp afforded,—that
we would be allowed to share with himself and
men the military stores and provisions supplied by the U. S. Government ; and, most of
all, we might rely on his friendly advice in conducting all our *purely military* operations.

The two first *conditions* were scarcely nominal. They only required that we should sign
a pledge that we would " abstain from the violation of the chastity of women", and that
we would conduct the Revolution honorably.
The third simply required a pledge of obedience to the orders of our properly constituted
officers.

He insisted at some length on the imperious
necessity that all should solemnly pledge implicit and unconditional obedience to the proper officers, which now became essentially necessary to success ; and after expatiating on
the vast importance of conducting honorably
the enterprise that was destined to become a
brilliant example to the oppressed throughout
the world, of a people though few, who have

by the mighty impulse of Equity's inspiring
principle, overthrown the rapacious powers of
usurpation, avarice and governmental oppression ; and, by instituting equal liberty of assuming a higher and more honorable system of
government among the enlightened and free.

After having again pledged his honor to
stand by us, at least until Gen. Castro should
have been overcome, he closed his propositions
and remarks by politely bowing to the soon-
to-be ex-commander, as if he would say, ' Will
you now have the magnanimity to second my
propositions'?

In reply to the Captain's proposition he said
that he believed the past honorable and unimpeachable conduct of the men of the garrison,
which had the esteem and confidence of even
many of our enemies, and the responded approbation and support of all present, could not be
refused, even by Captain Fremont, as a sufficient guarantee for the future, so far as the first
and second conditions were concerned. But
since we had but recently suffered the defeat of
all our well devised plans, through a want of
confidence in the ability of our highest officer
in command—and, too, through disobedience
of orders given, whereby our enemy had es-

caped an otherwise certain overthrow, and out
friends collected south of the Bay had been dis-
persed, and their leaders made prisoners, it was
admitted to be of the highest importance that
those to whom we had committed, or to whom
we shall hereafter commit the responsibility of
directing our combinèd efforts, might possess
so much of the confidence of the governed, as
would enable them to carry into effect at least
their commands. And inasmuch as Capt. Fremont had prepared a solemn pledge, calculated
by its provisions to give confidence to those in
command, and to bind us closer to the fixed
and publicly declared object of our Revolution,
a motion was made, in conclusion, to appoint
a committee to draft an appropriate PLEDGE,
to be subscribed by every man before he might
further participate in the perils or honors attendant upon the establishment of such a system of government, as shall secure to all the
free enjoyment of rational liberty.

The generous feeling of the assembly immediately responded by electing the last speaker
their said committee ; whereupon the prudent
sense of the privy council suggested the propriety of electing two persons more to join said
committee, *from the council of friends,* in ar-

ranging an affair upon which so much depended.   Thus strengthened, the said committee
retired to consider the subject of their charge,
under an injunction of brevity from the privy
council.

At the committee's assembling and proceed-
ng to business, it appeared that the adjument-
ative portion thereof were decidedly in favor
of setting aside all that had been done in the
cause, and for making the era of the Independence of California to commence with the command of Capt. Fremont.   It was true that
two of the three composing this committee
were selected from Capt. Fremont's Company,
neither of whom had hitherto taken any active
part under our Flag—who had each been nom-
inated by the other—who were in no manner
interested in anything that had been done under our Flag, farther than any other of Capt.
Frcmont's men ; neither of whom had signed
our articles, or otherwise identified themselves
with our cause.

Under these circumstances it was easy to
conceive and to understand the motive of these
representatives of the secret council : and, also,
it was easy to understand why they were elected by a body of men to which they at the time

did not belong. And it was easy, also, to represent the wishes and interests of that body,
whose right it was to be represented in a matter that only concerned themselves, to wit :
what shall be the *form* of that pledge which
they were disposed, of their own free will, to
offer to Capt. Fremont, in exchange for his
proffered *three overtures*—in ratification of the
proposed treaty of alliance, " offensive and de-
fensive", by which, according to his own statement verbally made, we were to make joint effort against " the common enemy."

Therefore it was worse than useless to further argue any difference that might exist in the
views of the primitive portion of the committee and its adjunct portion, than to understand
the position of each ; as it was reasonable to
suppose that the original assembly of " Bear
Men, *who were Bear Men*", would be at liberty to sustain such a report as would truly represent their wishes and interest.

Accordingly each of the component portions
of the committee drafted a resolution and
pledge suiting the views of each, which were
forthwith reported by its Chairman to the re-
assembled convention, in accordance with the
established rules of conventional assemblies ;

although not without a serious attempt, on the part of the adjuncts, to seize the chair. They appeared satisfied, however, with the impartiality of the Chairman, in the discharge of his duty as reporter of the committee's doings.

The Report of the majority was first read, and their views, as far as expressed in the sitting of the committee, were fairly represented.

It was proposed by the first article of the majority report, to annul and wipe out all that had been done up to the 5th of July. The reasons urged in defence of this article were : 1st, the 5th of July immediately follows the 4th day of July, the anniversary of American Independence ; and, 2dly, as Capt. Fremont was to be our *advisorary* leader, it would enable him to " begin with the beginning", and that his name and influence would add more advantage to the cause by being thus associated ; and, 3dly, it was proper that, in changing the ' administration', there should be a new organization throughout : or, more definitely, that we who are out of office may have a chance to get in.

After followed the Report of the minority. which——[Thus abruptly " ends the chapter.

CHAPTER XVII.

EDITORIAL REMARKS.—"THE CONQUEST OF CALIFORNIA" UN-
DER THE BEAR FLAG GOVERNMENT, AN ASSURED FACT.—
MR. IDE'S BUSINESS HABITS AND QUALIFICATIONS.—HIS
PUBLIC EMPLOYMENT.

THE WAMBOUGH LETTER brings this " History of the Conquest of California" down to
about the commencement of hostilities between
the United States and Mexico, in 1846. Before this state of war between us and his own
government was known by Gen. Castro, then
the actual head and commander of the Mexican authorities in California, (it appears by
Mr. IDE's statement), Castro had taken himself and his dilapidated military forces across
the Bay, on his way to Mexico, and had thus
" escaped due punishment for the murder of
Fowler and Cowey". Thus it also appears,
that on or about the 5th of July, when the
new " administration" took possession, and the
" change of government" was accomplised, the
civil and military authority of Mexico had been
thoroughly " wiped out"—California was not,

and had not been, from the 15th of June to
the 5th of July, under Mexican rule. She *was*,
what her rude "national" Flag had from day
to day proclaimed, "THE CALIFORNIA REPUB-
LIC." During these twenty days there was no
obstruction, by a conflicting party, to the exercise by the Bear Flag Government, of its entire functions and prerogatives of National Independence. For a greater part of this time,
and especially at its close, it was, as Mr. IDE
truly remarks, "in quiet, and for the time, in
undisturbed possession of all California north
of the San Joaquin River. All that was necessary was to have pursued our victory, to have
made it complete." These facts andc onsider-
ations (we think, from our stand-point), war-
rant the conclusion, that on the 4th of July,
1846, the " Bear Flag Government" had effect-
ually *conquered* California—had, to all intents
and purposes, wrested that province from the
mother country ; and would have maintained
that stand with " complete success," had there
been no " uwarrantable interference" from outside quarters, and without a change of ' administration' or Flag, until she had voluntarily
applied, as she eventually did, for admission as
one of the States of the American Union.

Those who were well acquainted with the subject of this memoir well know, that he was not the man to " put his hand to the plow and look back." As in scaling the Nevada Mountain, the year before, on his way with his emigrating train to the " land of promise", he undertook a job which his companions thought impracticable, but which proved a notable success, so did he succeed most wonderfully in another far more adventurous undertaking, which not only his boon companions, but his outside friends at first view deemed impracticable.— Although better qualified by education and experience to wield the broad-axe and hammer than the sword and helmet of the " commander", yet, when by accident the latter were put into his hand, what he lacked in skill for their use, he made up by sleepless vigilance and indomitable courage, resolution and perseverence —such as initiated the command, " Now take the Fort !"

AS A PRIVATE CITIZEN,

Mr. IDE was respected by his neighbors and acquaintance. He took a lively interest in their welfare, as by reference to pages 25-6 of these 'Sketches' it is stated that he ' took great

interest in politics ;   and, while in Madison,
O., he wrote a great many articles of agreement
for his neighbors, and was often consulted by
them on occasions of disputes occuring between
them about rights of land, division-lines, and
other misunderstandings'—thus acting as a genial and mutual friend, without fee or reward,
as ' a peace-maker' among them.

He started in the race of business-life, at the
age of twenty-one, with no other 'capital' than
a pair of stalwart arms and hands, and by the
use of them, and a judicious investment of
the fruit of their labors, at the age of about 56
he was in possession of what he considered a
" competency of this world's goods", for himself and family—as he then stated in a letter
to one of his brothers at the East.

But it was ' otherwise ordered' than that he
should remain here long to enjoy this "competency."   He died at Monroeville, Cal., on the
19th of Dec., 1852, aged 56 years, 7 months
and 12 days, after an illness disabling him for
the duties of his office of only about one week.
He held, at the time of his decease, the office
of County Judge for Colusi Co., by election,
and, by appointment, he officiated as Judge of
Probate, County Treasurer, County Surveyor,

County Clerk,—and, *exofficio*, as County Recorder and County Commissioner. We understand the sallary and perquisites attached to all these offices amounted to about $ 2,000 per annum.

His county, (I am informed by a California correspondent) was at that time nearly as large as the State of New Hampshire. He held these several offices, (or a great part of them) about 20 months, to the day of his decease.— My correspondent adds : "By the exercise of his influence, sound judgment and financial tact, he kept the county free of debt, at a time when extravagance and misrule, in most of the other counties, were piling up debts which are burdens upon the people's shoulders to this day. The County of Colusa had no jail at the time Judge IDE was appointed,'and no money with which to build one. There was no very convenient way for confining persons brought there for trial, in criminal cases, without the expense of day and night keepers. In the spring of 1852 Mr. Ide related to a friend who called on him, what he did to obviate this inconvenience, somewhat as follows: 'I have tools which I brought with me over the Plains, and some I brought by steamer, on my last trip

from the East. I will get some good bar iron
from San Francisco, and some bolts, and will
build a cage with my own hands.' " And this
writer adds : " He did so, with some assistance by the local smith, perhaps. He drilled
the bars and bolted them together ; thus making a safe and durable cell for the confinement
of prisoners. He placed this cage under the
dense and comfortable shade of a monster oak
in front of a building which, at that time, and
for that place, was a ' first-class Stage Hotel,
and the county Court House'. No guard was
required, and it needed no ventillation. It was
a healthy as well as a secure place for detaining
the accused while awaiting trial. It was a success—a necessary and inexpensive structure,
saving the County much expense in the line of
public buildings. Some years afterwards, when
the County Seat was removed from Monroeville, this cell or cage was also moved ; and
even now, after the lapse of so many years, it is
doing duty as a cell in the splendid new brick
Jail, at Colusi, Colusi County."

In further response to the Editor's inquiry,
this correspondent writes : " Some thought
Judge IDE's death was hastened to give opportunity for robbery. I do not think so. It is

true there were suspicious circumstances in relation to his last sickness, which gave credence to such a belief in the minds of some of his friends.   He was living away from his family: his wife having died about two years previously, and his children residing at a great distance on his Rancho, were none of them with him during his short confinement with the small pox   He had the key of the county safe under his head at the time of his death, I have been told.   The man who attended him during his sickness took said key and robbed the safe. It was known at the time how much money there was in the safe belonging to the County. The thief was pursued—finally caught, and all the County's money recovered—but no more. Mr. Ide was known to have money of his own in the safe, but how much no one knew.   None of his money was recovered ; and the thief, by the connivance of some one who was, perhaps, his confederate in the plunder, escaped the second time, and was never re-taken.

" Mr. IDE was buried at Monroeville, where was once the site of Coiusi Co. Court House ; but at the present day there are no buildings there, and the land they stood on is occupied as a wheat field."

Mr. IDE's plan for "civil service" rules, under his "administration", as explained by his third *stipulation* of principles, (see page 145), which were to prevail under the new government, for the time being, at least, viz : that its prominent public offices should be occupied by that class of philanthropic, patriotic citizens who could not be enticed by *the love of money* "to corruption, fraud and dishonor", shows that he was a full-blooded *radical* politician, of the strictest sect of the present day: but with this difference of developement : while the modern 'radicals' *preach* high-toned patriotism, and *practice* the contrary, he *practiced* what he preached—for we are credibly informed that, for his month or more indefatigable labors while organizing the "Bear Flag Government", and superintending its operations, and for his four or five months' services under Capt. Fremont, in his expedition down the coast in pursuit of Don Castro and his handful of men—for all these public services, "civil and military", he never asked or received of the Californian or of the United States' government, any compensation for his *time*, if, indeed, his necessary personal expenses while in the U. S. service were provided for him.

Mr. IDE was a man of temperate, industrious and frugal habits, and of an enterprising business propensitiy. Soon after his arrival in California he purchased a three-mile-square tract of land, situated in the pleasant valley "at the head of navigation", on the Sacramento River, some 60 miles above the city of Sacramento, on which he afterwards made extensive improvements. During the early stage of the "gold excitement", he and his oldest son and a son-in-law spent a few months " in the mines"; and they then retired " for good" from that branch of industry—satisfied with an amount of about $ 25,000, as the result of their labors therein.

We have not at hand the data from which to gather much information as respects his private pecuniary affairs ; but will, on this point, quote a few sentences from a letter of his to a brother, in 1851, then living in Illinois. " I do not seek more wealth ; but simply wish to exchange what I have for cash, that I may leave California once for all. I sell slowly— not half as fast as my stock increases. I have collected about $ 6,000 since I came home.*

* From a nine or ten month's visit among his relatives and friends at the East.

I have tried to sell out all, at once ; but few porsons have the means to buy 1000 head of cattle, 150 horses, and 30,000 acres of land. My cattle are appraised at $ 30, oxen $ 75, each, horses at $ 70, and land at 25 cents per acre*—making some $ 50,000. The tax is one per cent—the snug little sum of $ 500, which is more than one-tenth the revenue of the County—from all of which not a farthing's benefit is derived by any person except office-holders—two-thirds going to defray State expenses."*

We have now about concluded these " biographical skeches of the life" of a useful citizen, whose premature death was a severe loss to his surviving children, a large circle of relatives and friends, as well as, (prospectively), to any community in which his future lot might have been cast. He was the poor man's friend and adviser—and, in every sense of the word, a *sincere* Christian.

We propose to devote a considerable portion of the remaining pages of this volume to extracts from Mr. IDE's letters to his friends, af-

* In 1878 the occupant of this Rancho wrote the Editor that it was appraized for the assessment of taxes at $50,000, —was valued at $ 70,000, and his taxes on it amounted to between 16 and 17 hundred dollars.

ter he had been sometime a resident of California. The casual reader—not a relative, or an
acquaintance of his—will find many interesting incidents of pioneer life briefly treated of,
in these extracts—always bearing in mind, that
the letters they are taken from were written
for the friendly eye of the recipient, only.

But we will first introduce, as more particularly connected with his relation to California
as a devoted advocate of its "Freedom and Independence", extracts, at considerable length,
from an " Address to the Citizens of California", which, on account of his previous connection with them in their privations and strug-
gles, he thought it proper and incumbent on
him to send them.

CHAPTER XVIII.

EXTRACTS FROM A CIRCULAR ADDRESSED TO CALIFORNIANS,
—AND FROM SEVERAL OF HIS PRIVATE LETTERS.

In his Address to the " CITIZENS OF CALI-
FORNIA", dated at the City of New York, May
28, 1850, which he had printed in circular form
and distributed among his acquaintance and
friends in California, then engaged in inaugur-
ating a State Constitution and Government,
Mr. IDE makes an earnest appeal to their patriotism, magnanimity and self-respect. It is
too long for insertion entire here ; yet it is too
characteristic of the man—who had been charged (by men of so high standing, we are informed, as to require some attention by way of refutation), with *want of fealty* to his own patern-
nal government. We therefore give the few
extracts from it that follow :

" Do you still hesitate to secure the appointment from
among yourselves, by your own free suffrage, of such
servants as may be employed among you for the general benefit? *   *   *   Will you still linger, that your
country's dearest interests may be longer merged beneath the party strifes of a far-off people, who have

little knowledge of, and less interest in the prosperity of your own homes?"

"It does not become your humble servant to recount his services, nor to ask anything, individually, at your hands. He was not introduced into a responsible position by any contrivance of his own. But amid confusion and want of order, he chose to stand—to die—by a fixed resolve, rather than to prolong—to forfeit exis·ence, by the degradation of the spirit of FREEMEN—the profanation of the Temple of Liberty.

"When the voice of the half-lingering sons of Freedom, by united acclamation, uplifted that rude ensign of Unity and Equity—then were broken the manacles of usurpation: then, as it were, was a NATION born! By no premeditated conspiracy was it designed; by no stealthy fraud was it sustained; by no unhallowed ambition was it propelled. It shrunk not from the performance of duty from fear of the consequences. The heart of every freeman was given to it; the peaceable citizen received its protection. The vile usurper of the authority of Mexico and of your rights fled from the first touch of its constancy: yet designing artifice and insatiable avarice quaked, and plotted its ruin. It bowed in respect to the 'Father of Liberty'; yet it enveloped its dignity amid the folds of the parental robe. It is now reported back to you for safe keeping.

"Which of your towns or villages did not surrender to your citizens, for the establishment of your own independent sovereignty? When the last act of the drama was 'played',—the taking of De Angelos—it was a proper expression of your sovereignty.

" Will any of your opponents (if there may be any),
instance the taking of Monterey ?   So did that honorable Commodore [Stockton] frankly acknowledge, that
he found no other government than yours in the country ; adding, ' to you, sooner or later, must the country
be surrendered.' Neither was there a vestige of Mexican authority found afterwards in your whole country ;
especially within any comeatable distance of your constituted authority : for Mexico had ceased for a long
time to maintain her authority among you.   You have
never, in an organized capacity, or otherwise, alienated
your sovereignty.   Your whole country has possessed
a name and an identity ; with laws, customs and usages
long established, and peculiar to the interests of its citizens, which cannot be changed to the slightest diminu-
tion of the properly vested rights of the former inhabitants, without the grossest violation of common justice
and national law.

" Mexico never claimed to exercise a property-right
in your soil, your mines or your unoccupied lands.   She
never sought to enrich herself by selling ' acres' not her
own—all were the rightful inheritance of the citizens.
She gave, in compliance with such laws and usages as
still constitute a part of your personal property-rights,
those lands to such citizens (or strangers as might desire citizenship) as were pleased, in accordance with
their vested rights in those laws and usages, to ask for
the same.   Nor were those laws and usages subject to
change or alteration by the Mexican government, being
founded in the nature and fitness of things—on the self-
evident fact, that the earth is the common heritage of

MAN, to be acquired by possession and USE, instead of *arrogance, force or fraud.*

" What of the ' Fifteen Millions'? Mexico could not, under any circumstances, have sold you. Had the strongest governmental ties, cemented by the most amicable relations, have existed, the bare conception of the thought of such falsehood would have been a sufficient quitclaim and transfer to you of INDEPENDENCE. Will any Californian sacrifice his interest in the AMERICAN NAME ?—his exhiliarating hope in the proper extension of equal liberty, which can only be based on a proper regard for the just rights of individuals; of individuals associated in communities; of individuals composing the densely inhabited district, or the sparcely peopled desert; of individuals composing a *sectional* State, delegate, or ' *Confederate*' government? INDIVIDUAL RIGHTS! for the want of a clear and comprehensive knowledge of which, THE AMERICAN UNION, even now, hangs trembling, like the scathed leaf to the fruitless bough, amid the frosts of winter!

" Mexico received no money on account of your dependence. Let not your country now pay tribute to a distant and dissimilar land, whose people neither know nor regard your interests. What interest have you in the quarrels of Mexico? Or, what interest had Mexico in the matter of disposing of your sovereignty ? Are you to be bought and sold ' like sheep in the shambles' ?

" Rather encourage the settlement of your own country, and reward your own patriots, who pledged their lives for the support of your common liberties ; and give those Ranchos, and the 100 varas of mining lands

to such as ask for them, as all your sons have the right
to claim and receive, according to long and well established law and usage;—and thus encourage your sons
to protect, defend, enrich, beautify and populate your
own country—your children's HOME!"

DESCRIPTION OF THE CALIFORNIA INDIAN CUSTOMS.

In a letter to one of his brothers dated at
Sonoma, June 25, 1847, Mr. IDE gives the following account of the habits and mode of life
of the native inhabitants of the land, as he
then found them :

I have a hundred Indians to employ and to clothe:
and one half of them are now unemployed. Their labor is to cultivate the soil, to ditch, fence, build and improve the same lands over which their fathers have
spent their lives in idleness and nakedness for thousands
of years. They have hitherto increased beyond the
ability of the country, by its natural productions, to
support them. They have, apparently, never cultivated
the smallest plant, tree or shrub. They have subsisted
on fish, acorns, roots, clover and many other kinds of
grass—berries, and the flesh of the elk, deer, antelope,
rabit and smaller quadrupeds—and quails, which are
very numerous.

They live, in the rainy season, in conical tents, about 10
feet in diameter, covered with thatched mash of leaves,
sticks, reeds or rushes. They make floats or rafts [bal-

sies] of bull-rushes [tula]. The women wear an apron,
or bunch of willow bark, like a mop, which is made fast
about the hips by a cord of the same material, and
extends downward from a foot to 18 inches, in a profuse
pile of strings before and behind.

The men are entirely naked, except they sometimes
throw an antelope skin over their shoulders. They still
exist, as in former times, in small tribes [Ranchorees] of
from 100 to 4 or 500 men, speaking different dialects,
and are frequently enemies to each other. They look
to the white man who owns the land they inhabit as
their 'Great Chief,' and expect him to defend them from
the attacks of their neighbors, and also from their natural enemy, the Grizzly Bear, whose flesh they refuse
to eat—for the reason, as they believe, that he was once
human, but became beastly in consequence of his disposition to eat human flesh.

In the time of the year for clover, (of which California produces spontaneously 12 different kinds), they resort to the most favored spots, and dwell in booths
made of bushes. In the season for fish they dwell ·in
thick willow groves, on the low banks of the rivers,
and sleep in beds of sand. In time of oats-harvest the
squaws gather large quantities by swinging a basket
made of the bark of roots against the tops of the ripe
grain, a part of which falls into the basket. In time of
acorns, the squaws gather immense quantities, which
they put in store-houses made of small sticks interwov-
en with willow bark, which they keep for winter use.
These acorns are their corn, which is pounded, sifted,
and made into various kinds of bread.

These Indians are required by a law of California to

clothe themselves, and their services belong to the man who furinshes them with the means for clothing, till all arrears are paid. We generally employ the boys, and when they prove faithful we clothe their fathers, who only work in the wheat harvest. The word of the landholder is the Indian's law; but the owner is not to do him any injustice. He is the Indian's governor, and may punish him according to certain rules : but he cannot sell him, or take away his children without his consent. These Indians are voracious eaters. They have nothing to sell that will command spiritous liquors, and consequently, they are not drunkards; but they are " the slaves of *tobacco*" !

I have given you this concise history of the natives of the land, in part for the purpose of explaining my own situation. I have now two* farms which I have purchased and paid for. The first is situated at the head of steamboat navigation on the Sacramento River, which I selected as the most favored site for a "city of the Sacramento valley", on account of its beauty, and the sandy nature of its soil, which renders it dry and free from mud in the winter, and green and fertile in the summer—on account, also, (and more especially), of the vast amount of pine timber in the vallies above, on the River, which can be most conveniently sawed there, and of the fertility of the Upper Valley, which must be supplied from some point near this by land-carriage. But it is not yet time to talk of building cities, *where families are from five to ten miles apart!*

* A few years subsequent to the date of this letter, Mr. IDE informed the Editor that he did not get "a valid title" to the second " Farm" he here refers to.

THE PEACEABLE INDIANS, AND LYNCH-LAW.

We have before us another letter from JUDGE
IDE to a nephew of his, in his off-hand racy,
and familiar style, from which we give a few
extracts, showing how Indians can be civilized
by kind treatment, easier than by the "shot-
gun"; and how "Lynch-law" has been organized, and how it has operated in times past. It
was written to a young man who, in 1861, enlisted in Captain AUSTIN'S company of Sharp-
shooters in the war of the great Rebellion, and
was killed in the battle at Yorktown, Va., April
5, 1862. This letter was in answer to his in-
quiries respecting California, as a place for his
future residence.

"Monroeville, April 20, 1851.
"Not having room enough in the "Main Sheet," I
put up a "jib", just to finish my story, and sign my
name on.
"The Indians that come from the Mountains say that
they could not live with their mountain companions, unless they would join them to steal horses and cattle; so
they came down to live with our Indians, that we
might *know* that they were good men. They say that
they have often seen us while we were hunting in the
mountains, and were afraid of us; so they hid in the

thick bushes: but after we were gone, they went back
to their house, and found that we took nothing away
with us, nor did we injure anything of theirs; therefore
we were friends and good men. They say that their
companions laugh at them, and call them cowards.

"They asked us to let them see us shoot, and went
off a hundred yards and set up a cane in the ground,
and said they wanted to see if we could cut it down so
far off. So William took his rifle and cut their cane
down with a ball. This pleased them much—giving us
to understand that they would not join the mountain
Indians, but would fight for us, and work for us, and—
wàl–o–men kï–nŋör bö–hok hörŋen—i. e., they would
live with us, on hire, a long time.

"Now dont be alarmed about the 'Indian difficulties'.
We have not been in the least terrified. I have, alone,
chased a hundred of them: but now the leaders of the
war party are dead, and many of their followers are
crippled, and I think they will not again disturb us.

"But I must close: this is *Court-day*, and as I am
one of the Associate Justices, it is somewhat necessary
that I should attend. I suppose that some of the nabobs
of your country will be 'horrified' to hear, that such a
person as myself should be 'dubbed' with the title of
'JUDGE'; but strange things happen in California. It
is undoubtedly very improper; but so it is, and we must
put up with it the best way we can.

"Well, we must 'live and learn.' *Judge Lynch* was
becoming very popular in the northern mines, and men
were quite often hung. Stealing the value of twenty
dollars is now made, by legislative enactment, grand

larceny, and grand larceny is punished by hanging.—
And further : a jury of twelve qualified voters are made
'judges of the law and of the facts'; so there is not
much for *Judge Lynch* to do, but just call the Court to
order, by appointing the officers—as it is impossible, in
such a floating population as we have here, that any *local* officers should exist.

"It is thought that the new law, called the 'hanging
law', is beginning to restore order by *establishing disorder*. How that is to be brought about we shall soon
see. The hanging goes on bravely, and none appear to
be hung amiss. When they come to the hanging point
they confess more than is laid to their charge. But this
is an unsocial subject. * * * [He then gives an account of his financial, farming and mechanical operations, and closes with]

" Fare-thee-well.   Love to all who inquire for
" WILLIAM B. IDE.
" JOHN S. M. IDE, Claremont, N. H."

—

" Ide's Rancho, July 23, 1851.
" I am very lonely,   James and Daniel are absent on
an expedition against the Indians, who are becoming
very troublesome to white people.

" At my nearest neighbor's at the east, across the Sacramento, about one mile distant, a man named James
McKenney was shot while lying asleep in his bed, on
the 17th inst., at 10 o'clock at night, and died on the
19th. The arrow entered the lower part of the abdo-

men, a little forward of the left hip joint, and ranged
so as to lodge the point of the arrow against the inside
of the pelvis.   The only remedy decided upon by the
attending physician, was to cut open the body, take out
the entrails, wash them, sew them up and put them
back, after having removed every foreign substance;
—then sew up the body, and cover the wounded part
with some light, adhesive plaster to exclude the air and
water—then bathe constantly with cold water, and apply glysters, as they did for two days; and if these operations could not save the man, there was no remedy.
A surgeon was also called, who said it ' was *too nice a
job for him*' : but I was in hopes he would recover, as
he was free from pain.   This is the fifth man who has
fallen by the Indian's arrow, this summer, within a
short distance of my house—four of them died and one
recovered.   Three Indian thieves have been shot by
white men, within the same distance and time.

" The Indians are gathering together from all quarters at a place east of the River, about six miles north
of my house, as we are told by a man who came down
last evening—in numbers aggregating some 7 to 10 hundred men, women and children.   Another man reports
having seen 150 or 200, on their way thither from the
south of this.   All these are understood to be valley Indians, who have for three or four years been friendly to
the settlers ; but the conduct of the foreign miners has
been such toward them, in common with that of the
Mountain Indians (their enemies), that little or no dependence can be placed on their friendship.   If they
become enemies, they will be far more dangerous than

the Mountain Indians, as they know all about our business, occupation, &c., and where they can most successfully lie in wait for us.

"James and Daniel have been gone five days. I heard
from them two days ago. They had had a battle, but
owing to their party having got divided, only five of the
men were engaged in it. They had the advantage of a
good piece of ground, where they could charge on the
Indians with their horses. The fight lasted an hour or
more. It was difficult to say how many opposed them
—probably from 50 to 100. They were quite sanguine
in the attack—came up knife in hand; but soon took
to the bush. Our men brought off one prisoner, and re-
reived a slight scratch of an arrow.

THE BOYS' FIGHT WITH THE INDIANS.

" A few weeks ago we had another battle, in which the
Indians were beaten, with the loss of 8 or 10 killed, and
15 or 20 wounded. But the most ludicrous was the
' war' declared expressly against myself, by a *Rancheric*
of Indians, living on the low hills back of my farm.—
This war was contrived and headed, if not declared, by
one of my neghbor Shareid's buckeries [horse-riders].
He ran away from his employer and joined the aforesaid
Rancho of Indians, and made known his plan. He said
that two men should go down to my place—find me,—
go close up and *shoot* me; but *he* would not go, because
I should know him. Others would not go, for the same
reason. At length two Indians were found who did not
know him they intended to kill, and very safely con-

cluded that I did not know them.　After having taken
the necessary directions they set off.　＊　＊　＊　Our
heroes came down, and finding a man encamped near
my house, they shot two arrows into his back and fled.
Learning their mistake, a few days after they sent five
others who said they knew me, and would kill me sure.
So they came, and were discovered by my little Indian
boys, who gave the alarm.　I was not at home; but
Daniel and Lemuel (being all the white folks at hand),
armed for the fight and went out—but the Indians had
fled.　The next night, between daylight and dark, they
came again.　So Lemuel, Daniel and Thomas Crafton*
took the field—and, sure enough, this time they got into
a fight.　Lemuel and Tommy lost all relish for the fun
when the arrows began to whiz, and fell back in the
rear, and took shelter behind Daniel, holding on to his
clothes, in order to prevent his dodging away from before them ; but Daniel succeeded in wounding one of
the enemy, and in inducing Lemuel to fire his gun, which
he did without taking aim, and Thomas fired his in like
manner, without effect, except to encourage the enemy,
who, (taking advantage as they supposed of the unload-
ed guns), rushed on to the charge with knife in hand :
but Daniel had his gun loaded again, and Lemuel and
Tommy, seeing the Indians were about to lay hold of
them, took their former place in the rear, and so disturbed Daniel, that he missed his aim, threw down his
rifle, shook off the boys at his back, and sprang forward
upon the enemy—drawing his revolver, he put it right

* The boy mentioned in Mrs. Healy's account of the emigrating company of 1845.

to them, discharging his five shots so suddenly, that the
hindmost one of the retreating enemy felt the search-
ing influence of the little weapon on his naked knife,
before he had time to finish his triumphant hurrang!—
Thus ended *that war.*

"The boys, seeing the Indians turn their backs, did
not pursue, but returned to the house, one fourth of a
mile from their "glorious field of battle." The next
morning the Indians were all gone. They were all
wounded, to say the least—either in body or mind."

A MULTITUDE OF PUBLIC OFFICES.

"Monroeville, Colusi Co., Cal., Nov. 9, 1851.
"DEAR BROTHER:

"I am seated in the office of the County Clerk of
Colusi county, where I am at present, by virtue of the
elective franchise been made Judge of the county Court,
civil and criminal, President of the Commissioners'
Court or court of Sessions for said county, and Judge
of Probate ; and, by appointment duly recorded, I am
made the County Clerk—Clerk of the District Court,
(9th district) Clerk of the County Court and of the court
of Sessions, Clerk of the Probate Court, county Recorder and county Auditor. These several offices at present
limit my official duties: but I suppose I shall, *just to
accommodate our floating population,* be compelled to
serve as 'Treasurer, Deputy Sheriff, Dep. County Surveyor'—and very probably as Coroner and Justice of
the Peace—and, possibly, as Dep. Notary Public.

"This account may excite some surprise; but I will

explain : nine-tenths of our population are here to-day,
and, to-morrow—are somewhere else.　Our county is
about 75 miles in extent on the Sacramento River, and
about 30 miles wide.　Our population are like birds of
passage, except their migrations are not exactly period-
ical. . All the circumstances which make it difficult to
obtain responsible and permanent county officers com-
bine to make these officers necessary.　At present ten
individuals pay more than three-fourths of the taxes
paid within the county, and comprise nearly all its permanent residents.　These men, as a general thing, re-
side on their Ranchos, to attend to their private affairs,
and are the only residents of the county who are able
to give the requisite bonds.　At the polls the non-resi-
dents (when they unite), have the elections as they
please; and the usual result is, that transient, irresponsible persons are elected, and *bonds* of the *like character*
are filed.　Last year the 'sovereign people' elected for
County Judge, (who is by law the acceptor or rejector
of all official bonds), a dissipated lawyer who, of course,
accepted such bonds as came to hand; and the administration of public affairs, financially, went on swim-
mingly for a few months—all the offices were promptly
filled—bonds filed, and gin, brandy and wine-bottles and
glasses occupied the place of stationery.　The records
of the courts became unintelligible to sober people; not
a court of any kind, except justice of the peace courts,
was held within the county, (except the Court of Sessions. and that was uniformly conducted by the *Senior
Justice*, while the presiding Judge was otherwise employed.)

" The ' property-holders', as we are called here, refused to pay their taxes, on the ground of the insufficiency
of the official bonds; and the good Host at the county
seat became tired of his boarding customer in the post
of County Judge.   Next followad a proclamation from
the Governor, ordering the election of a person to fill
the office of Judge.   Judge —— resigned, and the election resulted in the choice of one of the ' property-
holders', [your brother].   And a further result was, that
LEGAL bonds are required, which transient persons cannot procure.

" Another provision of the law is, that all public offices, except that of justice of the peace, shall be kept
open at the county seat, from 10 o'clock until 12, and
from 1 to 4, each day, except Sundays, new-years, Christ-
mas and election-days; and none of the county offices,
separately, will pay a person who can furnish the requisite bonds, for keeping these office hours.   But ten or
twelve county offices, combined, will serve to amuse for
awhile the present incumbent—and will also *interest*
him not a little to keep down expenses; or at least to
prevent profligacy in the public expenditure.

THE BEAUTIFUL CALIFORNIA SCENERRY.

" Thus and so are my public duties explained.   Monroeville is in the heart of the largest valley in California, about 20 miles from my lower Rancho.   It is surrounded by rich and fertile lands on all sides, extending
far and wide.   The little valley of the Connecticut af-
fords no such scenery.   It may be said to surpass ours in

beauty. The hills, the valleys, the mountains are there contiguous, and are seen and contemplated at one circumscribed view; but here at Monroeville is one extended view of fertile, alluvial intervale bottom. In the distance beyond, arise the indistinct hills, and further on are successive ranges of mountains, towering one above another, until the lofty forests are seen capped by ever-present snows—which in winter rush down to the verge of the hills and invigorate the grateful breezes; while *Flora* paints the earth at our feet. The wild geese have come from the north to feed upon our valleys, and the bears have come from the mountains to feed upon the grapes that entwine the trees along the streams of the valleys. The antelope still bounds upon the plains; the deer scud amid the foliage of the leafy trees, and the elk herd in the valleys between the hills. Such are the rural scenes on this ' Pacific Slope.'

THE DARK SIDE OF THE PICTURE.

" But now for the 'dark side of the picture.'—No Church-bell calls together its solemn assemblies! In fine, nothing but the rude haunts of dissipation supply the place of schools, academies and colleges. Ox-teams and mules make up the locomotive power, in the main. But improvements are being made. We have already passed some of the evils attendant, more or less, upon all newly organized governments: still there is nothing very flattering in the civil and political prospects before us, and less in the moral aspect ahead. Nearly all the enterprise of the country serves to corrupt and demoralize our transient population. 'Transient'! in that one word much is lost: but as it respects morals, much is gained—as, when nothing but vice is learned and promoted in a community, the oftener that community is changed the better.

" Last night, while the rain was pattering against,— not the window, but against—the rawhide hung up to keep the storm out of my sleeping-room, a good old man whom I had known for two or three months past, came to my door and awoke me from a quiet sleep— saying, 'Judge, I must leave you; I am going home: here are the books you gave me. I have recorded but one case therein : I must resign the Justiceship: where shall I lay the books and papers ? the stage is waiting.' On the table, I replied. ' Good-bye, Judge', said he— Good-bye, dear Sir, and may peace and prosperity go with you, said I. Sad were the reflections of the hours that followed! *My* peace was indeed gone! The blear contrast was full before my mind—while in my ears sounded the harsh and tumultuous voices of the *scholars* of intemperance and crime, as they at that moment issued from their gaming haunts, pistol and knife in hand—screaming vengeance unearthly! But while the noise gradually died away in the distance, as the weaker party fled, long were the hours that intervened, e'er the morning light gave other scenes to enliven the sleepless mind. But I will content myself as well as I can, until April, 1853, when I shall (if I live), be free again. And, in the mean time I hope to improve my mind somewhat by the study of Law. I have'nt a very high regard for lawyers, generally. Nevertheless I can study their books by way of amusement, and, perhaps,

qualify myself a little better for my present employment.

"About thirty days ago sentence of death was passed upon a horse-thief tried before the Criminal Court of Colusi County. This morning was laid upon my table an Order of Commutation from the Governor, to fifteen years service in the State's Prison. The same man is charged with highway robbery, and will in all probability be brought up by writ of *habeus corpus* for trial again at Colusi."

THE CONDITION OF PUBLIC AFFAIRS.—EXTRACTS FROM TWO LETTERS TO HIS MOTHER.

"Monroeville, Dec. 3, 1851.

"Last year the whole interior of Colusi county fell a prey to lawless marauders and thieves, to suppress which 'lynch-law' was resorted to, to supply the defects of such systems of law as were, in the exigencies of the case, imported from, and alone applicable to, other communities—differing as widely from ours as light from darkness.

"And again : the attempt to remedy this second evil of hanging through the impulse of passion, instead of the former tardy imported system, by organizing government among ourselves, has given rise to another serious evil. The salaries of officers, it was thought, should be such as would pay our best men for their services—especially, as ordinary men frequently obtain in the mines a great remuneration for their labor. So, the offices became more lucrative than the mines. And as all American citizens were allowed to vote in our Democratic State, on the first day of their arrival here, the whole business of legislation, and the execution of our laws, became a matter of speculation, and was forthwith, in most counties, seized by the hordes of Eastern fortune-hunters, who failed not to apply the power thus obtained to their own advantage. There are thousands of worthless men seeking office for its emolument, who have not the slightest interest in the welfare of the country: and the consequence is, that the resident citizens are ruined by taxes, besides being saddled with debts. All our adjoining counties are in debt, some twenty to fifty thousand dollars. But we are better off. Since I have been elected to the office of County Judge, I have abated, in a great measure, these evils in our county. I have declared the proceedings of former officers illegal, and have withheld payment of sallaries ; and, so far as I know, or have reason to believe, I am sustained by legal men in the courts above. By these means, and a rigid economy in county expenses, our county is out of debt."

"Monroeville, January, 17, 1852.

"I am engaged at the county seat, and have not been home for three months. I have the whole management of our county affairs. I hold two Courts per month, besides Justice Courts. I have consented to serve my county as their Probate and County Judge, and Presiding Judge of the Court of Sessions, that I may have it in my power to counteract that system of speculation in public affairs that has nearly ruined some of the counties. Ours is the only county in the State that is not in debt more than three-fold its yearly revenue.— The scale of taxation is the same throughout the State, and I hope to save over one thousand dollars of our yearly public revenue for some public utility. I am regarded with all that respect I can desire—all classes pay due deference to their Judge; but I have few confidential friends, and no adviser in whom I can confide."

—

A FEW WORDS (IN 'CONCLUSION'), TO THE FRIENDS AND RELATIVES OF THE SUBJECT OF THIS ''BIOGRAPHICAL SKETCH."

We are in possession of a large package of Mr. IDE's letters to his friends, from which additional and equally interesting extracts might be made. And yet we have made greater use of these, even, than we should have done, had we not been dependent on them, chiefly, for information respecting his business affairs, and his official duties. By correspondence and other means, the Editor has sought access to the contemporary public workers of 'Governor' IDE, and others who were among his personal acquaintance; and he has done so, only to be assured that almost all of them have, with him, " passed that bourne from whence no traveler returns." Under these cirumstances, (it being now about twenty-eight years since his decease) these letters are our only available resource for the due performance of this part of our duty.

At the time, (about two years ago), when we commenced our labors on this work—and, indeed, not until some eighty pages of it were in type—we knew nothing of the existence of the Wambough Letter, which occupies so large a portion of these pages. Our friends will therefore please excuse our seeming missuse of a few of those pages, by refering in them to events which are amply discussed in said Letter.

But it is useless for us to undertake to enumerate, and apologise for, all the discrepances and blunders, (typographical or otherwise) that some of our qicksighted criticising friends may discover. If we were to do so, the only honorable course would be to shoulder them all, by informing them that the EDITOR, alone, is *responsible* for them, so far as the compilation of the material, setting the type, reading and correcting the proof-slips, and making the type ready for the press, is concerned : and, if he was inclined to study out an apology or excuse for any short-coming of duty in these several employments, the only one he could offer would be, that *the frosts of eighty-five winters* may

have somewhat impaired his mental and phys-
iscal capability for such employment.

As this little book is intended as a memorial offering to the memory of a beloved Father,
by his only surviving Son and Daughter,* and
by his two surviving Brothers, to be placed in
the hands of so many of his other relatives and
their friends as may obtain copies of it, but a
small edition of will be printed : it being, in a
degree, devoted to a subject, as its title imports,
in which the general reader was not expected
to feel much interest. Yet, could he become
well aware of the fact, that it contains many
*"Scraps of California History never before
published"*, the case might be different.

Children of WILLIAM B. *and* SUSAN G. H.
IDE.

	WHERE BORN.	WHEN BORN.
James Madison,	In Keene, N. H.,	May 2, 1822.
William Haskell,	"	February 10, 1824.
Mary Eliza,	"	October 29, 1825.
Sarah Elizabeth,	"	November 1, 1827.
Ellen Julia,	"	January 14, 1830.
Susan Catharine,	in Woodstock, Vt.,	August , 1832.
Daniel Webster,	in Madison, O.,	March 6, 1835.
Lemuel Henry Clay,	"	December 24, 1837.
John Truman,	" near Springfield, Ill.,"	February 28, 1840.

THE INSCRIPTION.

To the Relatives of the late William B. Ide
and their posterity, of the " third and fourth",
and succeeding "generations", this book is respectfully inscribed. One, two, or more hundreds of years hence, should it be so long preserved in their family archieves, it will be read
by them with greater avidity and satisfaction,
than by any of their *anticipated* 'ancestry' of
the present greneration. With this suggestion
it is submitted to their perusal in the hope that
they will charitably overlook or condone any
short-comings of duty they may have discovered in the course of its perusal.

S. I.

Who Conquered California ?"
—OR—
Is it not time that "some pages of American History" were "re-written"?

" AN AUTHENTIC HISTORY OF THE CONQUEST OF CALIFOR-
NIA,"—Is the head-line or running title of a 140-page Book
just published by SIMEON IDE of Claremont, N. H., containing that part, only, of the " Biographical Sketch of the Life
of William B. Ide" which relates to his History of the " Bear
Flag Republic", and which is of more especial interest to the
general reader than the biographical part of the work. The
Editor says in his Preface :   " The Question,—' Who Conquered California ?' is of trivial interest, no doubt, to the
present generation; but the fidelity of History has something
to do with it, notwithstanding.   Another question, however,
not of personal significance, but intimately connected with
the discussion of this, *is* of vital importance, in a national
point of view, and deserves the attention of all good citizens
and of statesmen, especially ; and that question is,—Which
of the two conflicting ' plans of conquest'—that of Mr. Ide, or
that of his ' adviser' and active competitor, the renowned
Capt- Fremont—was the most judicious, praiseworthy and effectual ?"

The Editor of the San Francisco DAILY BULLETIN, in an
alaborate review of this " History," says : " It is of absorb-
ing interest.   If it should be found to stand the test of rigid
historical criticism, it would go far toward diminishing the
importance of the services of General Fremont in the acquisition of California.   The facts brought out are not at all in
his favor."

The publisher has recently received other commendatory
notices : among them, one from the Boston *Literary World*,
the Editor of which says, it " is an important contribution to
California History ; going to show, as it does, that *not* John
C. Fremont, but William B. Ide was the true ' conquerer.'"
And at the close of the article this Editor adds : "This narra-

tive, founded entirely on original authorities, deserves the careful attention of scholars. If its statements are to be received—and we see no reason why they should not be—they compel the re-writing of some pages of American History." "*If* its statements are to be received," says this writer. So far as the credibility or truthfulness of "its statements" is concerned, it is proper to state the fact, that parties most directly interested in their refutation, if incorrect, have for a year or two past been in possession of copies of the work: and if "its statements" cannot "stand the test of rigid criticism," they are, as good citizens—and in self-defence, it may be—bound to make it known. We *invite*, rather than *shun*, such a "test." *

The New York "GOOD LITERATURE—A Weekly Review of American and Foreign Publications,"—says of this work:

"Discussions concerning the conquest of California for the United States have been carried on for nearly forty years; and though there no longer exists the keen interest they once aroused, the *Historical question is one of importance.* The claims of Gen. Fremont as the pioneer conquerer have been more than once disputed; and a sharp attack on them is once more made in a 16mo volume of 139 pages, published in Claremont, N. H., by SIMEON IDE. * * * The book, which chiefly consits of a recently discovered manuscript written by the late Mr. Ide, claims that the entering wedge which severed California from its old position, and prepared it for becoming a part of the U. States, was driven by Mr. Ide; and that his plans were so far carried out before Fremont undertook the direction of affairs, that the subsequent military acts were needless. The little book is a historical monograph which should not escape the attention of collectors of Americana."

---

* The publisher respectfully requests any one into whose hands this book may fall, any valid evidence they can produce, going to disprove any statement of essential facts and occurrences, as narrated by Judge Ide in his Wambough Letter. It is believed his character for honesty and integrity will "stand the test" of the most rigid scrutiny.

Who Conquered California ?

READ THE FOLLOWING PAGES, AND THEN YOU WILL KNOW :

FOR THEY CONTAIN

THE MOST PARTICULAR, THE MOST AUTHEN-

TIC, AND THE MOST RELIABLE

HISTORY

OF

THE CONQUEST OF CALIFORNIA, IN JUNE, 1846,

BY

THE "BEAR FLAG PARTY."

EVER BEFORE PUBLISHED.

WRITTEN

BY ITS ORGANIZER AND LEADER,

THE LATE

HON. WILLIAM BROWN IDE.

CLAREMONT, N. H.

PRINTED AND PUBLISHED BY SIMEON IDE.

WHO CONQUERED CALIFORNIA?

PREFACE.

THE design of this little book is not to provoke controversy, nor to build up or pull down the public reputation of any one. The question—"Who conquered California?" is of trivial interest, no doubt, to the present generation; but the fidelity of History has something to do with it, nowithstanding. Another question, however, not of personal significance, but intimately connected with the discussion of this, *is* of vital importance, in a national point of view, and deserves the attention of all good citizens, and of statesmen, especially: and that question is—Which of the two conflicting " plans of conquest"—that of Mr. Ide, or that of his " adviser" and active competitor, the renowned Capt. Fremont, —was the most judicious, praiseworthy and effectual? The friends of the first named personage contend that the conquest of California was peaceably and fully assured by the ' Bear Flag Party,' before the latter assumed the lead, and that without the sacrifice of life or treasure; and that the measures adopted by it to effect that object were by far preferable to those proposed by the Captain—thus confirming the theory, that in all cases of

controversy between individuals or nations, a conciliatory line of measures is preferable to a resort to those
of violence and bloodshed.

We believe the good citizens of this republic *have really* a deep interest involved in this question, aside
from any considerations of a *personal* bearing. Captain
Fremont did, no doubt, indirectly aid the conquerors in
various ways; but,—as we have elsewhere remarked—
William B. Ide, (and *not* John C. Fremont, as has been
proclaimèd, and as is now believed by a vast majority of
the American people) was the originator and conductor
of that enterprise, from first to last. And why is it that
this misunderstanding has so long prevailed, if not from
the circumstance, that the one was a humble, unaspir-
ing mechanic in the common walks of life, while the
other was and is the recipient of high civil and military honors? Is it just, is it consonant with the free Republican principles of our political creed, to set in the
back ground, or entirely ignore in history, the benefi-
cent public services of our less favored sons by birth or
education, and transfer the fame and eclat of such services from them to others occupying a more conspicuous public position ? No, say we : " Let every tub
(high or low), stand on its *own* bottom."

CHAPTER I.

CALIFORNIA,—BEFORE ITS VIRTUAL CONQUEST BY THE " BEAR
PARTY," IN JUNE, 1846.—EDITORIAL REMARKS, INTRO-
DUCTORY TO WILLIAM B. IDE'S HISTORY OF THAT PARTY.

NATIONS, like individuals, in the course of
their history, pass through certain great crises
or epochs, which have an important bearing on
their future character. These epochs are not
regular, but intermittent ; and are often the
result of, what looks like accident ; though
doubtless, as in the phenomena of vegetation,
they have their hidden laws of growth and development. Hence, on perusing the history
of a people you will find periods of expansion
which have their origin, to some extent, in the
restless, impulsive life of society, and the thirst
for acquisition.

An epoch of this character largely affecting
the industries, the wealth and the commerce
of the American people, occurred in the year
1848, on the discovery of gold in California.
Previous to that time emigration to the Far
West had been going on, but confined to comparatively small limits ; not assuming a gen-

eral character stimulating large bodies of men
But the marvellous stories spread abroad by
the accidental discovery of gold on the American Fork, as it was called, of the Sacramento
River, caused the wildest excitement throughout the country. People everywhere, of all
classes and conditions of society—artizans, ag-
riculturalists, mechanics, merchants, doctors,
lawyers, and even ministers of religion,—were
suddenly arroused by dreams of untold wealth.
Vessels, crowded with enthusiastic adventurers, sailed from every port in the United States
for the newly discovered Eldorado ; and hundreds who registered their names for the voyage
full of hopeful and cheerful anticipations of
the future, went forth only to encounter hardship, disappointment, disease and death.

The course of history takes us back to the
local conflicts of the two or three years preceding this period of excitement, which was no
doubt hastened in its development by the occurrence of events which form the topic of discussion in this and in several of our succeeding
chapters. And, for the better understanding
of what is to follow, it may be well for us to
take a hasty glance at the civil and political
condition of California, at the time when these

events occurred. It is well known, that from its first settlement by Spanish adventurers from Mexico, no well-ordered system of national or provincial government had been established. Aristocratic "Dons," originally from Spain, formed a self-constructed oligarchy, by which the few emigrant and native laboring population were oppressed. This lordly race owned, or laid claim to, almost the entire domain of arable land—parcelled out as it was to them in 3-miles-square sections, known among the inhabitants, then and now, as *ranchos*. The laboring people there were in a condition but little better than that of the serfs of Russia, or the slaves of Virginia, in by-gone times. Common schools and the higher institutions of learning, and houses of public worship (unless there were here and there found at a Romanist *"Mission"*,) were unknown to them.

One of the peculiar grievances to which the emigrants from the States were subjected, was the arbitrary and oppressive exaction by their *"Alcaldes,"* or sole civil magistrates, of a per-capita tax from said emigrants, on taking up their residence among them. A correspondent of high standing in California, who took a conspicuous part in the troubles of '45, writes the

Editor, that Gen. Castro's threatened raid upon them was to compel the payment of this tax.

Hence it will be seen that a state of anarchy
and misrule confronted them at every step, and
that they could do no less than rise as they
did, for self-preservation, and attempt a " Revolution," by which they could " establish law
and order where none had existed before."

In the historical course of events, it is now
in order to invite the reader's attention to the
Letter of Mr. IDE, in succeeding pages. It
was probably written in the winter of '46-7 ;
as, during the " gold excitement" of '48-9, his
time was too much occupied at " the diggins"
to allow his attention to bygone events. Precisely *when* it was written is immaterial. After
it had lain over 30 years in obscurity, and after
the recent decease of his eldest son, James M.
Ide, it was found among his (J. M.'s) effects,
in a good state of preservation.

We have a reasonable guaranty, in the reputation of its writer for honest integrity in all
his dealings, of its truthfulness of statement :
and it is confidently believed that those of his
personal acquaintance who are still alive, and
who may be favored with its perusal, will do
his memory the justice to disabuse it of any

sinister or unworthy motive, in taking the part
he and his compeers deemed it necessary to
take in their "Revolutionary" movements of
'46. We entertain the opinion, furthermore,
that when the general reader, unbiased by
class, sect, or pre-national prejudice or attach-
ment, shall have thoroughly perused this document, and will take into consideration the situation of the country—the state of anarchy
then existing—he will cheerfully admit, that
however *unmilitary*, in the eye of gentlemen
skilled in warlike movements, their *modus op-
erandi* for the accomplishment of the object
in view—he will admit, I repeat, that *they did
accomplish it*. And we beg leave to make a
further suggestion—viz: that it might have
been a problem of difficult solution, for the
wisest adept in military science, or even in
"*path-finding*", to inaugurate a different line
of proceeding, by which that heterogeneous
population of Spanish, Mexican, Indian and
Yankee origin could, in less than one month's
time, by the well-directed labors of a handful
of men under the direction of an experienced
military leader, even, have been brought from
a state of bitter antagonism, into that of peaceful subjection to the United States' authority

—and that, too, at so trifling a "sacrifice of blood and treasure."

Suppose, for instance, there had been no *organized* resistance to Castro—that, as would naturally in that case have been the result, had not Mr. IDE, or some one else, promptly moved "among the emigrants," and got up the celebrated, *justly* "celebrated, BEAR FLAG PARTY" *organization*, setting at defiance the exterminating Proclamation of Gen. José Castro ; and that there had been a cowardly shrinking from self-defence—a "fleeing to the mountains for safety" by some, and a sort of gorilla, hand-to-hand warfare between pioneers and Castro's scouts by others, until they knew of the war between Mexico and the United States; what would then have been the condition of the contending parties ?

That such a state of warfare between the natives and emigrants then existed, we respectfully refer the reader to ante-pages 63 and 64*

---

* The reader will please bear in mind, that this reference is to these two pages of a work lately published, entitled:

"SCRAPS OF CALIFORNIA HISTORY: A Biographical Sketch of the Life of WILLIAM B. IDE, giving a minute and intersting account of one of the largest emigrating companies (3000 miles over land in 1845) from the East to the Pacific Coast," etc., in which are several extracts from the letters of W. M.

for ample proof—where Mr. BOGGS tells us of
the barbarous murder of two young Americans;
and that Americans, (not of the Bear Flag party), by way of *retaliation,* killed three peaceful Californians, " who had not taken up arms
against them, neither had they taken part in
the massacre of the two young Americans."
And what is added seems unaccountable : this
act of "retaliation" was performed by Kit
Carson, with Capt. Fremont's approval.

Had Gen. Castro remained a month or two
longer than he did, in the undisturbed possession of his fort, arms and military supplies, is
it to be doubted that he would not have used
them somewhat *successfully* in his threatened
exterminating process ? and thus have aroused the retaliatory energies of the U. S. government ; so that, when the actual state of war
between it and Mexico arrived, much "blood
and treasure" would have been expended on
both sides in California, before the return of
peace. Had there been the Bear Flag move-

BOGGS, Esq., of Napa City, Cal. (an acquaintance of Mr. IDE)
who obligingly furnished the Editor several historical incidents for said work—which he respectfully refers the reader
to, as a more readable and instructive book for the youth of
California and the East, than most of the thousands of the
sensational Story-books with which the country is floqded.

ment, or an organized opposition to Castro, and
no formal state of war between the U. S. and
Mexico, is there any reason to doubt the event-
ual erection of an Independent Republic on the
Pacific Coast? That war existed between
the two nations was not known in California,
until, by comparatively peaceful measures, this
province had been prepared, without the "loss
of blood or treasure", to become an "Independent Nation". The "Bear Flag Proclamation", (every word of which, Mr. IDE remarks
in his Letter to SENATOR WAMBOUGH, was
penned by him on the 15th of June, 1846, between the hours of 1 and 4, A. M.) was the
entering wedge, so to speak, that separated a
down-trodden people from allegiance to an oppressive oligarchy under which they had groaned from time immemorial. It annunciated
principles of government new and attractive.
It contained no vindictive or coercive threat ;
but, on the contrary, was persuasive and conciliatory. It approached the people as brethren, rather than as enemies. It was sought for,
circulated among and read by them so earnestly, that copies of it could not be written fast
enough to supply the demand. Its circulation
in Castro's camp, it is stated, had the effect to

withdraw from it one half (300) of his followers, and convert and transform them into peacable citizens, under the new order of things.

After due consideration of these and other
circumstances connected with " the conquest of
California", it is submitted to an honest, dispassionate and appreciative posterity to pass
upon the validity of William B. Ide's claim to
the merit of *upright intention*, at least, in doing what he did do, towards the " Conquest of
California", and the "*wisdom* or *unwisdom*"
of the measures he adopted to accomplish that
object. If he had been an aspirant for fame and
high place in governmental affairs, would he
have quietly yielded to the adroit manœuvreing and contriving of his "successor, in that
General Assembly" he refers to, at the close of
his narrative?—by which a "change of Administration" was effected, and " We, who are
out of office, may have a chance to get in."

It is deeply regreted that his narrative of
those proceedings ends so abruptly. Mrs. Healy thinks her Father gathered the main facts
and dates it treats of from a memorandum he
kept of events as they occurred, which he carried in his pocket. This memorandum-book,
(she says), her brother JAMES was robbed of,

—together with a sum of money—on his way to Utah, several years before his decease, and does not doubt that it contained an account of his experience in Fremont's expedition " down the coast", in July, August, September, October and November, 1846 : allusion to which by one of his brothers will have been noticed in our preceding pages.* And this suggests the idea, that inasmuch as that that "brother's" statement of what Mr. Ide told him about the occurrences under the "Bear Flag Government", during its brief existence, does not *essentially differ* from the version of the same transactions in his SENATOR WAMBOUGH LETTER, we may conclude that said brother's account of said "expedition" is substantially correct. Therefore we may give credence, also, to his statement that Commodore STOCKTON, as an authorized officer of his government, formally received the transfer of the Califor-

(These "Editorial Remarks, introductory", etc., are taken from the work entitled "*Scraps of California History,*" &c. (see the foot-note on pages 10 and 11). That book gives an account of Mr. Ide's three or four months' service under Fremont's command—from about the 6th of July to November, 1846—while engaged in the "sport" of following Castro down the Pacific coast, then on his way home to Mexico. This account was furnished the Editor of "a Biographical Sketch", etc., by his brother, to whom it was orally related in 1849.

nias to the United States, aboard his ship, by
the only governmental authority he then found
there ; and, in recognition of Mr. Ide's authority as Governor and Commander-in-chief, the
Commodore gave him the compliment of a reception, collation, etc., as before stated. And
we cite this circumstance as evidence that his
services in the cause of order and good government were duly regarded by that noble officer.

The Compiler of this memorial sketch of an
unpretending citizen and early pioneer of California has deemed it due his memory, that
his "Letter to Senator Wambough," giving a
minute account of the " Bear Flag enterprise,"
should be placed before the American people,
that they may be able to decide the question,
whether he, or Capt. Fremont, originated and
conducted this ' enterprise' to its successful issue. We believe the generally received opinion is, that the credit of it is due the latter.

This theory we recollect to have heard very
unreservedly advanced by a distinguished public speaker, the Hon. JAMES WILSON, an ex-
member of Congress from New Hampshire.
He had just returned to resume his residence in
his native town, (Keene, N. H.), after an absence of four or five years during the war of

the great rebellion, *in California,* where he no
doubt imbibed his views on this question.   He
gave, in several towns in N. H., very interesting lectures on California—geographical, mineralogical and historical—soon after his return;
and, while on the latter named branch of his
subject, he stated distinctly before a large audience among whom this writer was an interested
listener, that John C. Fremont was the originator and leader of the " Bear Flag Party", and
conqueror of California.

After having attentively read the circumstantial statement of the moral, industrial and
political aspect of affairs, and the account of
that short-lived " embrio Republic", from the
pen of Mr. IDE—written, as it undoubtedly
was, within a year of its " rise and fall"—the
unprejudiced and candid reader will find little
ground on which to base said lecturer's theory,
except on the presumption that Mr. IDE intentionally misrepresents the whole concern.   And
we leave it to the dispassionate judgment of
posterity to settle the question, as to *which* of
the two most conspicuous *" Heroes"*, the unpretending mechanic, or the renowned " Pathfinder", did the country the most valuable service in the " Conquest of California" ?

CHAPTER II.

MR. IDE'S EXPLANATION OF THE SITUATION OF AFFAIRS IN
CALIFORNIA, ON HIS ARRIVAL THERE IN 1845.

TO THE HON. SENATOR WAMBOUGH:

DEAR SIR:

BEING ever willing to contribute to the pleasure of those with whom I am associated, I am persuaded, although somewhat reluctantly, to comply with your request, by furnishing a detailed account of what is called the "Bear Flag Enterprise" or Revolution—embracing a copy or rehearsal of what was then written, or may still be among my papers ; and in such manner as truly to represent any matter or circumstance that may have led to its origin, unexampled success, sudden overthrow, and——total eclipse.

It will be with much diffidence that I engage in giving an account of the past ; which at best can serve but little other good than to awaken curiosity in the mind of some, with scarce the hope of its gratification ; while in the mind of others it will not fail to renew the memory of those scenes, and sharpen regret, that time has blunted and robbed of power to sting : but if duty require, I will sacrifice the happiness I choose and enjoy in hidden retirement ; and, regardless of consequences, frankly relate occurrences that may lead to a just estimate of the motives and designs of those concerned as actors ; being aware that if in aught I am mistaken, the means of correction are at hand.

Then permit me, Sir, to call in requisition your general knowledge of the situation of the two parties in their relation to each other, who were immediately concerned in, and affected by the " *Independent Bear Flag Nation*"—for in fact it was nothing short of National Independence to which it aspired—I say the two parties, native Mexican citizens and natives of other countries—including, more particularly, recent American emigrants.

Being, on one side, excited to jealousy by the then recent events in relation to Texas, and a manifest disposition of certain American gentlemen to re-enact the like scheme in California ; and by a determined resolution on the part of the other side, to assert and maintain

the unalienable right of all men to the enjoyment of life, liberty and personal security, and
to attain the right of honorable acqusition, use
and enjoyment of the comforts of life ;—there
were, apparently, two parties ; *but, in truth
and in verity they were one people.* They were
made enemies by their prejudices and jealousies ; but it was as apparent as the face of day
that they could be bound in the bonds of mutual friendship by their common interest and
common consent and fellowship.

Let us appeal to your own heart, dear Sir :
Is it not the interest of *all men*, everywhere,
to be protected by an honorable, just and liberal government ?

And again : Do not all men desire for themselves exemption from oppression, and the liberty of justly acquiring, enjoying, possessing,
appropriating and bestowing the honest avails
of their labor, according to their own pleasure ?
If so, then men are made enemies by oppression, injustice, jealousies or ignorance.   But
those who love true Liberty, and abide by the
unchanging law of justice, will subdue enemies
without protracted violence.

The above granted, it will be more easy, (or
less painful), to proceed through the tame and

lifeless narrative of simple matters of fact necessary to the formation of an opinion in relation to a matter, now no longer of the smallest
moment, only as the everlasting, self-evident
principles of self-government were concerned,
whereby universal peace can only prevail ; although the rehearsal can awaken to recollection
and measurable endurance, the cares and sleepless solicitude, the far distant hope that prom-
ises peace and glory to a Nation as extended
as the race of man, because built amid the
foundations of that liberty that delighteth itself in the *Balance of Truth.*

I would, Dear Sir, that another pen than
mine might gratify the curiosity, and subserve
the interest that has been awakened : but thus
to desire is but to shrink from the task your
favorable consideration has imposed upon me.

Then be pleased to bear in mind, that prior
to the year 1846 the peace, prosperity and quiet of the good citizens of California had been
deranged by eight successive Military Revolu-
tions, which had devastated almost entirely the
whole country, from San Diego to its northern
extremity.

It will be unnecessary to describe in particular this general ruin. It was everywhere ap-

parent—presenting itself sorrowfully, and forc-
ing its consideration upon the minds of all who
were capable of perceiving the extent of that
cruelty—of that depraved spirit of injustice,
tyranny and theft, which had tempted a portion
of its most enterprising citizens to abandon the
path of common honesty—to listen to the sug-
gestions of the deceptive policy of foreign artifice, and to seek wealth and distinction by
seizing, diverting and changing the fatherly
care of government to an engine of rapacious
piracy.

Thus, on an occasion like the one I am called on to describe, it was easy to imagine that
all good, honest and intelligent citizens of California were tired of this state of continued violence, injustice and misrule.

But, dear Sir, before we bring ourselves to
the consideration of the events which gave
birth, unexpectedly, to the " Independent Bear
Flag Nation", it will be well that we consider
the situation, origin and character of the few
that were destined to be crushed and annihilat-
ed by the fears and jealousies of an apparently
well appointed, overwhelming military despotism.——Then, Sir, let us remember that the
then recently arrived American emigrants were

no *Cuban volunteers!* They were not enlisted from the lounges of dissipation, nor drilled in the school of political intrigue and dishonesty. They came not to *provoke the Mexican authorities to "strike the first blow", in a war sought for the acquirement of that fair and shining land to which they journeyed.* They came not equipped and provided with military stores. In short, they came not as enemies ; but AS FRIENDS CAME THEY, with hearts burning with love of liberty—of that liberty that is founded on the immutable principle of equal justice ; that gives an equivalent for what it receives.

They were not, like your modern gold-hunters and squatters, prepared for *"fight or flight" ;* but bearing with them their wives, their children, their flocks and herds—their home, their *all* at stake ; prompted by no groveling desire to obtain something for nothing—to rob, to plunder those they might find possessed of wealth, happiness and peace.

They were collected and banded together, not by any preconcerted scheme of any kind, but by individual enterprise,—by long cherished love of that pure, unadulterated freedom, *known only to the just and the brave ;* to those who, for the sake of peace, plant their foot and build their habitation beyond the reach of political oppression, where nature smiles in holiest loveliness—where there is naught to entice those vile miscreants who prey upon the rights of others.

Then, kind Sir, please imagine the disappointment of those brave men, who, having conquered the difficulties of the untrodden, pathless Sierra Nevada; after having maintained their peace, unstained even by the blood of the untaught savage; and having with toil, privation and watchfulness, known only to those who have endured similar privations—who, having pierced the trackless wilderness, had arrived within sight of the ever shining vales they had thus sought; when, by the intervention of a self-constituted government, heated to madness by jealousies excited by designing emissaries, we were forbidden the usual hospitalities of the country, and " *ordered to return*"!

It is in vain to trouble you further to consider the situation of the newly arrived emigrants, when you remember that 13,000,000 of dollars had been offered and refused for the possession of the Bay of San Francisco, and

that the acquisition of the same had been un-
successfully sought by negotiation for more
than fourteen years.

But there was another class of citizens
concerned, who were principally of American
origin, and constituted about one-tenth of the
citizen population of California. They had,
in many instances, intermarried and become
associated with the native citizens, and enjoyed
their common advantages. Indeed, a portion
of them had become the merchants and finan-
ciers of the country ; and thus failed not, in
the genuine spirit of Yankeedom, to direct and
profit by those political impositions, change of
administration, and continued increase of tariff duties, by which, during ten years of increasing distress and ruin, the main body of the
people were made *miserably poor.*

But of this class the mass had fallen among
the oppressed ; and it appeared to be the pleasure of the more successful, to set the whole
community at variance—to increase public expenditure and tariff duties, which constituted
their principal stock in trade. Whatever
scheme the merchants proposed became the rule
of action ; for it was claimed they *"paid all
the people's taxes"* !

You cannot fail to remember the preconcerted seizure and ironing of every American, except T. O. Larkin and a very few others—the plot to scuttle the vessel and throw them all, while in irons, into the Bay of San Diego—the failure of the plot by the humane interposition of the better disposed portion of the native citizens—their subsequent five months' imprisonment at Mexico ; and, withal, that those favored merchants, (at least their leader), improved this favorable opportunity to collect inflated demands against these prisoners. It is quite impossible to trace, in written characters, the reflections that crowd the mind, in view of their hypocritical and murderous acts.

While the aforementioned causes, and numerous others of like character, were producing their legitimate fruits—fruits which were proprolific of seeds of new dissensions—Captain Fremont came among us ; who, after having provoked the assumed authorities of the country, left us to experience the wrath and retaliatory vengeance his acts had engendered.

Immediately after, (about the first day of April, 1846,) Gen. José Castro, naturally humane and generous, caused to be issued and posted up at Sonoma and various other places—

the temporary residences of the newly arrived emigrants—a proclamation, ordering " All foreigners, whose residence in the country was less than one year, to leave the country, and their property and beasts of burden, without taking arms," on pain of death.

It may well be supposed that this proclamation produced no little consternation among the recent emigrants. But the prudence and sagacity of some of the resident (American) citizens prevented much alarm, by proposing to the authorities to call the said emigrants together, and to instruct them orally. This was agreed to, and the citizen Americans were visited, and persuaded their new neighbors to dress themselves decently in California fashion, as far as possible, without loaned articles of clothing, and to attend respectfully and submissively the meeting. Thus cautiously was a meeting and separation effected at Sonoma, without producing a general rupture. But notwithstanding every effort, a large party of young men and two or three women, to escape the much expected scene of blood, left the country for Oregon.

Next came Lieut. Gillespie, who failed not to give cautionary advice in relation to a state of preparedness, on the part of all of U. States origin, but dissuaded from any kind of organization ; no, not even in the externals of an "Agricultural Society"; "for such", he said, "is the watchful jealousy of the Spaniards towards the last emigration, that the slightest attempt at organization in any shape, or by any name, would be but the signal for the massacre of the whole of the last emigration." He made known that he should, as soon as possible, recall Capt. Fremont ; and suggested that his camp would be the means of temporary protection : or, if matters came to the worst, to effect a retreat to the States.

CHAPTER III.

FIRST UPRISING OF THE EMIGRANTS.—CAPT. FREMONT'S PLAN
OF "NEUTRAL CONQUEST".—INTERVIEW WITH THE CAP-
TAIN AND COMMENTS THEREON.

ANOTHER month rolled on, and Capt. Fremont came not ; for the snows were not yet
fully melted in the mountain gulches of the
Sierra Nevada.   The Oregon company were
long gone.   Forces were every day increasing
under Gen. José Castro at San Juan Baptista.
Six hundred armed men were known to be
foaming out vengeance against a few foreigners.   Everybody spoke of and felt the impend-
ing danger—admitted that organization and
resistance was desirable ; but all agreed that
it was impracticable.   A want of confidence in
the ability of any man among us to conduct
such an enterprise was everywhere apparent
and fully expressed, and a—a " certain fearful
looking-for of judgment and fiery indignation,
that would devour the adversary", should we
fail of success, bound and paralized the energy of that portion of our *friends* who were so
miserable as to possess more wealth than they

could *swallow at a meal.* " What was to be
done ?   Were they to risk their lives, and the
lives of their wives and children in the fath-
omless snows of the Sierra Nevada ?"   Oh,
no, Sir, no.   This was impossible : the snows
were melted.   It was the 6th of June, and all
eyes were turned to watch the approach of
Fremont ——He came !—the glorious era !—
memorable day !—when it was determined, as
we were informed nearly a year after by Col.
Benton's letter to Congress, to " *Overthrow the
government, and conquer California at once !*"
But pardon me, my dear Wambough, for thus
darting away to the consummation of such a
scheme, without describing the *modus operan-
di* whereby this was to *have been,* before coming to the subsequent plan of operation by
which it *was* accomplished.

I am requested to give such papers, among
my cast-off memoranda, as may be in point :
then read : " Notice is hereby given, that a
large body of armed Spaniards on horseback,
amounting to 250 men, have been seen on their
way to the Sacramento valley, destroying the
crops, burning the houses, and driving off the
cattle.   Capt Freemont invites every freeman
in the valley to come to his camp at the Butes,

immediately; and he hopes to stay the enemy, and put a stop to his"—— (Here the sheet was folded and worn in-two, and no more is found). This document was not signed by Capt. Fremont, nor by any person in his legal company ; else it would have been legal evidence of unwarrantable interference in the difficulties brewing in the country, which *he uniformly and unequivocally declared he should refrain from.* This letter came to hand by an Indian "agent", on the 8th of June, between the hours of 10 and 11, A. M.

You may be assured there was no hour of deliberation—not a moment; the horse bounded back to the cabin ; the rifle, pistols and ammunition were, by every inmate of the house, produced at the door ; one brief sentence gave the parting advice to the fond wife and listening, excited and wondering children, while the blanket was being lashed to the saddle. Every house in the valley was visited ; but not one was found willing to leave his *goods,* not his *wife,* (for there were only two within the valley)—and we hastened to the camp of Capt. Fremont, where we arrived at break of day on the 10th, and, by dint of apparent acquiescence, learned "THE PLAN OF

CONQUEST"; which was quite simple and easy of accomplishment—and here it is : First, select a dozen men who *have nothing to lose,* but *everything to gain.* Second, encourage them to commit depredations against Gen. Castro, the usurper, and thus supply the camp with horses *necessary for a trip to the States.* Third, to make prisoners of some of the principal men, and thus provoke Castro to *strike the first blow* in a war with the United States. This done, finish the conquest by uniting the forces, and " marching back to the States."

The foregoing constituted the whole of the " first edition" of Capt. Fremont's *plan of neutral conquest* of California.

And here I would beg a moment's indulgence, that I may the more fully show the true position of the " Bear Flag nation", so far as relates to any influence Capt. Fremont may have had in its origin or organization.

I do not wish to impugn his motives or conduct, but have no doubt he acted honestly in accordance with what he conceived to be the will of his superiors. Nevertheless, we must speak the whole truth, and say that the aforementioned plan was fully presented to us, with the advantages [it would bring, to wit :

a war between Mexico and the U. S., and the conquest and union of California with them.

Capt. Fremont, while we were alone in his markee, on the evening of the 10th, rehearsed the above plan, humanely providing that none who had anything to sacrafice should be implicated therein ; and asked the opinion of his auditor, who said in reply, that " it would be a long time ere he would consent to, or join with, any set or company of irresponsible persons, who first commit an outrage, and then dishonorably leave the country and others to settle the difficulty, or endure its consequences." Capt. F. remonstrated against this reply ; and especially against the reflection of dishonor cast on himself—went on to show that the emigrants had received great indignities from Castro, and would be justified in any measure they might adopt for their safety— went on to say, that if the emigrants waited to receive the first blow, all hope in resistance would be in vain ; and cited, in support of his argument, the seizure of all Americans that had taken place, as herein before mentioned.

I then informed him that no personal reproach was intended ; that he, (Fremont), as an accredited American officer, was supposed to act in obedience to his instructions from his superiors ; but that we, although beyond the protecting shield of the U. States' flag, still cherished the memory of the AMERICAN NAME, the honor of which was yet dearer to us by far than any rewards of falsehood and treachery dishonorably won. Whereupon Capt. F. became exasperated. Rising hastily he said : *"I will not suffer such language in my Camp; it is disorganizing!"* and went immediately out.

Thus ended all intercourse, on our part, with Capt. Fremont, until the 25th of June, when, in due course of events, his next salutations will be given. A few minutes after his departure Mr. King came into the markee, and politely invited us to another tent, and very soon commenced asking : " Suppose the men succeed in taking the horses, what will you in that case propose to be done?" The reply was, " When the breach is once made that involves *us all* in its consequences, it is useless to consider the propriety of the measure. We are too few for division. *In for it, the whole man! Widen the breach,* that none can stand outside thereof. *Down on Sonoma! Never flee the country,* nor give it up while there is an arm to fight, or a voice to cry aloud for Independ-

ence. But let truth and honor guide our
course. The United States may have cause of
war against Mexico ; but that is nothing to
us. We have cause of war and blood—such
as it is impossible for the United States to
have received." " Good !" cried Mr. King,
and ran out to repeat the sentiment. " Good !
Hurrah for Independence !" cried the whole
camp ; and several persons, among whom was
KIT CARSON, begged of Capt. Fremont their
discharge from the service of the exploring expedition, that they might be at liberty to join
us. This was peremptorily refused. Fremont,
in my hearing, expressly declared that he was
*not at liberty to afford us the least aid or as-
sistance; nor would he suffer any of his men
to do so; that he would not consent to discharge any of them, as he had hired them expressly for, and needed their assistance on his
journey over land to the States; that he had
not asked the assistance of the emigrants for
his protection; that he was able, of his own
party, to fight and whip Castro, if he chose,
but that he should not do so, unless first as-
saulted by him; and that positively he should
wait only for a supply of provisions,—two
weeks at farthest, when he would, without fur-*

*ther reference to what might take place here,
be on his march for the States."*

Scarcely were these statements made, ere it
was reported and acclaimed : " The horses are
coming !"—and on they came ! All was animation in the camp.   Capt. Merrit (for it was
understood it was he who was to be the leader
of this little band of heroes), made report that
he had followed his *instructions*, as given by
the "*advice*" of Capt. Fremont, and had surprised the guards and captured the *whole* band
of 250 horses—had offered to give back the
arms of the guard ; and, for "fair play", to
fight the battle over again, at 50 or 100 yards
distance. This favor being refused, he had generously given each man his arms and two horses ; and boldly directed the released prisoners
to tell Gen. Castro " if he wanted his horses,
to come and take them."

This conduct was highly applauded by Capt.
Fremont, (who, a moment before, would not
and dare not, on his honor, offer us the least
protection or assistance). The said horses were
acknowledged to be the rightful property of
the twelve men who so valiantly had captured
them, and were delivered over to the care of
Capt. Fremont for safe keeping, while their

new owners might acquire new spoils in the direction of Sonoma.

It was 12 at night, and all possible haste was made to be off, as it was known that the men who had been imprudently released would, in all probability, separate and spread intelligence of the rising of the emigrants, and of the taking of government horses, in every direction ; and it was more than probable, that the garrison at Sonoma might be *alarmed,* rather than *surprised.*

CHAPTER IV.

THE PARTY LARGELY REENFORCED BY NEW RECRUITS—THEIR
MISTAKEN NOTIONS EXPLAINED.—WHAT HAPPENED ON
THEIR ARRIVAL AT SONOMA.—MR. IDE MADE COMMAND-
ER-IN-CHIEF, "BY ACCLAMATION," AND TAKES THE FORT,
INSTANTER.—THEIR INCIPIENT MOVEMENTS UNDER THE
"INDEPENDENT BEAR FLAG GOVERNMENT".

JUST about sunrise on the 11th of June, '46,
thirteen mounted men, armed with rifles and
pistols, crossed the Sacramento River, a little
below, or at the mouth of Feather River.
Much time was spent in procuring fresh horses,
and no accessions were made to our forces that
day. We supped at Gordon's, on Coche Creek,
who gave us a bullock; but was too deeply interested in our enterprise to join our party just
then. At night we groped our way over the
mountain pass, and ere the sun had become
oppressive, we were safely at the Rancho of
Major Barnard. He, also, allowed us to kill
and eat a fat bullock ; but, like the other dear
friends, was too fond of the goods of this life
seriously to think of dying in defence of others.
Here or hereabouts were a considerable num-

ber of newly arrived emigrants, and the day
was spent in obtaining recruits. Much time
was spent in procuring as many as swelled our
number to *thirty-two;* and on the 13th, at 11,
P. M., sleep and drowsiness were on the point
of delaying, if not defeating our enterprise.
We were 36 miles from Sonoma. The sleepless energy of some arroused their companions
by representing the danger of delay, and half
an hour's debate turned the scale in favor of
immediate action, and all *put* for Sonoma for
dear life, as fast as our jaded horses could carry us, so, if possible, to arrive there by a rough
path away from the traveled road, before the
day-light gave notice of our approach.

And now, dear Sir, as it will be some little
time before we get there, I will improve the
time to state the views of the party as to the
object of their intended visit.

It will be borne in mind that none of this
party, save myself, were present when the sentiment of INDEPENDENCE was so heartily cheered in the camp under the Nevada mountains ;
nor was it reasonable to suppose that any of
them were informed by any of Capt. Fremont's
men, that his plan was to provoke an attack
on Castro's camp, *before he left for the States,*

to take along with him the offenders, to save
them from certain destruction. It was known
that Capt. F. possessed the unbounded confidence of those twelve men, and also that most
of them desired to avail themselves of the opportunity for a safe return to the States, in the
service of the United States, at $ 60 per month
for the trip. The subject of *Independence* was
only talked of as an event that might occur ;
and no one of them seemed to understand that
the taking of Sonoma formed any part of our
errand there.

And, moreover, Capt. Fremont, who is allowed to be proverbially cautious and prudent,
gave his directions—or rather " advice",—in
such manner as to avoid legal testimony in any
matter of interference in California politics,
(which he invariably and solemnly disavowed)
that it was impossible to prove, authoritative-
ly from him responsibility for any line of conduct by our party ; but every one, (especially
those of the " twelve"), seemed, as if by intu-
ition, to undertand that our only business was
to capture and convey to Fremont's camp Gen.
M. G. Vallejo, Don Salvadore Vallejo, Col.
Prudshon and Capt. Jacob P. Leese, if practicable, and if not, to drive off another band of

horses, or commit any other act of violence, in its nature calculated to provoke pursuit and attack in the proper quarter.

Fully impressed with the importance of this mission of benevolence and good will towards the sleeping and unsuspecting gentlemen to whom we were about to pay our respects, we took timely precaution to swear certain of our number against the commission of violence against either of those gentlemen. This step was considered proper, as we were aware there were certain *breathings of vengeance* against some of them, in the minds of a few of our party.

It was known that Doct. Semple, who was an active and conspicuous leading man of the host, was in favor of Independence, *instanter;* but we knew of none willing to *push* the measure. Under these circumstances it was thought prudent not to broach the subject generally, until some crisis should call the principle into immediate action.

Thus circumstanced, we arrived at Sonoma; and, after reconnoitering the place, and notifying our friends of our object in seizing the aforesaid gentlemen, and having secured the captain of the guard whom we found a little

way out of town, we surrounded the house of
Gen. M. G. Vallejo just at daybreak, on the
14th.   William Merrit. Doct. Semple and
Mr. Knight, (who took wise care to have it
understood on all hands that he was forced into the scrape as an interpreter), entered the
house to secure their prisoners.

Jacob P. Lease, an American by birth, and
brother-in-law of Gen. Vallejo, who lived near
by, was soon there, to soothe the fears, and otherwise as far as possible assist his friends.
Doct. Salvadore was also found there, and Col.
Prudshon was also soon arrested and brought
there. After the first surprise had a little subsided, as no immediate violence was offered,
the General's generous *spirits* gave proof of
his usual hospitality—as the richest wines and
brandies sparkled in the glasses, and those who
had thus unceremoniously met soon became
merry companions ; more especially—the weary visitors.

While matters were going on thus happily
in the house, the main force sat patiently
guarding it without.   They appeared to understand that they had performed all the duty
required of them, and only waited, that the
said prisoners might be prepared and brought

forth for their journey, and——waited still. The sun was climbing up the heavens an hour or more, and yet no man, nor voice, nor sound of violence came from the house to tell us of events within : patience was ill, and lingered ill. "Let us have a captain," said one—a *captain*, said all. Capt. Grigsby was elected, and went immediately into the house. The men still sat upon their horses—patience grew faint ; an hour became an age. "Oh ! go into the house, *Ide*, and come out again and let us know what is going on there !" No sooner said than done. There sat Doct. S., just modifying a long string of articles of capitulation. There sat Merrit—his head fallen : there sat Knight, no longer able to interpret ; and there sat the new made Captain, as mute as the seat he sat upon. The bottles had well nigh vanquished the captors. The Articles of Capitulation were seized hastily, read and thrown down again, and the men outside were soon informed of their contents. Pardon us, dear Doctor—we will not make an exposition. It is sufficient to say, that by the rule of opposition, they gave motion and energy to the waiting mass, and all that was necessary was to direct the torrent and guide the storm.

No one hitherto in authority had thought of seizing the fortress, or disarming its guard. Capt. Grigsby was hastily called, and the men demanded of him that the prisoners should be immediately conveyed to the Sacramento valley. Capt. G. inquired, " What are the orders of Capt. Fremont in relation to these men ?" Each man looked on his fellow, yet none spake. " But have you not got Capt. Fremont's name in black and white to authorize you in this you have done ?" cried the enraged Captain— and immediately we* demanded, that if there were any one present who had orders from him, either written or verbal, he declare the same. All declared, one after another, that they had no such orders. Thereupon the Captain was briefly but particulary informed, that the people whom he knew had received from Gen. Castro, and others in authority, the most insolent indignities—had been, on pain of death, ordered to leave the country ; and that they had

* The modest writer of this Letter, it will be observed, invariably uses the pronoun *we*, instead of *I*, in refering to what he had snid or done ; and the Editor has not felt himself at liberty to change his phraseology in these cases, as it may be necessary for the reader to do, mentally, in order to a correct understanding of what HE *said* or *did.*

resolved to take the redress of grievances into
their own hands ; that we could not claim the
protection of any government on earth, and
were alone responsible for our conduct ; that—
(Here the Captain's " fears of doing wrong"
overcame his patriotism, and he interrupted
the speaker by saying, " *Gentlemen, I have
been deceived; I cannot go with you; I resign
and back out of the scrape.* I can take my
family to the mountains as cheap as any of
you"—and Doct. S. at that moment led him
into the house. Disorder and confusion prevailed. One swore he would not stay to guard
prisoners—another swore we would all have our
throats cut—another called for fresh horses,
and all were on the move—every man for himself ; when the speaker [Mr. Ide] resumed his
effort, raising his voice louder and more loud,
as the men receded from the place, saying :
" We need no horses ; we want no horses.
Saddle no horse for me. I can go to the Spaniards, and make FREEMEN of them. I will
give myself to them. I will lay my bones
here, before I will take upon myself the igno-
miny of commencing an honorable work, and
then flee like cowards, like thieves, when no
enemy is in sight. In vain will you say you

had honorable motives ! Who will believe it ?
*Flee this day, and the longest life cannot wear
off your disgrace!* Choose ye ! choose ye this
day, what you will be ! We are robbers, or
or we *must be conquerors!"*—and the speaker
in despair turned his back upon his receding
companions.

THE LAST WORD—NOW THE BATTLE !

With new hope they rallied around the desponding speaker—made him their Commander, their Chief ; and his next words commanded the taking of the Fort. Joy lighted up
every mind, and in a moment all was secured :
18 prisoners, 9 brass cannon, 250 stands of
arms, and tons of copper, shot, and other public property, of the value of 10 or 1200 dollars, was seized and held in trust for the public benefit.

Arrangements were immediately made for
putting the garrison in a complete state of defence. Tools suitable for fortification, and for
supplying a well of water within our walls ;
and a liberal stock of provisions were procured
on contract—pledging the public property now
in possession for future payment. But that
portion of our forces who still adhered to the

"neutral conquest" plan, with the four gentlemen, the afore mentioned prisoners at Sutter's
Fort, were allowed to remain under the protection of Capt. Fremont, where every comfort was
granted them that their situation allowed.

Thus and so was the "Independent Bear
Flag Republic" inaugurated. Other circumstances might be given ; but not to change its
character. What dear friend of Capt. Fremont will hereafter claim that the taking of
Sonoma, or the hoisting the Independent Flag,
or any other act that grew out of the same,
constituted any part of his plan for the conquest of California ? If any of those twelve
men who took the horses had have had any
idea that Fremont desired the seizure of the
garrison, think you they would have sat on
their horses more than two hours, within pistol shot of the Fort, and never thought of taking possession of it ? or think you that if Capt.
F. had designed the capture and hoisting the
Independent Flag, he would not have so instructed his three champions, who were the
leaders of this force, up to the very moment
of the recalling the scattering soldiers, and the
appointment of the Commander by the people,
who ordered the taking of the Garrison ?

CHAPTER V.

HOW THE BEAR FLAG WAS MADE.—THE COMPANY ORGANIZED. THE COMMANDER ADDRESSES HIS MEN.—HIS REASONS FOR ISSUING A PROCLAMATION—ITS TEXT IN FULL—NOTICE OF ITS PUBLICATION ADDRESSED TO COMMODORE STOCK-TON, AS A U. S. OFFICER THEN DAILY EXPECTED ON THAT COAST.

NEXT, (if you will be pleased to exercise patience enough), we will consider the circumstances tending to its unexampled success, as we trace, step by step, its history to its first acquaintance with Capt. Fremont, and thence to its finale.

After the return of the three leaders of the party of the primitive plan of neutral conquest, and seven others had " left us alone in our glory," the said " Bear Flag"—made of plain cotton cloth, and ornamented with the red flannel of a shirt from the back of one of the men, and christened by the words " California Republic," in red-paint letters on both sides—was raised upon the standard where had floated on the breezes the Mexican flag aforetime. It was on the 14th of June, '46. Our number was *twenty-four*, all told. The mechanism of the flag was performed by Wm. Todd of Illinois. The grizzly bear was chosen as an emblem of strength and unyielding resistance. The men were divided into two companies of 10 men each. The 1st artillery was busily engaged in putting the cannon in order, which were charged doubly with grape and cannister. The 1st rifle company was busied in cleaning, repairing and loading the small arms. The Commander, after setting a guard, and posting a sentinel on one of the highest buildings to watch the approach of any one who might have the curiosity to inspect operations, directed his leisure to the establishment of rules of discipline and order, and of a system of finance, whereby all the defenceless families might be brought within the lines of our garrison and supported. Ten thousand pounds of flour were purchased on the credit of the Government, and deposited within the garrison ; an account was opened for the supply of beef, on terms agreed upon : and a few barrels of salt constituted our main supplies. Whiskey was altogether a contraband article.*

* Mr. Ide was a life-long " Te-totaler" and " Temperance Advocate," of the straightest sect.—Ed.

After the first round of duties were performed, as many as could be spared off guard were
called together, and the situation fully explained to the men by the Commander of the garrison. It was fully represented that our success,
nay, our very life, depended on the magnanimity and justice of our course of conduct, coupled with sleepless vigilance and care.

But ere this we had gathered as many of
the surrounding citizens as possible, and placed them between four strong walls—they were
more than twice our number. The Commander chose from these strangers the most intelligent—by the aid of an interpreter went on to
explain the cause of our coming together—our
determination to offer equal justice to all good
citizens ; that we had not called them there
to rob them of their liberty, or to deprive them
of any portion of their property, nor to disturb their social relations one with another,
nor yet to desecrate their religion. He went
on to explain the common rights of all men,
and showed them that those rights had been
shamefully denied them by those heretofore in
authority ; that the Missions had been robbed,
and the general prosperity of the country destroyed ; that we had been driven to take up

arms in defence of life and the common rights
of man ; and that we had pledged our lives to
the overthrow of injustice, and the establishment of such government as should give freedom to commerce, and that should collect its
revenues of those, who, by their improper conduct, make governments necessary for the protection of all good citizens.

He went on further to say, that although he
had, for the moment, deprived them of that
liberty which is the right and the privilege of
all good and just men, it was only that they
might become acquainted with his unalterable
purpose : and, that having made them thus
acquainted, " without waiting to know whether you approve or disapprove—whether you
are disposed to regard us as friends or enemies
—we will restore you the liberty of which we
have deprived you, after we have convinced
you"—(and here he assumed all the fierce, determined energy of manner that such an emergency was calculated to inspire)—" that as
enemies we will kill and destroy you ! but as
friends we will share with you all the blessings
of liberty, and all the privileges that we ourselves can hope to enjoy." " Now, dear Sirs",
he continued to say, " go and prepare your-

selves for the battle !   We are few, but we are
firm and true.   We have not come to hold
forth deceitful appearances.   Go.   You are
free as the air of heaven.   Receive us as friends,
and assist us to give liberty to your country
and countrymen ;   or, meet us like brave men,
according to your own time and pleasure."

Although the address was not the twentieth
part interpreted, yet the importance of success
in the measure, to persons circumstanced as we
were, gave expression that would have been understood by every nationality and tongue under
heaven ;   and the *Spaniard,* even, embraced
the Commander as he pronounced the name of
WASHINGTON.   There was a glow of feeling
beaming from his eye, that defied all hypocra-
cy, as he said, " Suffer my companions to re-
remain until we complete a treaty of peace
and friendship, and then go and come as friends
—only that we be not required to take arms
against our brethren."

By the unanimous vote of the garrison all
the powers of the four departments of government were conferred, for the time being, upon
him who was first put in command of the fort;
yet *Democracy* was the ruling principle that
settled every measure—*Vox Populi*, our rule.

On the evening of the 14th, after every precaution for security for the night coming had
been taken, the subject of issuing a Proclamation was discussed; and, notwithstanding ar-
guments were used tending to show that we
were bound by a proper respect for the rights
and interests of all honest and good citizens of
California, to represent ourselves as to our doings and purposes, yet a very large proportion
of our men were against making any public
representation of our situation and intentions,
until our numbers should have been increased
to something like a force adequate to the undertaking. But how were our forces to be aug-
mented, and who would come to the assistance
of those who were only represented as robbers
and rebels? Would our enemies be pleased to
represent us truly, and in such a character as
would induce others to incur the like responsibilities? Or, would Capt. Fremont volunteer for us such kindly assistance, after having
pledged his honor and the honor of his country to remain neutral?—and, besides, he had
declared his intention to leave the country
within two weeks, and that in our own hearing. Were we to believe that Capt. Fremont
would hold out, publicly, false pretentions?

Those who would have entertained such an opinion, without cause, of an officer of a government they delight to honor, must have been virtually destitute of any just sense of honor themselves. But all would not do. It was contended by some, notwithstanding all his pretentions to the contrary, that he would yet consent to become our leader. So it was urged that no proclamation should be made until Capt. Fremont, Doct. Mearch, or some other person of distinction, could be persuaded to join us.

So, here we were ; by our flag proclaimed " The California Republic"! twenty-four self-consecrated victims to the god of *Equal Rights* —unknown by any mortal being, except ten men who had dissented from our plan of operations, and fled to the protection of Fremont's camp, (except 30 or 40 Spaniards, who had, from a brief acquaintance, sworn fidelity to our cause), exposed not only to the wrath of 600 armed men, whom we were compelled, in order to avoid the just imputation of violence and crime, to defy in open fight, but to the unmingled scorn and contempt of all honorable men, whether Mexicans or Americans, if we failed to represent our true character, and the cir-

cumstances which compelled us to assume such
an unusual position. Was it prudent to delay
a just representation to the public ear? to that
community which had equal rights with ourselves to a representation in any system of government we might establish? Was it prudent
thus to delay what it immediately concerned
everybody to know, until the happening of an
event which might never occur? Who or
what circumstance was to call to our aid that
august personage capable of duly and honorably representing to the public favor our benevolent designs?

Under these circumstances, and impressed
with these views, it was believed that any representation was preferable to none ; and our
Commander [invested with "all the powers of
the four departments of the government", it
will be remembered], JACKSON-like, "assumed
the responsibility" of performing his duty, "as
he understood" his obligations to all concerned, and drew up, on the morning of the 15th,*

* This was the EIGHTH-DAY morning since, "between the
hours of 10 and 11, A. M.," he had left his family to arouse the
emigrants to action in self-defence ; but they fled to Oregon.
The two days thus spent, and then the four or five more days
and sleepless nights while organizing the 'new government',
(his relatives believe), was a strain upon his physical powers
of endurance, materially shortening his useful life.—EDITOR.

between the hours of 1 and 4 o'clock, the following

"PROCLAMATION,

"TO ALL PERSONS, INHABITANTS OF THE COUNTY OF SONOMA AND COUNTRY AROUND, REQUESTING THEM TO REMAIN AT PEACE; TO PURSUE THEIR RIGHTFUL OCCUPATIONS,— WITHOUT FEAR OF MOLESTATION.

"The Commander-in-chief at Sonoma gives his inviolable pledge to all persons in California, not found bearing arms, or instigating others to take up arms against him, that they shall not be disturbed in their persons, property, religion, or social relations to each other, by men under his command.

"He hereby most solemnly declares the object of his movement to be,—first, to defend our women and children, and his brave companions in arms, who were first invited to this country by a promise of lands on which to settle themselves and families; who were promised a Republican government; who, when having arrived in California, were denied even the privilege of buying or renting lands of their friends; who, instead of being allowed a participation in, or of being protected by a Republican government, were oppressed by a mil-

itary despotism ; who were even threatened by
proclamation of one of the principal officers
of the aforesaid oppressive government, with
extermination, if they would not depart out
of the country, leaving all their property—
their arms and their beasts of burden ; and
who were thus to be despoiled of the means of
defence or of flight—and were to have been
driven through deserts inhabited by hostile
savages to certain death.

" To overthrow a government which has
robbed and destroyed the Missions, and appro-
priated the properties thereof to the individual aggrandizement of its favorites ; which has
violated good faith, by its treachery in the be-
stowment of public lands ; which has shame-
fully oppressed and ruined the laboring and producing inhabitants of California, by their enormous exactions of tariff on goods imported into
the country :—this is the purpose of the brave
men who are associated under his command.

" He also declares his object, in the second
place, to be,—and he hereby invites all good
and patriotic citizens in California to assist
him—to establish and perpetuate a liberal, a
just and honorable Government, which shall
secure to all, civil, religious and personal liber-

ty ; which shall insure the security of life and
property ; which shall detect and punish crime
and injustice ; which shall encourage industry,
virtue and literature ; and which shall foster
agriculture, manufactures and mechanism, by
guaranteeing freedom to commerce.

" He further proclaims that he relies upon
the justice of his cause—upon the favor of
Heaven—upon the wisdom and good sense of
the people of California, and upon the bravery
of those who are bound and associated with
him by the principle of self-preservation, by
their love of Liberty and by their hatred of
Tyranny—for his hope of success.

" And he further premises that a Government, to be prosperous and ameleiorating in its
tendency, must originate among its people :
its officers should be its servants, and its glory
its COMMON REWARD !"

" (Signed)   WILLIAM B. IDE,
                            Commander.
" Head-Quarters at Sonoma, }
    June 15th, A. D. 1846." }

A letter was also written, during the night,
addresssd to Commodore STOCKTON, who was
daily expected to be at the Bay, informing
him—and intended, by the earliest possible

means, to inform the world in general, so far
as it was interested, and the Government of
the United States, through its officers, in particular—that we had been compelled in self-
defence to appeal to arms ; that we had possessed ourselves of the fortress of Sonoma—
had set up a Flag of Independence, and were
determined, whether victorious or otherwise,
to approve ourselves not unworthy the sympa-
thy, at least, of those who labor for the glory
of the American name.

And let me remark, dear Sir, that this letter (a copy of which I still have, and have no
doubt of the present existence of the original)
did not, in the remotest manner, ask for or intimate that we desired assistance ; but it was
intended to notify, in due season, the officers
and Government of the U. States that we had,
agreeably to the universal and immutable right
of all men, claimed the right of self-government for the good citizens of all California ;
that we had solemnly, by an appeal to the last
resort, abjured all connection with the government of Mexico, its protection and liabilities ;
—that although other nations might have just
claims upon Mexico, they could have no claim
upon the sovereignty of the people of Califor-

nia ;—that we had recorded our establishment, and notified our seizure and possession. And farther : lest the well known desire, on the part of the United States' Government, to possess itself of the Bay of San Francisco should tempt the officers of said Government to commit an unwarrantable and inglorious interference in our affairs, *in violation of the one principle that hath given peace to the world,* we had, in a timely manner, incorporated in this same *" notice",* most sincerely and unequivocally, that we would embrace the earliest *honorable* opportunity to unite this fair land with the land of our birth.

It was honestly and implicitly believed on our part, that the U. S. officers, whom we were proud to believe were men of deathless honor, would rejoice to acknowledge our right to Independence, and so far become our friends as to conquer any inward aspiring after individual renown as conquerors of California, and still continue to adhere tenaciously to that just sense of national honor which prompted the *Reply to the above mentioned Notice.*

CHAPTER VI.

ARTICLES OF AGREEMENT AND TREATY STIPULATIONS ARRANG-
ED.—SYMPTOMS OF DISCONTENT AMONG THE MEN OF THE
GARRISON—A CHANGE OF " COMMANDER" TALKED OF.—
THE LETTER TO COMMODORE STOCKTON FORWARDED BY
WILLIAM TODD—CAPT. J. MONTGOMERY, OF THE U. S. SHIP
PORTSMOUTH, RETURNS BY LIEUT. MISSROON A FRIENDLY
LETTER—CAUSING THE COMMANDER, HOWEVER, NOT A
LITTLE DISQUIETUDE.

But it is proper to return to the history of
events, in the order in which they transpired.
Every moment that could be prudently spared from the duty of overseeing the guards, at
very short intervals, (as most of the men had
been deprived of sleep, and some of us for five
days and nights in succession), was devoted to
writing—as we had no clerks or printing establishment. The remainder of the night was
spent in drawing up such articles of agreement
and treaty stipulations, as were most likely to
enlist the good will of all good citizens of California, without respect to the circumstance of
any peculiar origin of its inhabitants.

These treaty stipulations•were based on the

independent right, self-existent in every individual, to cast off at pleasure any former obligation to governments, that experience might demonstrate as unproductive of the best good of the governed ; and to remain isolated, if consistent with their circumstances and pleasure : or, if necessary to secure protection and peace in the enjoyment of that just Liberty which is, ever was and ever will be the immutable birth-right of all men, to associate themselves voluntarily for the present necessity, under such regulations as may best guarantee the protection sought. * * *

But not to stop to make our last appeal in behalf of equal Liberty, we will simply inform you that, in addition to the preceding statement, the stipulations provided, First : That no individual division of the public property should be allowed, but that such should be sacredly held as security for the faithful payment of the just value of such articles of provisions as necessity demanded for the common support of such as should, without pecuniary consideration or hope of other reward than the con-, sciousness of having freely given their devoted services to the cause of Independence, and the the establishment of such government as the good sense and wisdom of the people of California might desire.   Secondly : That Commerce should be free—that no impost should be levied or collected—that frauds and crimes only should be taxed, and that without license! Thirdly   That, the supreme direction of the affairs of Paternal government should be entrusted to those alone, whose generous philanthropy and patriotic regard for the welfare of their children, in common with the rest of their fellow-countrymen, and the race of men in general, would enable them willingly and cheerfully to do so, without enlisting the corrupting influence of the love of money.   That no governor, president, legislator, member of assembly, council-man, or Senator, (if you please), should ever be enticed to corruption, fraud and dishonor, by the love of money.   Fourthly : That all involuntary taxation of the virtuous, industrious, self-governing freemen of California, or any other people whom we would account worthy of our fellowship, should never be allowed or practiced—that whenever taxation shall be necessary, (except as punishment for the infraction of the moral principle of honesty, justice and equal rights) it shall be between contracting parties equally free to choose or refuse. Fifthly : No persons shall ever be compelled, contrary to their free will, to bear arms, or otherwise to serve the cause of Liberty : for that would prove that its people were unworthy of its blessings ; or, that those blessings were no longer worth enjoying. And, lastly : All good friends, (Spaniards and native Californians), who had taken a solemn oath that they were pleased to support our Independent principles and Flag, were on their part, according to their request, excused from bearing arms against any of their brethren who might not understand, or believe in the sincerity of our professions, or our determined resolution to make a virtue of the stern necessity which had compelled us to assume responsibilities so unusual and unlooked-for ; and voluntarily promised that they would write to their friends and acquaintances throughout all the country, and inform them as to the nature of our intentions, and persuade them not to resist us ; and they further voluntarily agreed to furnish us with any supplies of provisions, or other articles we might stand in need of for the public service, on the conditions we had proposed ;—and, further, it was stipulated and agreed that receipts should in every case be given, signed by the Commander of the garrison ; and that no gift, not even the smallest trifle, should be accepted by any of the soldiers, individually or collectively, lest it should be infered that, in some event, extortion, through fear of violence, should have been practiced.

It was not without the greatest difficulty that these stipulations could be interpreted to the understanding of the first Alcalde of the District of Sonoma ; and still more difficult to make him see how and by what magic the wheel or postule of government was to be made to operate without the aid of the love of money. It became necessary to dissect each sentence, and reduce it to its simplest form, ere it could be interpreted into Spanish, and by another interpreter changed back to English again, which was considered necessary in order to any certainty of understanding.

There was another difficulty of no inconsiderable magnitude, which was a want of proper understanding on the part of many of our own men, of the policy or principle of action necessary for success. That portion of our little band of heroes who at first enlisted for plunder and flight to the States, who proposed to tear down and pillage the house of Gen. M. G. Vallejo (as it was known that he had charge of a large amount of money in his house) still earnestly contended that a Spaniard had no right to liberty, and but very little right to the enjoyment of life.

You will not, therefore, dear Sir, be surprised to incredulity, we hope, when you are informed, that after a portion of the men had exhibited the most surprising vigilance in capturing all the Spaniards, and even some others whose love of freedom was considered questionable, and thrusting them indiscriminately within the walls of the callaboose ; that after the Alcalde had been taken from thence by the Commander—not without the most earnest remonstrance on the part of a large portion of our " Independent Freemen"—that after they had witnessed the assurance that the said Alcalde gave of his approbation of our cause ; after they had refused their consent to the publication to the world of our intentions, lest it might be the means of hastening our indiscriminate destruction ; when you are informed that the release of one man was sufficient to fill them with consternation—to fill their minds with distrust as to the sagacity and ability of

their leader to conduct an enterprise fraught
with such terrible consequences ;—we add,
when you are also informed that it became
necessary to conduct these friendly negotia-
tions without the camp, and without the full
knowledge of the garrison, you will not be surprised that it was by a great sacrifice of feeling on their part, that the garrison continued
their Commander in office.

But on the other hand it was acknowledged
that no fault could be found with his watchful
care in providing for the maintenance of that
security of "*persons*", now become so apparently necessary ; and, as he was the only man
then present that could command with that
determination and decision necessary to insure
obedience, it was again agreed, that until a
more suitable man could be found, he should
be sustained.

Early in the morning of the 15th of June it
was deemed necessary to send an ambassador
to the Bay, to carry the letter heretofore spok-
en of to Commodore STOCKTON, if he were
then arrived ; and if not, to deliver it to him
who should be highest in command in the U.
S. Navy then present. But as no man might
be found willing to risk his life in going to the

Bay of San Francisco (to Yerba-Buena) simply to carry a letter, it became necessary to
make other and more important business. It
is necessary and right, sometimes, to take advantage even of the fears, as well as of the
bravery of those with whom we have to do.
That the fears of the men of the garrison, after the first moments of excitement had subsided had prevented, and would continue to
prevent desertion, and to bind them close to
the loaded cannon, and to the 250 loaded muskets, was easy to understand ; but how to
compel an individual, by the same fear, to travel 50 or 60 miles through an enemy's country,
was a problem not so readily solved.

The men of the garrison were accordingly
summoned to attend, and the circumstances of
our situation were recited ;—positions upon
the neighboring hills were pointed out, where
Gen. Castro might plant his cannon ; and, in
case of the want of a sufficient supply of powder, we might be greatly annoyed : and the
men of the garrison were informed that a letter had been prepared for Commodore STOCK-
TON, and a volunteer was necessary to carry it,
and take charge of anything that might be
sent back in return.

William Todd, whom circumstances afterwards proved to be a brave man, volunteered
to go—who was conducted on his way immediately by the Commander of the garrison, beyond the guard lines, where he received the said
letter and full information in relation to the
existence of the Proclamation and treaty stipulations, which had been partially made known
to the Alcalde before refered to, and the hopes
of the Commander were communicated in relation to the same. He was then charged in
relation to his journey ; and, withal, to be sure
not to ask for anything from the men or officers of the ship where he delivered the letter,
as the letter contained all the business of his
mission ; but simply to take whatever (if anything) was put into his hand, and be sure to
make his way back by another route than the
one he pursued thither.

The balance of the 15th, the 16th and 17th,
was spent in translating and re-translating the
simple elements of the articles of the treaty
of peace and amity, and of the Proclamation,
by so many of the men as could be spared from
the general oversight of the garrison.

The men were divided into 4 night guards
of 6 men each, and into 8 day guards of 3 men

each. One half of the men were at all times,
by day, employed in camp duty—the other
half guarded and slept ; and the Captain, who
was never counted anywhere, served as officer
of the day and night. The camp service consisted in cleaning the muskets, providing wood
for cooking, bringing in provisions and cooking.
Roast beef, fried pan-cakes and cold water served us for rations.

We received no intelligence from abroad the
first four days ; and such had been the vigilance with which our camp was guarded, that
none were known to approach it near enough
to be at all acquainted with our means of defence, and to escape. Every opportunity was
embraced to make ourself and our plan of government known and approved by our prisoners ; for which purpose we took occasion to
make them understand it was necessary to detain them a few days.

On the evening of the 17th came back Wm.
Todd, and with him Lieut. Missroon, of the U.
S. ship Portsmouth, bearing a letter from his
Capt. J. Montgomery. He was bearer of verbal dispatches, which for prudent reasons were
not written, but refered to and authorized by
written documents from Captain Montgomery.

It appeared on investigation, that our messenger, after having delivered the letter, and waiting some time, and nothing was said about any powder, thought it necessary, notwithstanding his orders not to ask for anything, to inquire if any powder was to be sent ; and the letter, which was written to be read before the garrison, contained the following sentence :— "Although we have ample means to defend ourselves from any attack that can be made on us by Castro, by the use of small arms, we have not a sufficient quantity of powder to withstand for any considerable length of time, an attack by the use of cannon".

Thus, under these unfortunate circumstances, it was easy for our good Capt. Montgomery to mistake the real design of the letter, (which it is true was written in haste, but with care), and which contained no intimation that we desired of him the slightest assistance—no, not "so much as one charge of powder"—which to have asked would have been the begging our own destruction, and inviting that unwarrantable inteference we feared, and which afterwards ingloriously arrested our progress, defeated our plans—caused disobedience of our orders, and ourself to be bitterly, and, else,

justly reproached by more than a hundred of
our companions who knew us only by our
Proclamation—who had secretly organized under Weaver, Bird and others on the south side
of the Bay—waiting in vain, because of the
disobedience of our orders, for that assistance
which it was abundantly in our power to have
given—whereby Castro's main army would
have been suddenly and wholly defeated.

But to reserve this part of our history for
the leading subject of another division, we will
rehearse from recollection Capt. Montgomery's
answer to our said "Letter of notice", which
he unfortunately not only failed to understand,
but failed, for nearly six months, to deliver to
Commodore STOCKTON.

Capt. Montgomery's letter bore date June
16th—and, after the usual compliments, went
on to say, that he was "here as the legal rep-
resentative of the Government of the United
States of America—having in charge the proper interests and peace of its citizens engaged in commerce," etc., and it was more than
his gallant ship was worth to give us so much
as one charge of powder. He responded, very
handsomely, to the sentiment that it is right,
on every proper occasion, to resist oppression

by all honorable means ; and that it was the
settled policy of his Government always to acknowledge any authority they might find in
power, without considering the legitimate
rights of the contending parties—said he was
happy to learn by my messenger, that we had,
by Proclamation, secured the proper rights and
peace of the inhabitants of Sonoma and country around, and hoped that the same humane
course of conduct would characterize all our
future operations.

Capt. Montgomery closed 'his letter by saying he had not time to communicate all he
would say in answer to my letter ; that he was
in expectation of important news from Mexico
or the United States, and refered us to any ex-
planations Lieut. Missroon might make, which
were thereby made a part of his communica-
tions to me.

Lieutenant Missroon, after we were quietly
seated in a room by ourselves, read the said
letter, and went on to explain and say that, as
officers of a Government at peace with Mexico,
to assist, or in any way to interfere in any revolution that might be going on in any country
where they might be present, would justly subject their Government to dishonor, and them-

selves to be disgraced and driven from the service of their country : but that, in the event of war with Mexico, his Captain had instructed him to say that he would supply any amount of ammunition we might be in need of, and would also place the half of his men under my command, and coöperate with his ship against the common enemy.   He then asked for a copy of the Proclamation of the 15th. He was informed that we had no clerks to perform our writing, and that one would be handed him at the time of his return.   He thanked me, and said he would direct the clerk of the ship to copy and circulate it.   He took his leave, and agreed to meet me at sunrise, at my room next morning.

I gave charge of the guards, for the first time, to Capt. Sears and Lieut. Ford : after writing until 11, went quietly to rest for the first time since the 8th of June, and slept until sunrise. These matters are of trivial importance ; but they show how much labor was performed in order to avoid what was conceived to be *a dishonorable act.*

CHAPTER VII.

THE LIEUTENANT INTERVIEWS THE GARRISON, AND FINDS IT STILL DISTRUSTFUL.—THE COMMANDER INDULGES A LITTLE DESPONDENCY, FOR A MOMENT.—THE MEN APPROVE THE PROCLAMATION, AND ALL ARE JUBILANT IN VIEW OF THE SITUATION.—AN ATTEMPT TO DRAW A FIGHT.—CASTRO'S SECOND PROCLAMATION.—TWO YOUNG MEN INHUMANLY MURDERED BY HIS MEN.—THE FIRST AND ONLY FIGHT WITH THE ENEMY.

A LITTLE after sunrise came Lieut. Missroon, whose every expression indicated that a sad change had come over his mind in relation to the subject of our Independence. He said, sorrowfully, that he had been talking with the men of the garrison, and it was thought best not to put out any proclamation ; and that something might be done by way of relieving us from our disagreeable situation---but as he continued to speak in sad, sorrowful tones, we tossed the copy of the Proclamation of the 15th we held in our hand, which by its dangling motion caught his eye, despite his sorrowful abstraction of mind. "What have you got in your hand, Sir?" said he--his voice a little

elevated by curiosity. "It is a copy of the
Proclamation, Sir ; and as it is already published, and as the men of the garrison so seriously disapprove thereof, it is very proper that
they should know what it is, that they may
be able to provide a timely remedy for the evils
it may otherwise cause. Will you be so kind
as to take it up to the garrison and read it to
them ?" Lieut. Missroon very gravely reached
out his hand, without saying a word, and took
the copy ; his countenance indicating more of
sadness and pity than before, as he slowly
opened it and began to move his eye along the
lines.

This was a moment of horrid apprehension !
Was it possible that the men of the garrison
were to be taken on board the ship, and all our
labor in proving to the world, that *we scorned
death and danger in any shape, rather than
be shown up to the world as a band of Mountain thieves and robbers ?* With what inde-
scribable anguish did we trace each kindling
emotion in the mind of the Lieutenant, as he
slowly and carefully passed his eye to the end
of it. But this horrible suspense was of short
duration : it required no word of promise, nor
word of any kind—nothing but the language

of *the soul, the life of men,* was capable of removing the apprehensions which had prompted our mind to the endurance of sleepless vigilance,—which was first quieted the evening
before, by the assurances of Capt. Montgomery's letter, that the U. S. officers would not
interfere,—to be thus horribly renewed !

Hitherto not a single voice (except Montgomery's) had spoken encouragement—not a
man of influence came to our assistance. Four
days had passed, and the men of our little garrison were only brave when wound up by the
*melodious sounds of Liberty aud Independ-
ence,* to become cold and desponding again, as
soon as the excitement of action was past. If
left to ourselves we would at least prove by
our blood poured out, and by our written documents sent abroad, that we were " no base
band of robbers, bent on mischief."

But, my dear Wambough, we had cherished,
in our more cheerful moments, a brighter hope
than this. We knew with positive assurance,
that the whole country was groaning to be delivered from that excessive tariff taxation that
had reduced our exports to less than nothing,
and had left us to clothe ourselves, our wives
and children, in skins or fig-leaves, if we would

maintain independence of lordly merchants. We also believed, in all sincerity, that if some man, even an entire stranger, would present us even the hope of a desirable change before the public mind, *that one general crowding to the uplifted standard* would render all "individual" entreaty and persuasion to adopt our cause unnecessary.

It was therefore that we neither importuned nor begged of a single individual, even to lend a listening ear to our plan ! *If the whole mass moved not,* in answer to our appeal, it was more honorable *to die singly and alone,* rather than involve others in our fate.

The men of the garrison were already equally involved with ourself—(only, as, perhaps, the head of their leader might ransom *them*) ; but not one single man had thus involved himself through any persuasion of ours.   Other *persons* and other *motives* had tempted them to enter the vortex.——But stop !—We must confess our guilt, as well as plead our innocence !   Truth, like the diamond, is always bright and clear ; and the darkest crimes are deprived of half their turpitude by frank confession, and the other half is more than canceled by unfeigned contrition and forsaking.

One solitary man (and others may have been in his situation) vehemently, in the anguish of his soul, accused us of having deceived him, and of having thus involved him in rebellion. What have we said, what have we done, thus to deceive? was the anxious inquiry. You were along with them. Guilty, we plead. But *we* were involved in the consequences we could not suppress. If *we* could not " gather up the flood in a basket", *we* might, perchance, run along before it, and, at some favored point, direct its course, and change the evil—the " *partial* evil"—to " *universal* good."

Now we were so simple as to suppose that he, whom chance and necessity had placed in the brief and uncertain command of the enterprise—he who had conceived and unwaveringly sustained it—would encounter the applause, the stupid gaze of all the world, by such an act. It was well known that he was charged with entertaining designs more base, more hostile to the interests and wishes of the good people of California, than even the plundering and robbing the house of Gen. Vallejo ! He had been charged by Capt. Fremont with being a Mormon, and his scheme was denounced as an artifice to betray the whole country into the

hands of the Mormons! and it was known
that most of the garrison believed the *foul
slander!*

It was fully known, also, that the men of
the garrison had the most unbounded confidence in these United States officers, and that
they looked to them for protection ; and it
was also known that, if the plan of Independence could be suddenly presented to the public,
it would enlist the bone and sinew—and it was
fondly hoped—the *minds* of all such as were
capable of understanding the difference in favor of conquest, by extending just and benevolent principles of government, and that of violence, bloodshed and political murder.   And it
was fondly hoped there would at least be found
one of noble and upright intentions, who might
be willing to wear the honors, while we might
still be permitted to perform some part of the
labor necessary to the establishment of a government more humane, more honorable, more
just and more enduring, and less oppressive,
than any government that had hitherto arisen
and fallen here in California.   We had indeed
promised, in behalf of its citizens, *union* with
the land of our birth, at the earliest honorable
opportunity—not by the devastation of blood,

nor by the more ignoble system of purchase, but by the more exalted principle of universal and equal liberty and freedom of choice by the people; which remains to be more fully explained as we proceed in our narrative.

" Hope springs eternal in the human breast ;"

And hope sprang up in our mind, the moment hope seemed to rise in the mind of the Lieutenant ; and hope spake thus : " If he reads it before the garrison, and approves it himself, (and he will read and approve), it will make no difference whether they discover merit in it or not : if he approves they will approve, and we shall find means to circulate it: and when the people begin to flock to the standard, there will be a time for action ; the mass will be in motion, and it will be easy to direct it, if no counter current springs up—if no vile interfer ·ence defeat our aim."

—But the Lieutenant has finished the reading. With the smile of joy he says : " I *will* read it to them"! He hastened with a long and bounding step back to the garrison—which said to us, (mentally), " The battle 's won ; we 'll triumph still, *in spite of 'fears of Mormonism' !"*

Not long after the Lieutenant returned and said : " Every man has approved the Proclamation, and has sworn to sustain its principles !"—and from this moment that instrument became the test by which to approve our friends and condemn our enemies. Joy and animation were enkindled in every heart : even he who had denounced " the damned Mormon as less deserving of respect than a dog", smiled again, and yielded service with cheerfulness and joy, and furnished incontestable evidence *that it was best not to have punished with death so trivial an offence as ' Mormonism.'*

The first business was to send out the Proclamation, and also a Letter written by our friend, the liberated Alcalde ; and a trusty man of known ability was dispatched southward with said copies and letters. Brooker penetrated successfully his way as far as Monterey ; gave copies to known and faithful men ; spread the copy of the Alcaldes's Letter even within Castro's camp, and the Proclamation was written and re-written, and sent as far as San de Angelos.

It was a fact worthy of note, that within three days of the arrival of the Alcalde's Letter and the Proclamation at Santa Clara, then the Head Quarters of Gen. Castro, more than half of his army deserted. Men were sent in every direction with the Proclamation, and it was not until our men were reduced to nearly one half our original number, that we received the first accession to our force.

A party, on the 19th in the afternoon, arrived from the neighborhood of Napa Valley and Cash Creek, and as José Castro had, as early as the 18th, sent out a proclamation calling on all good Californians to unite, and with one bold effort, "fall on and kill the Bears of Sonoma, and then return and kill the whelps afterwards", it was deemed prudent to collect all the unprotected families, and support them within the garrison at the public expense, so long as the services of the husband or father were required for the common security.

It was known that a party of 70 or 80 of Castro's men were "cruising" about our neighborhood, and the danger to unprotected families was imminent; and therefore it became necessary to divide our forces in such manner as that the safety of the garrison should not be endangered. Accordingly, Capt. Sears, of the "1st Artillery", and Lieut Ford, commander of the

"1st Rifle Company", were left in charge of the Fort, with about 20 men, in addition to those expected and known to be making preparations to join us. Selecting the husbands, fathers and relatives of those defenceless families, the " General in Command" started before the dawn of day, with an escort of 10 men, for the aforementioned purpose. Proceeding cautiously along we discovered, a little after sunrise, a party of about 25 or 30 Spaniards, and made preparation for a meeting, by improving a path on the opposite declivity of the hill, so as approach unobservedly ; but our wary opponents disappeared. This circumstance convinced our leader that any attempt to get a fight, (just for a sample of what could be done, so as in the main to avoid bloodshed), could not be effectual, unless the enemy were allowed to have an advantage of 'five to one' : and even then a retreat must be feigned. This conclusion he formed from the fact, that he knew that not more than one-third of his small force had been seen by the enemy. The next day (21st) the families were returned in safety.

Gen. Castro's proclamation, which breathed out death and slaughter against even the infant that had a drop of American blood in its veins, greatly assisted us in getting together our forces. Even those who a few days before were unwilling to leave the care of a few calves, were not only ready to leave their stock and ranchos, but their houses and household stuff, and to bring their families, instead of " taking them to the mountains", by by-paths, and in the night-time, to the protection offered by our garrison.

On the 19th of June Thomas Cowey and George Fowler, two young men of peaceful dispositions were sent to Doct. Bails, a distance of about 20 miles, to obtain a keg of powder which had been purchased. They received particular instructions as to the manner of proceeding, and of avoiding danger : but having proceeded more than half way very cautiously, and meeting no enemy, they took the main road, and traveled as at other times. They were discovered and captured without resistance—having trusted the promise of the enemy, that if they would give up their arms, they should receive no harm. They gave them up, and died like martyrs! They were tied to trees and inhumanly cut in pieces, in a manner too horrible to relate. *This was the first blood shed in the Conquest of California*—an

exemplary measure of the consequence awaiting all who might be weak enough to think of
retaining life by the surrender of their arms,
in a conflict with such an enemy. But this
vile act of his gave strength to our nerve, and
sharpness to our flint.

On the 21st our force was hourly increasing.
All our prisoners in the callaboose had signed
the " treaty stipulations", and been discharged ; and it is not yet known that any of those
Spaniards who made treaty with " the Bear-
Flag-Men", ever after violated their engage-
ments.

As our numbers were now somewhat increased, and there were men who had families dependent upon their daily labor for their support, an effort was made to establish some system of monthly pay for the service : but as we
had no other means than the securities of the
public properties, and none of these were in any
manner immediately available, it was foreseen
that any system of monthly pay would serve
but to increase our financial difficulties : it
was resolved that there should not be made
any distinction between one man's services and
another's, and that no one should be allowed
an individual perquisite, except rations for

himself and wife, and children under the age of twelve years.

It was further resolved to recommend and pledge ourselves, that there should be given to each man who had not already that amount of land, at least one square league of choice land, as a bounty for which he was to consider himself always bound to defend his rights, in common with his fellow-countrymen ; or, to acknowledge himself unworthy of citizenship.

And again : it was resolved that the Mission property should be considered public property, except so much of it as had been properly vested in the several churches ; and that all persons who were known to have received any portion of these properties be required to account for the same ; and that every transfer of any of this property, wherein a valuable and complete consideration had not passed t) some authorized agent of the Mexican Government, shall be considered void. It was considered that these means would be quite sufficient to defray expenses.

On the 23d of June we learned that another of our messengers, (William Todd), had been captured by means of the treachery of a guide that had been employed to conduct him to a

settlement on the coast; and great fears were
entertained that he would also be cut in pieces,
(as the two American young men had been)
by the Spaniards who had Todd in custody—
they being 88 strong.

Now it was certain that the only way to rescue Todd, was to get a fight and whip the enemy, and thus enable him to make his escape
at the same moment that the enemy should
make his escape. At this time we could have
met him, man to man, besides guarding our
Fort ; but to have sent such force after them
would have caused the death of our comrade.
So, as the only means of the thing sure, our
Commander selected, one by one, until there
were 18 men in the row. Capt. Ford, then 1st
Lieut. of, and in command of the 1st company
of Riflemen, was selected to carry into execution the especial Orders of (not " General Fremont", for he knew nothing of the matter), but
of another man who was understood, at this
time, not to be on the most friendly terms im-
aginable with that noble officer.

This little band of 19 men, after having
been made up, as nearly as possible, on the ra·
tio of 1 to 5 men of the garrison, was especially charged as to the importance of understand-

ing and obeying orders. The design in particular was to save the life of Todd ; but the
practical utility and importance of properly
conducting this manœuvre was set forth in un-
mistakable terms. The Lieutenant received
orders to "conduct his men cautiously along,
without fatiguing the horses, until he should
discover himself to the enemy ; then halt, and
as soon as the enemy began to be in motion,
retreat to the nearest clump of trees, and every
man get down and tie his horse fast. Then
mark out the distance of 100 yards, and let it
be understood by every man where the line of
the circle shall be, that there may be no mistake. Then let no man fire before the enemy
reach the well-known line. Then be careful to
take, each one, your man—but be cautious not
all to fire at once, lest they rush upon and cut
you to pieces before you can re-load. Make
no calculation for mounting your horses, nor for
running away. The Spaniards can outrun you,
therefore *don't fight them by running.* Remember that *this day is to decide the fate of
every one of us!* If you do your duty like
men this day, and we be faithful to ourselves,
and follow up its advantages, you will not be
again called on to engage in fight, until the full

conquest of all California is achieved. But if,
on the other hand, you yield like cowards this
day, *not a man of us can save his life!* And
now, if there is a man among you in whom I
have been mistaken in thus putting your bravery and good conduct to this severe test, let him
speak, and I will fill his place. Will you carry
out these orders at the expense of your life, if
need be ?" " *We will do it!*" said the gallant
Ford. " Have you a man with you that you
cannot trust your life with ? Are you all satisfied ? Is every man ready to go and do his
duty ?——Then go ! and not a man of you
will be harmed"—and they bounded away.

There was felt no little anxiety as to the result ; especially as we thought the life of Todd
was at stake, and his release depended on an
entire rout of the enemy. We had heard that
Gen. Castro had already crossed the Bay,
and as he was allowed, even by his enemies, to
be a wily adversary, it was fully believed that
the operations of his advance party, whom Lt.
Ford was sent to encounter, were intended to
draw out our forces in a western direction,
while Castro, with his host (for we were not
yet informed of the fact that half of his men
had deserted him), would, in that case, sud-

denly fall upon our defenceless garrison from the east. Therefore it was, that the " Commander-in-Chief" remained at the garrison, and made all necessary preparations for such a movement by Castro : but (as we soon afterwards learned) he had sufficient occupation for his tact at generalship, to keep down and overcome a formidable party that had organized in support of our Proclamation of the 15th, on the south side of the Bay, under the superintendence of Weaver and Bird. Capt. Grigsby, who was first elected Captain before the taking of the Fort, and who resigned through fear of being found in a state of "unauthorized rebellion", came back from a visit to Capt. Fremont's camp, and begged of the men to be reinstated ; and was elected captain of the 1st Company of Riflemen ; which office he held until the 5th of July.

On the afternoon of the 24th Lieut. Ford came back, bringing Todd with him, and made report to the Commander, in these words :

"I have done exactly as you ordered. *We have whipped them, and that without receiving a scratch.* We took their whole band of horses, but owing to the fact that about one half of the men retreated with all possible

haste, I did not think best to encumber ourselves by taking the whole band. So we only
picked out each one a good horse, and thus
supplied the place of the horses we had killed,
and have come back without bringing the
whole band." "Very well done! I did not
order you to bring the horses : I only told you
that you never mind the killing a few horses,
for you would easily get more. You have done
all that I expected of you. *You have given
tone and character to the Revolution. We
have only to follow up this example and the
work is done.*"

CHAPTER VIII.

CAPT. FREMONT'S FIRSF VISIT—IS A BIT CENSORIOUS—CHANG-
ES FRONT, AND IS A TRIFLE LAUDATORIOUS —HIS WHERE-
ABOUTS FROM THE 11TH TO THE 25TH OF JUNE.—THE ,
GENERAL ASPECT OF THEIR AFFAIRS SERIOUSLY CONSIDER-
ED BY THE COMMANDER.—NARROW ESCAPE OF FREMONT
AND PARTY.—THE MURDERERS OF FOWLER AND COWEY
ESCAPE DUE PUNISHMENT, THROUGH FREMONT'S INTER-
FERENCE.

ON the 25th of June, at 2, P. M., came Capt.
Fremont with the whole of his forces, amounting to 72 men. Doct. Semple hailed us with
joyful greeting, and frankly confessed that a
few days since he had no confidence in any
man among us capable of conducting the enterprise ; but since the event of the 24th he was
willing to risk his life anywhere that such a
man as Lieut. Ford might lead the way.

Amid the general congratulations of the occasion, Capt. Fremont came up to me, and,
without any other salutation, in a sarcastic and
commanding tone, (looking me steadily in the
face), said, " Who wrote that Proclamation for
you ?" and continuing his " stern gaze" a mo-

ment, and perceiving that not the least˙notice
was taken of his insolence, he indignantly said,
" H-ah !—your name was to it !" and left me
as abruptly as he came. The inference to my
mind was instantaneous, and to the effect that
however I might refuse to expose an accom-
plice in that offensive act, if there had been
one, he was determined that *I* should not escape his wrath. But in a very few minutes he
re-appeared, changing his whole line of attack,
and I have every reason to believe that ere this
he had *changed his whole plan for the " Conquest of California"!* But as, in the events
of warfare, plans, and especially indefeasible
purposes, are subject to alterations and change,
no farther notice would have been taken of
these trivial demonstrations, had a tithe of his
professed devotion to the cause of Independence been genuine.

But to proceed, dear Sir. If you will be
patient, I will tell you the whole tale, so far
as it came to my personal knowledge; although
we have somewhat difference of version from
what has been published instead of the truth,
about this matter : and if in aught there is
exaggeration or mistake, as I said before, the
means of correction are at hand. It has been

said that "truth should not at all times be
spoken"! But we consider the path of truth
the only path of safety—ah, and of glory, too!
But we will not contend for glory, since, like
a shadow, it fleeth from its pursuer.

We were about to say, that after a few moments Capt. Fremont came in again, and accosted us in a most civil and graceful manner,
this time, (as it became a *gentleman*)—said he
was happy to see and understand that the
Proclamation was all it could have been ; that
every word was as he would have it, so far as
it went ; that we had done ourselves immortal
honor ; that in style of diction it would compare favorably with the best writers in the
States ; and only regreted that we had not
made the insult and abuse he* had received a
part of our grievances :—and went on to say

* The " insult" here alluded to happened in this manner :
As Capt. Fremont, with his surveying party, on the 3d of
March, 1846, was encamped at Hartwell's Rancho, he received a threatening missive from Gen. Castro, " by the hands
of a Mexican officer, who was backed by 80 lancers, well armed," ordering him to " return with your party beyond the limits of this Department"—warning Fremont if he did not immediately comply, Castro would take measures to compel him
to quit the country.   This mandate was thus officially communicated to Fremont on the 5th of March, and on the 6th

that he would receive it as a great favor, in case Gen. Castro should write or do any act or thing that might call forth another Manifesto, that we would not forget to do him (Fremont) the justice to set forth the insults he had endured at Castro's hand. To this we agreed, and we separated in mutual friendship; at least as sincere as were his unbounded professions of friendship for the success of our labors for unalloyed INDEPENDENCE !

Seeing that we had succeeded in saving the life of William Told, and as we had learned that about 80 of Castro's men were on duty, this side the Bay, we determined to send a sufficient force to hunt them down so closely as to prevent their re-embarkation across the Bay. Lieut. Ford was sent in command of this expedition, with orders not to turn to the right

he entrenched himself, with his little band of assistants, on the summit of Hawk's Peak, 30 miles distant from Monterey. This place—2200 feet above the level of the sea—he fortified with fallen trees, &c., and stripped one of them of its limbs and foliage, and suspended on it, 40 feet from its base, the American Flag. Castro raised a force of about 200 men, and marched them off to dislodge his disobedient visitor; but he took especial care not to go within rifle range of his fortified encampment, and finally abandoned the undertaking.—[*From a California newspaper.*—ED.]

or left from pursuit, so as to suffer them to escape. Capt. Fremont said in our hearing that he had come down, *not to take any part in the matter;* only to see the sport, and *explore* about the Bay : and that he would be pleased that our party should accompany him—or, that he would be pleased to accompany our party—which, we cannot certainly say—but so it was they all set out together, and so anxious were all hands to "see the sport", that it was with difficulty we could persuade 75 men to remain to guard the Fort.

On the morning of the 26th this "pleasure" party left—in number amounting to about 134 men.—Large numbers continued to flock to our standard, and to record their names in support of Independence—pledging themselves to support the principles of the Proclamation of the 15th of J une.

Before entering upon the doings of the said "pleasure party", it may be well to give an account of all we knew (by report) of Capt. Fremont's operations from the 11th to the 25th of June. And here, as we knew nothing by personal observation, you will compare it with other testimony.

We were informed that Capt. Fremont continued his preparations for his journey to the States until the 17th, when he learned that a party had seized the Fort at Sonoma ; and, as it was not reasonable to suppose that Gen. Castro would pass by so small a force as that at Sonoma, to attack the larger force at Johnson's Rancho, more than 100 miles further off, the only chance to provoke that attack, which was, according to his instructions from the Executive Departmeat, to constitute and be, in effect, a Declaration of War, on the part of Mexico, against the United States, was to move down nearer to the liabilities. So, on the 18th he moved to Sutter's Fort, and informed Capt. Sutter that it was necessary to take possession of his Fort, and if he thought fit to yield peacable possession, it would save the disagreeble necessity of taking it by force. Capt. Sutter gave possession, and Gen. Vallejo and his companions were put under guard there.

Here Capt. Fremont waited for a few days, expecting that the garrison at Sonoma would soon be overthrown, and that the much desired assault upon the United States' Flag would soon be made, to rescue the much loved and esteemed Gen. Vallejo and his friends.

But while preparations for the said attack,

and further provision for his journey across the
Plains were being made, he received a letter
from Lieut. Ford, informing him that the men
of the garrison had no confidence in the ability of Mr. Ide to manage matters at the Fort
at Sonoma ; that they were in great danger of
being betrayed into the hands of the Spaniards ; that such an inference was drawn from
the supposition that the Commander had erred
in his conditions of peace with the neighboring
Spaniards.   (At the time this letter was sent
we had no knowledge thereof, as it was sent by
that weekly messenger that was provided by
the hospitality of the Americans, to convey letters from the families of the said prisoners to
Gen. Vallejo and companions, and from said
prisoners to their families, weekly.)

Intelligence of this was soon communicated
to the Commander, and every effort was made
to convince the men of the garrison that our
interest, as well as moral obligations, forbade
that we should refuse to others the same rights
and liberties that we claimed for ourselves, and
that we must not, if we desire the best good
of the inhabitants of California, think of lay-
ing hold of the right to govern by the iron hand
military force, but by the might of such equit-

able principles as we could plainly show were calculated to unite the masses in one common effort to extend the knowledge and blessings of true Liberty.

Lieut. Ford, (as we were informed by an officer who had seen the said letter) begged Capt. Fremont, by all means, to come down and make his camp in the immediate neighborhood of Sonoma. Whether this letter had pith and pathos sufficient to dissuade Capt. F. from all his public protestations against involving himself, his men or his Government, in any unwarrantable and dishonorable interference in the internal difficulties of the people of a nation then at peace with his Government, (as far as was then known by us), or whether a desire to avail himself of the honor of provoking the Mexican authorities to open the floodgates of that war which fate had destined to be the messenger of *peaceful Liberty* to so much of the Mexican domain as it might be desirable to "annex" to the Union, in order to obtain, or rather to *retain* the balance of political power in favor of "the cherished institutions of the South", we will not presume to affirm ; but will state distinctly, that up to the 25th, and even to the 5th of July, he had adhered

strictly to his neutral plan of provocation, according to what was fully understood among
the knowing ones to be in accordance with his
private instructions : and what course of conduct could be better calculated to exasperate—
to induce some unthinking agent of Mexican
authority (a subaltern of a friar, perchance), to
throw an unlucky shot at one of Capt. Fremont's "neutral and unoffending men", and
thus to have struck the chord discordant—that
had rung the tocsin of war, involving in its
consequences *a hundred thousand lives!* If
he who, by the favor of Heaven and persevering study, has seized the lightnings and directed their course, shall be thought worthy the
admiration of his surviving race, in how much
higher estimation shall he be held, who may
introduce a successful mode of conquest, without the shedding of blood—of extending Liberty to the suffering sons of civil oppression
and slavery ?

But pardon me, dear Sir, and I will return
to the narration of another series of events as
they occured, and which imperceptibly produced our overthrow.

Perhaps you would have considered the 5th
of July the zenith of our glory! Not so, dear

Sir. It is true that numbers came pouring in up to the 5th. This continued increase of numbers was the effect of that quiet influence of motives, designs and principles, silently set in motion, which could not be supposed to cease to act, on the commission of the first error, nor yet on any change of the general plan. But you will recollect that no action was had reflecting the least credit to our enterprise, after the arrival of Capt. Fremont at Sonoma : and if we had been ten days in establishing a reputation for our cause, which was capable of enlisting the whole energy of the country in its support, and which did enlist hundreds who had no knowledge of us, except by the one common appeal made to all alike—to enemies as well as to friends—ten days more were fully sufficient to effect an entire revolution, and to divert and change the current of that general interest which none other had power to awaken.

These prefatory remarks bring us to consider the events and circumstances which changed the character of our enterprise, and presented California to the United States as a trophy of that species of conquest that wallows in the blood of murder, or of that ignoble traffic that makes the price of Liberty the price of blood,

—instead of presenting the same fair land on terms of honorable compact and agreement,— such as all the world can participate in without loss or dishonor, by the free, frank expression of voluntary consent and good will of the parties.

We will now refer to a little incident illustrative of the feeling of all California, at that time, on this subject. The native Californians were democratic in feeling, scorning subjugation by conquest; but not ignorant of advantages that might have been secured to all California by an amicable union with the United States. After taking the garrison at Sonoma, and after confidence had been established by the equitable course pursued, the highest official officer of the District of Sonoma, on seeing our flag, said to me: " Why did you not raise the United States' flag ?" I said we had no right to do so ; that the United States' Government would justly punish us should we do so, and return within its jurisdiction : but that we would raise an Independent Flag, and become a united and free people ; and then, by peaceful agreement, unite ourselves to the United States by treaty—and *then*, (and not till then) we would hoist the United States'

Flag. He heartily replied, " Buena ! then will my people dance all day ! !" But such a day of glory to the free institutions of America was not then at hand.——Yes, we would have gladly " danced", also, *rejoicing*—" Old men and maidens, in the dance together", if we might have been allowed to behold the peaceful triumph of just principle, rather than the triumph of Buena Vista and Sierra Gorda !

On the evening of the 28th one of our men intercepted a letter addressed to certain citizens of Sonoma, giving intelligence, that early on the morning of the 30th Gen. Castro would invade Sonoma, and put to death every soul found there, without distinction, except the " Grande Oso", whom they intended to chain and convey to the other side of the Bay, for the amusement of their women and children. All the Spanish people came and requested of me permission to leave the town, which was positively refused. After much unavailing persuasion they ceased to importune ; but a short time after a request was presented, that all the women and children, both American and Spanish, might be allowed to congregate in one house, and that the Spanish men might be allowed to take shelter in the callaboose. To

this we agreed. The women and children were
hived in the back apartment of Gen. Vallejo's
house ; and as the night came on, all were ready
for the expected attack.   The two 18-pound-
ers, double charged with canister shot, guarded
the main entrance, and 7 other pieces of artillery were in using order, and so arranged as to
be available at short notice at any point whither an attack might be made. The 250 loaded
muskets were divided among the men, and so
placed as to be within convenient reach.   The
rifles, all fresh capped, were ready—the guards
were strictly charged, the matches were always
burning at night.

About 4, a. m., or a little earlier, our guards
came in and reported having heard the tramping of horses in the distance. Every man was
called to the position intended. The signal for
the fight, the onset, was agreed on. The 18-
pounders were first to answer the report of my
rifle—each officer had his orders at what particular distance the enemy should be allowed
to approach, before he might engage in the
fight. And as we well knew that if the enemy
were to succeed at all, it would be by a sudden
charge ; therefore we placed a trusty guard,
whose duty it was to reserve each a loaded

musket, only to be used in such an emergency.
Thus prepared, in less than one minute from
the first alarm, all listened for the sound of
the tramping horses—we heard them coming !
—then, low down under the darkened cañon,
we *saw* them coming ! ! In a moment the
truth flashed across my mind : the Spaniards
were deceiving us ! In a moment orders were
given to the captains of the 18-pounders to reserve fire until my rifle should give the word ;
and, to prevent mistake, I hastened to a position a hundred yards in front of the cannon,
and a little to the right oblique, so as to gain
a nearer view. " Come back ; you will lose
your life !" said a dozen voices. " Silence !"
roared Capt. Grigsby ; " I have seen the old
man in a bull pen before to-day !" The blank-
ets of the advancing host flowed in the breeze.
They had advanced to within 200 yards of the
place where I stood. The impatience of the
men at the guns became intense, lest the enemy came too near, so as to lose the effect of the
spreading of the shot. I made a motion to lay
down my rifle. The matches were swinging—
" My God ! they swing the matches !" cried
the well known voice of *Kit Carson.* " Hold
on, hold on ! we shouted—'tis Fremont, 'tis

Fremont !" in a voice heard by every man of both parties, we cried—while Capt. Fremont dashed away to his left to take cover behind an adobe house ; and in a moment after he made one of his most gallant charges on our Fort : it was a noble exploit ; he came in *a full gallop, right in the face and teeth of our two long 18's !**

Thus ended this 'glorious' battle ; and thus were our plans defeated ; and thus escaped

* The account of this affair, as given on pages 69, 70 and 71 of the "BIOGRAPHY OF WILLIAM B. IDE," a work we have before refered to in these pages, which was put in type some months before the existence of this " Wambough Letter" was known to the Editor, and which was related by Wm. B. Ide to his brother about two or three years after its occurrence, agrees substantially with the foregoing, as will be seen from the following extracts from those pages :

" Not long after this rather unique military exploit of the Bear Party, one of their men picked up, on the street, a letter addressed to a citizen of Sonoma, notifying him that Don Castro's party was preparing to make a raid upon the Fort very soon. This notice coming to the Governor in an apparently authentic shape, he set about making preparations to give the Spaniards a warm reception. Fremont, with a small company of his surveying party and a few other emigrants, was at that time located at Sutter's Fort, and Brother was not expecting assistance from him.

'In the mean time every thing in the Fort was put in or-

those very men who cut in pieces George Fowler and Thomas Cowey, through the disobedience of our orders ; else had they have paid the
penalty justly due to so inhuman an act.   But
the officer in charge, on being interrogated the
reason why he had not left the Fort to the care
of him whose duty and privilege it was to have
defended it, until he had punished the murderers of Fowler and Cowey ? said " the advice
of Capt. Fremont had induced him to forsake
the path of duty." The party were immediate-

der. The cannon and small arms were loaded with cannister, balls or buck shot, as it was thought would render them,
respectively, of most service. Scouts were sent in different
directions to bring back to the Fort early notice of the approach towards it of any hostile force ; and with these and
other precautionary measures, the officers and men of the
Bear Flag party patiently awaited on their arms a short time
to see what would next turn up. Precisely how long they
waited, I dont recollect that my brother told me : but he
said that quite late one evening one of his scouts came hur-
riedly up to the Fort on horseback, and announced the enemy's approach within a short distance—it might be half a
mile or more : when the cannon were drawn out and put in
position in front of the Fort, the matches lighted—the men
inside the Fort formed in ' battle array,' with loaded arms in
hand, and all things ready for action.

" Thus prepared (brother told me), he gave orders to his
men not to fire until, by a given signal, he ordered them to
fire. He then went some ten or twenty rods towards the

ly ordered back to the pursuit of the flying
murderers of Fowler and Cowey ; and, after a
hearty breakfast, they departed and arrived at
the Bay in season to witness the embarcation
of Castro's men.

It appeared on investigation, that—First, a
letter had been addressed to Sonoma, intended
to fall into the hands of the garrison, in the
hope that I would recall the men under Ford
for the protection of the Fort ; but this having failed, the flying Spaniards drew lots among
their number, and three men, prepared with
letters in their boots, put themselves in the
power of their pursuers, threw away their arms

coming foe, and he soon heard a voice among them call out :
'*See ! their torches are lighted ! they 're going to fire upon us !*'
He knew the voice—it was KIT CARSON'S—and instantly
threw up his arms as a signal for them not to fire ; saying to
his men, at the top of his voice : ' *Dont fire ! It is Fremont !*'
' Thus, (said my brother) Kit Carson, who I knew was with
Fremont, probably saved us from a pretty bad disaster :—
which, had it happened, would have resulted from Fremont's
failure to give us seasonable notice of his coming.   His excuse for not doing so was, that he sent a man ahead for that
purpose, who, being a foreigner, did not understand his order.   And, as showing that Fremont took in readily the perilous situation of his squad, he hastily ' switched himself off
on a side track', out of harm's way, even if we had fired on
his party.' "

and fell on their knees, begging for quarter :
but the orders were to take no prisoners from
this band of murderers, and the men were shot
and never rose from the ground. But notwithstanding one of the men declared with his
dying breath, that he expected death—that he
came on purpose to die for the benefit of his
countrymen ; yet Capt. Fremont was either
deceived by the letters found in their boots, or
he deceived our men, by advising them to forsake the pursuit ;—in either case the strata-
gem took effect, and the murderers escaped.

CHAPTER IX.

CAPT. FREMONT AGAIN IN THE FIELD.—THE COMMANDANT'S
ORDERS DISOBEYED.—THE BEAR FLAG GOVERNMENT "IN
QUIET POSSESSION OF ALL CALIFORNIA."—THE U. S. OFFI-
CERS' PLANS—THE BEAR FLAG GOVERNMENT TO BE MADE
OVER TO THEM.—THE "GENERAL ASSEMBLY AND COUN-
CIL" CONVENE ON THE 5TH OF JULY—VOTE TO WIPE OUT
ALL PREVIOUS DOINGS OF THE BEAR FLAG PARTY, AND
RAISE THE UNITED STATES' FLAG, UNDER CAPTAIN FRE-
MONT'S COMMAND.

ON the 1st day of July came three men from
the opposite side of the Bay, and informed us
that all the Americans and other foreigners
were up and doing to spread our Proclamation,
and that a company of 100 were already collected in its support, and requested us to send
them arms.   A boat was provided, and arrangements made to mount a small piece of
artillery on board the boat, so as to secure the
safe conveyance of a party of 12 men in charge
of 100 muskets ; but before these arrangements were complete, Capt. Fremont returned

to Sonoma, and so advised as to defeat the measure.

It now wanted only two or three days to the 4th of July, and our order for the immediate embarkation of the 12 men with the arms, to the assistance of our friends, at the head of whom was Weaver, Bird and others, could not be enforced, because Capt. Fremont was opposed to it, and the measure was postponed until after the 4th. The 4th came like other days.

Two hundred and seventy-two men had signed our roll. We were in quiet, and for the time, in undisturbed possession of all California north and east of the San Joaquin River. We had taken possession of Yerba Buena and spiked the cannon there. All that was necessary was to have pursued our victory, to have made it complete.

It may have been considered very important to the interests of the United States, to have prevented the crossing of the Bay by our forces, and the consequent union and coöperation with our friends there, who had assembled in support of our Proclamation of the 15th of June, as such an event would have rendered the immediate conquest and success of princi-

ples inevitable ; and that, too, before any safe
plan could be devised for getting up the United
States" Flag. Although this conquest would
not have in the least retarded the union of California with the States ; yet it would have giv-
en the citizens of California the right of being
consulted as to the TERMS of the union ; and
what was and is of equal importance to those
who delight to cherish the honor of the Institutions of Liberty—it would have prevented
that foul stain of disgrace that attaches to that
very institution of liberty which we delight to
honor.

As relates to the next consideration of moment—which, indeed, may with truth be said
to have had more influence in determining
events than any other consideration whatever
—it is of inconsiderable importance *who* were
to be the renowned ' Conquerors of California.'
One thing was reduced to a moral as well as a
physical certainty : that if the current of pop-
ularity our cause had acquired, thus suddenly,
were allowed to proceed, it would have been
quite impossible for any force of the United
States authority, then within using distance,
to have kept up with it ; and, consequently,
all that glory which had so manifestly inspired

the hopes of its officers present would have been lost ! To prevent a catastrophe so appalling, it became necessary that the greatest exertions should be used to hurry up a pretext for hoisting the U. S. Flag, and, Commodore Jones-like, take possession of the whole country. Now, dear Sir, at what particular date this new plan of Conquest was matured, is more than we know ; but, nevertheless, we are able to leave it between ten days next preceding the 5th of July, '46. We were now no longer, in case of war with the United States, to be considered a free people, and regarded as allies ; but we were soon to be told that it was the policy of the United States Government (officers) to treat those as enemies, whom they might find in an enemy's country !

But before it was prudent to throw such an insult square in our face, it was necessary to place one of their number in command of our military forces ; and not only so, but it was also *imperatively necessary* to rely much on our love of country, and devotion to the best interests of the people with whom we were associated, else had they learned more of the nature and consequence of such an unwarrantable and uncalled for abuse.

If it is still necessary to state, in concise language, this *second* edition of the plan for the
conquest of California, ' revised and corrected'
by the joint labors of Lieuts. Gillespie, Missroon
and others, we will give it without fear of con-
tradiction. First, secure the command of the
Independent forces of the Bear Flag Republic.
Secondly, hoist the U. S. Flag, and follow up
to the entire conquest. Thirdly, if no war between Mexico and the United States ensue, sell
out all the military stores of the U. S. to the
Government of California, and obtain California by treaty with the new Government. But
in the event of a war, to seize and acquire the
whole by the right of conquest. And it was
admitted by all that the Government of the
United States would, as a matter of course,
cashier whoever might consent thus to violate
its honor, by becoming the leader of the said
Independents. Yet as a solace for his dishon-
or, (to use the language of our informant, who
was one of said U. S. officers), "he will be in
town with a pocket full of rocks."

Further to explain how, and in what manner, this plan was made successful, I will now
copy from my Journal written at the time, and
as I have hinted before : " Capt. Fremont op-

posed the sending men and arms across the Bay
—advised us not to believe every report—that
as one of our informants was an Englishman, it
might be a plan to entrap us : it was not best
to push our success too rapidly, as we would
endanger the safety of Sonoma. Only delay a
day or two—you may receive more information." Further on it is added : "From the
foregoing advice and other inducements connected therewith, it became impossible to convince our men of the danger which threatened
our unarmed associates on the other side of the
Bay : and delay ensued which caused their entire dispersion : while four of their number
were made prisoners—three of whom suffered
extreme cruelty ; but the fourth, who was my
second son, was released with the gift of a horse
and a passport, with the following expression of
Gen. Castro : 'I will not punish you ; I have
released you to convince your Father that I,
too, know how to perform a generous act.—
When I meet you on the battle-field, I will
ask you for your passport.' "
    You will recollect that that portion of the
men who were opposed to. making themselves
responsible for their own acts, at the time it
was determined to take possession of the Gar-

rison of Sonoma, departed to join Capt. Fremont. These men were again returned to Sonoma, and seeing all the good citizens of California were fast falling into the same fatal error which had well nigh involved themselves in
rebellion—from motives of prudence, and by
the advice of certain naval officers, resolved to
effect by artifice what could not have been
done by a fair expression of the voice of the
whole. They argued that if Capt. Fremont
could be placed in command of our forces, it
would amount to an alliance with the United
States ; or at least that he would be cashiered, and would remain with us. They seemed
fully to understand, that if Capt. Fremont
could be placed in command, we should at
once come under the protection of the United
States : while it is more than supposable, that
our very attentive friends of the U. S. marine
authority, in connection with their " Civil Engineers", had quite another object in the manœuvre—which may be more fully understood
from the narration of what follows :

Early on the 5th of July Capt. Fremont requested the " bear men", as the " Independents" were designated, to assemble ' *without
arms*', within a large room at Don Salvadore's

house, adjoining which was a smaller room capable of convening the Captain's Company—
who assembled there, *under arms*, to the number of 72 of his men, and 8 or 10 gentlemen officers from the U. S. ships then in the Bay. The
number of the Independents, in contradistinction, was about 280 men, without arms—a citizens' assembly, convened to deliberate on some
proposition expected to be made by Capt. Fremont.

The business was before the Independent
citizens, as a matter of course : but the Council was composed of their friends, and an armed sentinel, from Capt. Fremont's guards, kept
the door between the private Council-room and
the hall of the *Representatives* of the People.

This large assembly might properly be assimilated with the Legislative Assembly of
Vermont, in its first organization (the more
efficient arm of the government), while the assemblage of armed friends might prefigure the
Governor and Council of Vermont ; yet they
do not enjoy the *veto* power, but simply the
power of *suspension*.

Capt. Fremont, accompanied by Lieut. Gillispie and two or three others—officers in the
U. S. Navy—presented himself before the ' gen-

eral assembly', and opened the business of the
session by declaring—(not his determination to
conquer California, to be sure ; for he said he
should not, in any manner, intermeddle in the
affairs of California politics)—but his already
d-e-c-i-d-e-d resolution to conquer Gen. José
Castro, whom he violently denounced as an
usurper in the California government.   He
went on to say that his meditated expedition
against him could not be considered a violation
of the amicable relations existing between the
United States and Mexico.   He continued to
say : " I shall proceed to take Castro, and take
him with me to the States, whether you coöperate with me or not" :   and, in justification,
refered to the manner in which he had been
insulted by Gen. Castro.

After having sufficiently guarded himself
against any future imputation of unwarrantable interference, on his part, in those matters
which exclusively belonged to the citizens of
California, he said, that as *we* (connecting *his*
party with the assembly of citizens), have one
common enemy, he would state the conditions
on which he whould agree to make common
cause with us.

The advantages he proposed to confer on us

were : First, his unwavering support of our Independence, and of the principles and purposes set forth by our Proclamation of the 15th of June. Secondly, he offered us every facility his well supplied camp afforded,—that we would be allowed to share with himself and men the military stores and provisions supplied by the U. S. Government ; and, most of all, we might rely on his friendly advice in conducting all our *purely military* operations.

The two first *conditions* were scarcely nominal. They only required that we should sign a pledge that we would " abstain from the violation of the chastity of women", and that we would conduct the Revolution honorably. The third simply required a pledge of obedience to the orders of our properly constituted officers.

He insisted at some length on the imperious necessity that all should solemnly pledge implicit and unconditional obedience to the proper officers, which now became essentially necessary to success ; and after expatiating on the vast importance of conducting honorably the enterprise that was destined to become a brilliant example to the oppressed throughout the world, of a people though few, who have by the mighty impulse of Equity's inspiring principle, overthrown the rapacious powers of usurpation, avarice and governmental oppression ; and, by instituting equal liberty of assuming a higher and more honorable system of government among the enlightened and free.

After having again pledged his honor to stand by us, at least until Gen. Castro should have been overcome, he closed his propositions and remarks by politely bowing to the soon-to-be ex-commander, as if he would say, ' Will you now have the magnanimity to second my propositions'?

In reply to the Captain's proposition he said that he believed the past honorable and unimpeachable conduct of the men of the garrison, which had the esteem and confidence of even many of our enemies, and the responded approbation and support of all present, could not be refused, even by Captain Fremont, as a sufficient guarantee for the future, so far as the first and second conditions were concerned. But since we had but recently suffered the defeat of all our well devised plans, through a want of confidence in the ability of our highest officer in command—and, too, through disobedience of orders given, whereby our enemy had es-

caped an otherwise certain overthrow, and our
friends collected south of the Bay had been dis-
persed, and their leaders made prisoners, it was
admitted to be of the highest importance that
those to whom we had committed, or to whom
we shall hereafter commit the responsibility of
directing our combined efforts, might possess
so much of the confidence of the governed, as
would enable them to carry into effect at least
their commands.   And inasmuch as Capt. Fremont had prepared a solemn pledge, calculated
by its provisions to give confidence to those in
command, and to bind us closer to the fixed
and publicly declared object of our Revolution,
a motion was made, in conclusion, to appoint
a committee to draft an appropriate PLEDGE,
to be subscribed by every man before he might
further participate in the perils or honors attendant upon the establishment of such a system of government, as shall secure to all the
free enjoyment of rational liberty.

The generous feeling of the assembly immediately responded by electing the last speaker
their said committee ; whereupon the prudent
sense of the privy council suggested the propriety of electing two persons more to join said
committee, *from the council of friends*, in ar-

ranging an affair upon which so much depended.   Thus strengthened, the said committee
retired to consider the subject of their charge,
under an injunction of brevity from the privy
council.

At the committee's assembling and proceeding to business, it appeared that the adjument-
ative portion thereof were decidedly in favor
of setting aside all that had been done in the
cause, and for making the era of the Independence of California to commence with the command of Capt. Fremont.   It was true that
two of the three composing this committee
were selected from Capt. Fremont's Company,
neither of whom had hitherto taken any active
part under our Flag—who had each been nom-
inated by the other—who were in no manner
interested in anything that had been done under our Flag, farther than any other of Capt.
Fremont's men; neither of whom had signed
our articles, or otherwise identified themselves
with our cause.

Under these circumstances it was easy to
conceive and to understand the motive of these
representatives of the secret council: and, also,
it was easy to understand why they were elected by a body of men to which they at the time

did not belong. And it was easy, also, to represent the wishes and interests of that body,
whose right it was to be represented in a matter that only concerned themselves, to wit :
what shall be the *form* of that pledge which
they were disposed, of their own free will, to
offer to Capt. Fremont, in exchange for his
proffered *three overtures*—in ratification of the
proposed treaty of alliance, " offensive and de-
fensive", by which, according to his own statement verbally made, we were to make joint effort against " the common enemy."

Therefore it was worse than useless to further argue any difference that might exist in the
views of the primitive portion of the committee and its adjunct portion, than to understand
the position of each ; as it was reasonable to
suppose that the original assembly of " Bear
Men, *who were Bear Men*", would be at liberty to sustain such a report as would truly represent their wishes and interest.

Accordingly each of the component portions
of the committee drafted a resolution and
pledge suiting the views of each, which were
forthwith reported by its Chairman to the re-
assembled convention, in accordance with the
established rules of conventional assemblies ;

although not without a serious attempt, on the part of the adjuncts, to seize the chair. They appeared satisfied, however, with the impartiality of the Chairman, in the discharge of his duty as reporter of the committee's doings.

The Report of the majority was first read, and their views, as far as expressed in the sitting of the committee, were fairly represented.

It was proposed by the first article of the majority report, to annul and wipe out all that had been done up to the 5th of July. The reasons urged in defence of this article were : 1st, the 5th of July immediately follows the 4th day of July, the anniversary of American Independence ; and, 2dly, as Capt. Fremont was to be our *advisorary* leader, it would enable him to " begin with the beginning", and that his name and influence would add more advantage to the cause by being thus associated ; and, 3dly, it was proper that, in changing the ' administration', there should be a new organization throughout : or, more definitely, that we who are out of office may have a chance to get in.

After followed the Report of the minority, which——[Thus abruptly " ends the chapter."

CHAPTER X.

EDITORIAL REMARKS.—"THE CONQUEST OF CALIFORNIA" UN-
DER THE BEAR FLAG GOVERNMENT, AN ASSURED FACT.—
MR. IDE'S BUSINESS HABITS AND QUALIFICATIONS.—HIS
PUBLIC EMPLOYMENT.

THE WAMBOUGH LETTER brings this "History of the Conquest of California" down to
about the commencement of hostilities between
the United States and Mexico, in 1846. Before this state of war between us and his own
government was known by Gen. Castro, then
the actual head and commander of the Mexican authorities in California, (it appears by
Mr. IDE's statement), Castro had taken himself and his dilapidated military forces across
the Bay, on his way to Mexico, and had thus
"escaped due punishment for the murder of
Fowler and Cowey". Thus it also appears,
that on or about the 5th of July, when the
new "administration" took possession, and the
"change of government" was accomplished, the
civil and military authority of Mexico had been
thoroughly "wiped out"—California was not,

and had not been, from the 15th of June to
the 5th of July, under Mexican rule. She *was*,
what her rude "national" Flag had from day
to day proclaimed, "THE CALIFORNIA REPUB-
LIC." During these twenty days there was no
obstruction, by a conflicting party, to the exercise by the Bear Flag Government, of its entire functions and prerogatives of National Independence. For a greater part of this time,
and especially at its close, it was, as Mr. IDE
truly remarks, " in quiet, and for the time, in
undisturbed possession of all California north
of the San Joaquin River. All that was necessary was to have pursued our victory, to have
made it complete." These facts and considerations (we think, from our stand-point), war-
rant the conclusion, that on the 4th of July,
1846, the " Bear Flag Government" had effect-
ually *conquered* California—had, to all intents
and purposes, wrested that province from the
mother country ; and would have maintained
that stand with " complete success," had there
been no " uwarrantable interference" from outside quarters, and without a change of ' administration' or Flag, until she had voluntarily
applied, as she eventually did, for admission as
one of the States of the American Union.

Those who were well acquainted with the subject of this memoir well know, that he was not the man to " put his hand to the plow and look back." As in scaling the Nevada Mountain, the year before, on his way with his emigrating train to the "land of promise", he undertook a job which his companions thought impracticable, but which proved a notable success, so did he succeed most wonderfully in another far more adventurous undertaking, which not only his boon companions, but his outside friends at first view deemed impracticable.— Although better qualified by education and experience to wield the broad-axe and hammer than the sword and helmet of the " commander", yet, when by accident the latter were put into his hand, what he lacked in skill for their use, he made up by sleepless vigilance and indomitable courage, resolution and perseverence —such as initiated the command, " Now take the Fort !"

AS A PRIVATE CITIZEN,

Mr. IDE was respected by his neighbors and acquaintance. He took a lively interest in their welfare, as by reference to pages 25–6 of these ' Sketches' it is stated that he ' took great interest in politics ; and, while in Madison, O., he wrote a great many articles of agreement for his neighbors, and was often consulted by them on occasions of disputes occuring between them about rights of land, division-lines, and other misunderstandings'—thus acting as a genial and mutual friend, without fee or reward, as ' a peace-maker' among them.

He started in the race of business-life, at the age of twenty-one, with no other 'capital' than a pair of stalwart arms and hands, and by the use of them, and a judicious investment of the fruit of their labors, at the age of about 56 he was in possession of what he considered a " competency of this world's goods", for himself and family—as he then stated in a letter to one of his brothers at the East.

But it was ' otherwise ordered' than that he should remain here long to enjoy this "competency." He died at Monroeville, Cal., on the 19th of Dec., 1852, aged 56 years, 7 months and 12 days, after an illness disabling him for the duties of his office of only about one week. He held, at the time of his decease, the office of County Judge for Colusi Co., by election, and, by appointment, he officiated as Judge of Probate, County Treasurer, County Surveyor,

County Clerk,—and, *exofficio*, as County Recorder and County Commissioner. We understand the sallary and perquisites attached to all these offices amounted to about $ 2,000 per annum.

His county, (I am informed by a California correspondent) was at that time nearly as large as the State of New Hampshire. He held these several offices, (or a great part of them) about 20 months, to the day of his decease.— My correspondent adds : " By the exercise of his influence, sound judgment and financial tact, he kept the county free of debt, at a time when extravagance and misrule, in most of the other counties, were piling up debts which are burdens upon the people's shoulders to this day. The County of Colusa had no jail at the time Judge IDE was appointed, and no money with which to build one. There was no very convenient way for confining persons brought there for trial, in criminal cases, without the expense of day and night keepers. In the spring of 1852 Mr. Ide related to a friend who called on him, what he did to obviate this inconvenience, somewhat as follows : ' I have tools which I brought with me over the Plains, and some I brought by steamer, on my last trip

from the East. I will get some good bar iron
from San Francisco, and some bolts, and will
build a cage with my own hands.'" And this
writer adds : " He did so, with some assistance by the local smith, perhaps. He drilled
the bars and bolted them together; thus making a safe and durable cell for the confinement
of prisoners. He placed this cage under the
dense and comfortable shade of a monster oak
in front of a building which, at that time, and
for that place, was a 'first-class Stage Hotel,
and the county Court House'. No guard was
required, and it needed no ventillation. It was
a healthy as well as a secure place for detaining
the accused while awaiting trial. It was a success—a necessary and inexpensive structure,
saving the County much expense in the line of
public buildings. Some years afterwards, when
the County Seat was removed from Monroeville, this cell or cage was also moved ; and
even now, after the lapse of so many years, it is
doing duty as a cell in the splendid new brick
Jail, at Colusi, Colusi County."

In further response to the Editor's inquiry,
this correspondent writes : " Some thought
Judge IDE's death was hastened to give opportunity for robbery. I do not think so. It is

true there were suspicious circumstances in relation to his last sickness, which gave credence to such a belief in the minds of some of his friends. He was living away from his family; his wife having died about two years previously, and his children residing at a great distance on his Rancho, were none of them with him during his short confinement with the small pox. He had the key of the county safe under his head at the time of his death, I have been told. The man who attended him during his sickness took said key and robbed the safe. It was known at the time how much money there was in the safe belonging to the County. The thief was pursued—finally caught, and all the County's money recovered—but no more. Mr. Ide was known to have money of his own in the safe, but how much no one knew. None of his money was recovered ; and the thief, by the connivance of some one who was, perhaps, his confederate in the plunder, escaped the second time, and was never re-taken.

"Mr. Ide was buried at Monroeville, where was once the site of Colusi Co. Court House ; but at the present day there are no buildings there, and the land they stood on is occupied as a wheat field."

MR. IDE'S TOUR UNDER FREMONT, DOWN THE PACIFIC COAST.—
HIS CONTRACT WITH A SEA CAPTAIN, ETC.

We have elsewhere in these pages refered to
a work entitled, "*A Biographical Sketch of
the Life of William B. Ide*". Several of its
240 pages are occupied with an account of his
reception by Commodore STOCKTON, on board
his ship, then lying in the Bay—the ceremony
of transfering California, by its then reputed
'Governor', to the United States, the Commodore officiating as agent of the latter party—the
collation, etc., then following.   This account,
up to the time he applied to the captain of the
ship for his passage home, was furnished the
Editor of that work by a brother, to whom it
was related by said ex-'Governor' in 1849.

Soon after the U. S. Flag was hoisted at Sonoma, and the command of the garrison there
was tranfered to Capt. Grigsby ; and after Gen.
Castro had embarked for the southern section
of the late 'Republic', Capt. Fremont's first
step in the new government, it would seem, was
taken to retalliate on him the '*indignity*' that
the Commander failed to notice in his Proclamation.   For this expedition he needed an ac-

cession, from the ranks of the 'bear men', to
the small force he brought with him to Sonoma on the 5th of July—to obtain which it was
found necessary that their late Commander
should be of Fremont's party, in order to induce
any considerable number of the said 'bear men'
to go with him. Mr. IDE therefore thought it
his duty to his country to go—and he did go
and continue on duty with them, as a *private
soldier*, from about the 10th of July to the
1st of November, 1846—when he found himself four or five hundred miles away from
home, down on the southwestern coast of California, without money, and poorly provided
with clothing. A merchant ship lay near the
place where he and his comrades were dicharg-
ed, with the captain of which he engaged to
work his passage home. It so happened that
" Commodore STOCKTON, then around on that
coast with the U. S. ship Princeton, who had
called to pay his respects to the Captain"—
(we here quote, *verbatim*, from said account)
—" while walking arm-in-arm with him on
deck, saw my brother at his new vocation, and
said : ' Captain, do you know who that old
man there, (pointing to Mr. IDE), sawing wood
for you, is ?' ' No ; I did n't ask his name',

replied the Captain. 'Well, that is Governor
IDE, of the Bear Flag party.' 'Can that be
so ? do you know him ?' asked the Captain.
'Yes, I know him,' was the reply. Whereupon the Captain called his Steward and said
to him : 'Here, Steward, go tell that man
sawing wood, yonder, that the Captain wants
to see him at his office.'

"The above incident and coloquy came to
my knowledge through a different channel, as
I have before remarked. It was told to a friend
of mine by said Captain, to whom the Commodore introduced Mr. IDE : 'and on his said
introduction, he [Mr. I.], was made welcome,
not only to his passage, but to as good fare
and accommodations as his ship afforded.'

"At that time this Captain was on his way
to San Francisco, in the merchant service. In
1855 he had retired from a sea-faring life with
'a competency,' (as sea-faring captains sometimes do), and settled in a town near Boston,
where my said friend had an interview with
him in '55, during which the Captain related
the above incidents,—adding : that 'during
the passage he had frequent interviews with
WM. B. IDE, and had formed a very favorable
opinion of him.' And my informant added,

that this Captain, about that time, furnished
an article for the 'Boston Journal,' in which
he gave a short account of the Bear Flag enterprise, and dwelt particularly on what he
considered the important service Mr. IDE had
rendered his country by the part he took in
' the conquest of California'."

We cannot account for the abrupt manner
in which the Wambough Letter was closed, except for the reason that he considered his task
finished with the "total collapse" of the 5th
of July; and that his tournament under Fremont we have just alluded to was of little or no
account, in a historical or other point of view.
Yet it *is* worthy of note here, as conclusive evidence, that the discourteous treatment of his
former "adviser" did not in the least dampen
his ardour in the cause of " Equal Rights" and
good government. He took " not the least notice of his insolence" or slights,—conscious, as
he was, of the rectitude of his own intentions.
While he regarded Captain Fremont as an aspiring, youthful rival, he harbored no illwill
towards him. His conscienciously disagreed
with him, as to the correct course of proceedure
in that fearful emergency—the war with Mexico removed all cause for further disagreement.

Mr. Ide's plan for "civil service" rules, under his "administration", as explained by his third *stipulation* of principles, (see page 62), which were to prevail under the new government, for the time being at least, viz: that its prominent public offices should be occupied by that class of philanthropic, patriotic citizens who could not be enticed by *the love of money* "to corruption, fraud and dishonor", shows that he was a full-blooded *radical* politician, of the strictest sect of the present day: but with this difference of developement: while the modern 'radicals' *preach* high-toned patriotism, and *practice* the contrary, he *practiced* what he preached—for we are credibly informed that, for his month or more of indefatigable labor, while organizing the "Bear Flag Government", and superintending its operations, and for his four or five months' services under Capt. Fremont, in his expedition down the coast in pursuit of Don Castro and his handful of men—for all these public services, "civil and military", he never asked or received of the Californian or of the United States' government, any compensation for his *time*, if, indeed, his necessary personal expenses while in the U. S. service were provided for him.

NOTE

The following list is indexed largely to proper names, i.e., people and places. Where possible, we have indexed ideas and incidents. For the sake of consistency, all references to the "Bay" throughout both books have been placed under the heading "San Francisco". We have not indexed Governor Reagan's foreword, nor the publisher's preface, nor Dr. Gilbert's introduction. We believe the index to be as adequate as it can be, but if it should fall short of some expectations, The Rio Grande Press apologizes. It should be noted, perhaps, that as with most other historic documents published in the mid-1880's, the author often mentions a surname, but not a given name. Where Mr. Ide has done that in these two volumes, we have supplied the given name when possible. We have also indicated 'sic' to indicate that we have knowingly used an incorrect spelling in the index, but we have used the spelling as Ide used it. There may be some instances where Ide used the correct spelling, but usage and grammar have since changed it. In any event, we believe this index will be of considerable help to future users of these fine source titles.

-The Publishers

INDEX